Maker Innovations Series

Jump start your path to discovery with the Apress Maker Innovations series! From the basics of electricity and components through to the most advanced options in robotics and Machine Learning, you'll forge a path to building ingenious hardware and controlling it with cutting-edge software. All while gaining new skills and experience with common toolsets you can take to new projects or even into a whole new career.

The Apress Maker Innovations series offers projects-based learning, while keeping theory and best processes front and center. So you get hands-on experience while also learning the terms of the trade and how entrepreneurs, inventors, and engineers think through creating and executing hardware projects. You can learn to design circuits, program AI, create IoT systems for your home or even city, and so much more!

Whether you're a beginning hobbyist or a seasoned entrepreneur working out of your basement or garage, you'll scale up your skillset to become a hardware design and engineering pro. And often using low-cost and open-source software such as the Raspberry Pi, Arduino, PIC microcontroller, and Robot Operating System (ROS). Programmers and software engineers have great opportunities to learn, too, as many projects and control environments are based in popular languages and operating systems, such as Python and Linux.

If you want to build a robot, set up a smart home, tackle assembling a weather-ready meteorology system, or create a brand-new circuit using breadboards and circuit design software, this series has all that and more! Written by creative and seasoned Makers, every book in the series tackles both tested and leading-edge approaches and technologies for bringing your visions and projects to life.

More information about this series at https://link.springer.com/bookseries/17311.

The Evolune Metaverse

Meta-Avatars, Spatial Computing, and the Evolution of Humans with AI

Frank Lisitano
John Hickie

Apress®

The Evolune Metaverse: Meta-Avatars, Spatial Computing, and the Evolution of Humans with AI

Frank Lisitano
VELDHOVEN, Noord-Brabant,
The Netherlands

John Hickie
Eindhoven, Noord-Brabant,
The Netherlands

ISBN-13 (pbk): 979-8-8688-1587-4
https://doi.org/10.1007/979-8-8688-1588-1

ISBN-13 (electronic): 979-8-8688-1588-1

Managing Director, Apress Media LLC: Welmoed Spahr
Acquisitions Editor: James Robinson-Prior
Development Editor: James Markham
Coordinating Editor: Gryffin Winkler

Cover designed by eStudioCalamar

Distributed to the book trade worldwide by Springer Science+Business Media New York, 1 New York Plaza, New York, NY 10004. Phone 1-800-SPRINGER, fax (201) 348-4505, e-mail orders-ny@springer-sbm.com, or visit www.springeronline.com. Apress Media, LLC is a Delaware LLC and the sole member (owner) is Springer Science + Business Media Finance Inc (SSBM Finance Inc). SSBM Finance Inc is a **Delaware** corporation.

For information on translations, please e-mail booktranslations@springernature.com; for reprint, paperback, or audio rights, please e-mail bookpermissions@springernature.com.

Apress titles may be purchased in bulk for academic, corporate, or promotional use. eBook versions and licenses are also available for most titles. For more information, reference our Print and eBook Bulk Sales web page at http://www.apress.com/bulk-sales.

Any source code or other supplementary material referenced by the author in this book is available to readers on GitHub (https://github.com/Apress). For more detailed information, please visit https://www.apress.com/gp/services/source-code.

If disposing of this product, please recycle the paper

True success lies in the ability to rise from every setback with unwavering determination and enthusiasm.

Table of Contents

About the Authors

Frank Lisitano has spent over two decades dedicated to enhancing digital strategies and processes within Artificial Intelligence, IoT, Data Architecture, and the utilization of technology for Smart Cities and Analytics. Frank holds an MBA from the University of Liverpool and a master's in Machine Learning from Columbia University, with specialized research in Natural Language Processing at Stanford University.

During his career, Frank has contributed to many projects in various sectors, including roles at ThinkingMind as an R&D Specialist, Data and AI Architect at ASML, and consultancy positions at ING Bank, Shell, Jumbo, and Google.

As an avid entrepreneur, Frank set Evolune, which stands at the intersection of metaverse gaming and Web3 technology. This endeavor showcases his visionary approach to creating immersive, blockchain-powered gaming experiences, aiming to redefine user engagement and community building within the virtual realm. Through Evolune, Frank not only leverages his vast experience in digital strategies and AI but also underscores his commitment to exploring the future of digital interactions and gaming, positioning himself as a leading figure in the digital innovation landscape.

John Hickie is currently Director at Carrick Communications and has spent the last 30 years at the intersection of technology, communications, and technical writing. After graduating from the Limerick Institute of Technology with a degree in Computer Science, he started his career at Westinghouse Electric, writing instructional manuals for the US Air Force before moving to Sweden to work for ASEA Robotics (now ABB) and

BOFORS as a freelance technical writer. At Carrick Communications, John has worked extensively for Philips Electronics, working with almost every product division (Industrial and Consumer Electronics) as well as the Marketing Communications Group across the globe.

Since 2007, John has been providing writing services to a wide variety of international companies, including Omron, Fluke, FEI, Caterpillar Work Tools, Universal Electronics (One-For-All), DSM, PlasticsEurope, and SABIC.

About the Technical Reviewer

Artur Kireev holds master's degrees in Aerospace Engineering and Applied Mathematics and Computer Science, with a specialization in modern combinatorics methods. He worked as a Design Engineer conducting gas turbine engine simulations and as a Research Engineer developing modeling methodologies for biotechnological equipment. At ThinkingMind, he implemented NLP and Computer Vision algorithms. Currently, he works as a Data Scientist, focusing on forecasting models.

Introduction

Welcome to "Evolune," a far-reaching adventure set in the year 11000, where the frontiers of Reality, Artificial Intelligence (AI), Blockchain technology, and the Metaverse converge. In this advanced future, we explore the profound capabilities of a metaverse platform known as Evolune, which enables the jumping between universes. This realm is under the rule of the powerful King Duncan and his corporate empire, The Gnos. This narrative intertwines with a mission to secure the potent Evolune energy, navigate diverse planetary systems, and resist the tyranny of The Gnos.

As you step into the role of an astronaut, fighter, and scientist, this book serves as both a guide and a companion. Each chapter, depicted as a unique planet within the Evolune universe, delves into the intricacies of cutting-edge technologies. With a focus on Generative AI solutions, the revolutionary potential of blockchain, and the transformative capabilities of computational graphics, we embark on a journey to unravel these complex domains. Through a blend of immersive storytelling, detailed technical descriptions, and practical insights, the narrative is designed to demystify these technologies while integrating the lore of Evolune.

This book caters to a diverse audience—from Metaverse visionaries and blockchain developers to machine learning engineers and technology enthusiasts. The content herein is tailored to broaden your horizons and deepen your comprehension of these rapidly evolving fields. We discuss practical applications, ethical considerations, and visionary future directions of AI, Blockchain, and the Metaverse to equip you with the knowledge and skills necessary to innovate and excel.

Our ultimate aim is to inspire you to imagine and create virtual and immersive realities, where the lines between digital and physical worlds blur, opening a panorama of possibilities and innovations. Through real-world examples, code snippets, and engaging narratives, this book will guide you through the nuances of these technologies, empowering you to be a part of the next wave of digital transformation.

Embark on this grand exploration through Evolune, where technology meets deep-space storytelling, and each chapter unveils a new world of possibilities and challenges in the cosmos of technology.

How to Read This Book

To navigate this comprehensive resource effectively, the book is structured to unfold logically from foundational concepts to advanced applications.

Planet Celestor: Introduction to Artificial Intelligence and the Metaverse

The Rise of the Virtual Universe: Experience the evolution of virtual worlds as you traverse through the Turing Era, and witness the advancements in hardware and software that have shaped the digital cosmos.

Artificial Intelligence: The Backbone of Digital Realms: Explore the digitalization of services and the virtualization of hardware and services, including cloud computing and the rise of robotics.

The Metaverse: A New Frontier for Human Interaction: Discover how the Metaverse redefines human interactions and societal norms.

Planet Tibara: Generative AI Solutions for Creativity and Prediction

Revolutionizing Image Generation with AI: Dive into the transformative impact of AI on image creation across various sectors.

Text Generation and Natural Language Processing: Unpack the advancements in AI-driven text generation and its applications.

Predictive Analytics in Cryptocurrency Markets: Investigate how AI influences predictive analytics within the volatile cryptocurrency markets.

Planet Tenrai: Blockchain—The Foundation of Digital Trust

Exploring Blockchain Technology: Learn about the fundamental aspects of blockchain technology and its potential to revolutionize digital trust.

The Power of Smart Contracts: Delve into how smart contracts automate and secure transactions and agreements.

Blockchain in Action: Beyond Cryptocurrencies: Examine blockchain applications that extend beyond mere financial transactions.

Planet Epsilon: Synergies Between ML and Blockchain Technology

Enhancing Blockchain with AI Capabilities: Explore the integration of AI to bolster blockchain technologies.

AI-Driven Smart Contracts and Security: Analyze how AI enhances the security and functionality of smart contracts.

Real-World Applications and Case Studies: Study real-world implementations where AI and blockchain converge.

Planet Zeta: Unveiling the Metaverse and Digital Twins

Building Blocks of the Metaverse: Get familiar with the core components that make up the Metaverse.

Digital Twins: Bridging the Physical and Virtual: Understand the concept of digital twins and their application across various industries.

Practical Applications Across Industries: See how these technologies are applied in different sectors to solve real-world problems.

Chapter 6 covers the evolution and future of computational graphics.

Planet Eta: Navigating Legal and Security Landscapes

Chapter 7 delves into the legal frameworks and security measures that are critical in the governance and protection of AI, Blockchain, and Metaverse technologies. Explore the regulatory challenges and security protocols that safeguard these digital realms.

Chapter 8 dives into hyper-realistic graphic design, spatial computing, and their future implications.

Chapter 9 offers practical advice on integrating AI, Blockchain, and Digital Twins into real-world projects.

Chapter 10 looks forward to the future directions of AI and Blockchain, preparing you for the next big thing.

Epilogue

The Epilogue reflects on the implications of these technologies and the continuous evolution of the digital world.

Code Repository Access

To enhance your learning experience and provide practical insights into the technologies discussed in this book, we have established a comprehensive online code repository. This repository contains code snippets, detailed programming examples, and complete project templates that correspond to the strategies and technologies covered in each chapter. Whether you are looking to delve into Generative AI algorithms, explore blockchain implementations, or simulate environments within the Metaverse, this repository serves as a valuable hands-on resource.

Accessing the Repository

The repository is hosted on GitHub, allowing easy access and collaboration. You can clone the repository to your local environment, contribute by suggesting improvements, or simply use the code as a reference for your projects. Each chapter in the book has corresponding folders in the repository, ensuring that you can find relevant code easily and efficiently.

The repository is available here: `https://github.com/Apress/The-Evolune-Metaverse`

How to Use the Repository

1. **Explore by Chapter:** Navigate through the repository to find folders organized by chapter, allowing you to focus on specific areas of interest.

2. **Download Code Snippets:** Each folder contains code snippets that are directly applicable to the concepts discussed in the corresponding chapter. These snippets are ready to run with minimal setup, providing a practical way to see theories in action.

3. **Engage with Complete Projects:** For a more in-depth exploration, some folders include complete project setups that you can deploy and test. These projects provide a more comprehensive understanding of how different technologies integrate and operate in real-world scenarios.

4. **Collaborate and Contribute:** As an open source project, you are encouraged to contribute by providing feedback, suggesting improvements, and even adding your own examples that might help the community.

Benefits of Using the Code Repository

- **Practical Experience:** Transition from theoretical knowledge to practical application smoothly as you implement and manipulate the code.

- **Continuous Learning:** The repository is regularly updated with new examples and solutions, keeping you abreast with the latest advancements in AI, Blockchain, and the Metaverse.

- **Community Engagement:** Join a growing community of developers, engineers, and enthusiasts who are exploring these cutting-edge technologies. Engage in discussions, solve problems collectively, and share your insights.

As you journey through the pages of this book, the code repository will serve as a bridge between learning and application, making the complex world of AI, Blockchain, and the Metaverse accessible and engaging. Enjoy the hands-on experience and unleash your potential to create innovative solutions in the digital age.

CHAPTER 1

Planet Celestor: Introduction to Artificial Intelligence and the Metaverse

As John Lee's vessel sliced through the starry panorama toward the electrifying planet of Celestor, his mind raced. An astronaut for hire, John's strength and intelligence were assets Gnos Corporation had leveraged for years. Gnos, hailed as "mankind's savior," had built its empire on Evolune, a powerful energy source that unlocked pathways to other universes. Under the guise of peacekeeping, Gnos extended its reach, exploiting resources across countless timelines.

© Frank Lisitano, John Hickie 2025
F. Lisitano and J. Hickie, *The Evolune Metaverse*, Maker Innovations Series,
https://doi.org/10.1007/979-8-8688-1588-1_1

Figure 1-1. *John Lee on His Way to Celestor*

To the public, Gnos was a beacon of progress. Its headquarters, a
dazzling industrial city of towering skyscrapers and endless opportunity,
was a testament to the fruits of its "knowledge." They had mapped a
third of the Gaia galaxy, and their technological leaps were undeniable:
regenerative cells, nano-powered muscle fibers, and cerebral enhancers.
But John had seen the truth behind the polished veneer. He'd seen what
the "peacekeepers" did on their missions: they took, leaving devastation
in their wake. His idealism had been chipped away with every assignment,
but it was on Celestor that it would finally shatter.

To you and many others, Gnos is a beacon of hope. The sprawling
industrial city where Gnos is headquartered dazzles with bright lights,
myriad shops, massive skyscrapers, and seemingly endless opportunities.

Figure 1-2. *The City of Gnos*

After being forced to take a leave following an "accident" on his last mission, John was restless. A new peacekeeping force had been established on Celestor after a failed coup against its king, Ari IV. Gnos's official reason for a deeper presence was to stabilize the region; their real reason was to dig for precious materials—a recent operation having already poisoned the local sea life. "Necessary use of force," the report had read. "The local wildlife was highly aggressive."

John is an astronaut driven by the legacy of Duncan Lee, his idol and the head of Gnos. John has always been a good man, but the harsh reality of his missions has begun to show him the darker side of Gnos. He saw what really happened during the peacekeeping missions: the peacekeepers did nothing but take. He was naive until he met Anda on Celestor, where his perspective began to change.

Now it's John's time to go to Celestor. Forced to take paid leave after a little accident in Tenrai, the last two months have felt cold and sluggish. A change of scenery was necessary, and Gnos had introduced

3

a peacekeeping force based on Celestor after a failed coup against the current king, Ari the 4th. After a recent ammonia haul from a neighboring planet, Gnos decided to dig for precious materials, poisoning the local sea life in the process. "Necessary use of force. The local wildlife was highly aggressive," they said. John thought he was a local hero patrolling the streets of Gorand, Celestor's capital, at night. In fact, he was nobody, living in his safe bubble, but his life was about to change on that lonely night at the Prodded Cow Inn.

Welcome to Evolune

Welcome to Evolune, a journey through the fascinating and interconnected realms of Artificial Intelligence, Blockchain, the Metaverse, Data Management, and Cloud Computing. The first chapter of a technical book often sets the tone for the entire narrative. The best-written books always begin by exploring the history of their respective fields, providing a foundation upon which current advancements and future innovations are built.

However, historical overviews can sometimes feel like a dry recitation from a textbook, lacking the excitement and engagement that such revolutionary topics deserve. This chapter aims to present the history of hardware and software computing in a way that not only informs but also captivates the imagination.

In this chapter, the journey begins with a voyage through time, starting from the rudimentary tools of early computation and progressing through the monumental milestones that have shaped the digital age. The exploration will cover how the relentless evolution of technology has laid the groundwork for the sophisticated systems relied upon today.

From the mechanical calculators of Pascal and Leibniz to Charles Babbage's visionary designs for programmable machines, each invention built upon its predecessors, gradually increasing in complexity and capability. The narrative then delves into the electromechanical age, featuring devices like the Zuse Z3 and Harvard Mark I, which showcase the transition from mechanical to electronic systems that enabled faster and more reliable computation.

The advent of vacuum tubes marked the beginning of the electronic computer era, with groundbreaking machines like ENIAC and UNIVAC setting new standards for computational speed and reliability. The profound impact of Alan Turing's theoretical work, which provided a framework for understanding the capabilities and limitations of computing devices, will also be explored.

Moving into the personal computing era, the development of microprocessors such as the Intel 4004 enabled the miniaturization of computers and brought powerful computing capabilities to individuals and small businesses. Companies like IBM, Apple, Microsoft, and HP revolutionized personal computing, making it accessible and indispensable in homes, schools, and workplaces.

Finally, the modern era of computing will be examined, characterized by the rise of Graphics Processing Units (GPUs) and the transformative impact of cloud computing. These advancements have democratized access to powerful computational resources, enabling innovation and scalability on an unprecedented scale.

By understanding the history of hardware and software computing, valuable insights are gained into how humanity can harness these technologies to address complex challenges and create new opportunities. This chapter is not just a recounting of historical milestones but a tribute to the relentless spirit of innovation that continues to drive progress forward.

So, buckle up and prepare for an exhilarating journey through the annals of computing history. Welcome to Evolune!

The Metaverse: A New Frontier for Human Interaction

The Promise and Reality of Virtual Environments

Immersive digital environments, commonly referred to as the Metaverse, have emerged as one of the most ambitious technological frontiers of our time. Leading technology companies, particularly Meta (formerly Facebook) and Microsoft, have committed billions of dollars toward developing these virtual spaces where users can interact within computer-generated worlds. Yet the gap between vision and reality remains substantial.

The adoption curve has proven steeper than industry predictions suggested. Expensive virtual reality hardware creates a significant barrier to entry, while the content ecosystem lacks the depth and engagement necessary to justify the investment for most consumers. Users frequently encounter technical limitations that break immersion: network latency disrupts real-time interactions, motion sickness affects user comfort, and bandwidth requirements exclude those without high-speed internet access.

Economic models for these platforms remain underdeveloped. Revenue streams from virtual property transactions, digital item purchases, and immersive advertising have failed to generate the returns that justify continued massive investment. Meanwhile, governance challenges multiply as these platforms grapple with privacy protection, cybersecurity vulnerabilities, and the prevention of virtual harassment—issues that require new regulatory frameworks.

User feedback consistently highlights interface problems that make virtual interactions feel cumbersome compared to established digital platforms. This creates a retention challenge that compounds adoption difficulties, as early users often abandon platforms after brief trials.

Market Dynamics and Industry Challenges

The competitive landscape has created unintended consequences for
Metaverse development. Rather than collaborating on shared standards,
major companies are developing proprietary ecosystems that cannot
communicate with each other. This fragmentation prevents the network
effects that would make virtual worlds truly valuable, as users become
trapped within isolated platforms rather than participating in a unified
digital universe.

Building comprehensive virtual worlds demands coordination
and standardization efforts unlike anything the technology industry
has previously attempted. Current development approaches lack the
collaborative framework necessary to achieve this scale of integration.

Investment patterns reveal tensions between ambitious long-term
goals and market realities. Creating sophisticated virtual environments
requires sustained financial commitment over many years without
generating immediate profits. As market conditions have become more
challenging and investors demand faster returns, many companies have
reduced their Metaverse investments in favor of projects with clearer near-
term profitability.

This shift is particularly pronounced in the technology sector, where
economic uncertainty has prompted companies to focus resources on
proven revenue models rather than experimental platforms. The result
has been a scaling back of the most ambitious virtual world projects just as
they were beginning to mature.

Yet industry professionals remain committed to the vision's
transformative potential. They frame current obstacles as typical
challenges for emerging technologies, comparing the Metaverse's current
state to the early internet era when skeptics questioned whether online
services would achieve mainstream adoption. These advocates argue that
technological improvements, declining hardware costs, and expanding
content libraries will eventually overcome current barriers.

The development trajectory toward fully realized virtual worlds continues despite these challenges, driven by the compelling vision of interconnected digital spaces that could fundamentally transform how humans communicate, collaborate, and create. The next several years will likely determine whether these platforms can evolve beyond current limitations to become integral components of digital life.

John Lee's Digital Odyssey: A Window into Advanced Virtual Systems

By 2024, virtual reality technology has achieved remarkable sophistication, creating seamless bridges between physical and digital existence. This evolution becomes apparent through the experiences of John Lee, a Gnos Corporation astronaut, as he explores the technologically advanced planet Celestor. His encounters reveal how virtual systems have matured into comprehensive platforms for human experience and interaction.

John's introduction to these advanced systems begins with his exposure to hyper-realistic virtual environments powered by next-generation VR and AR technologies. Advanced haptic feedback systems and neural interface devices enable him to experience digital worlds with complete sensory immersion. The virtual representations he encounters on Celestor demonstrate how sophisticated these environments have become, featuring complex ecosystems, varied terrains, and inhabitants that respond naturally to interaction.

During his exploration, John discovers the ecosystem of organizations and individuals driving virtual world development. Major corporations including Meta, Snapchat, Unreal Engine, and Unity have built infrastructure capable of supporting millions of simultaneous users across vast virtual spaces. Creative professionals and independent developers have leveraged these platforms to construct experiences that challenge traditional boundaries between entertainment, art, and social interaction.

John's journey reveals virtual world applications that extend far beyond gaming and entertainment. He engages with training simulations that replicate hazardous space exploration scenarios, participates in global conferences that enable seamless international collaboration, and explores digital marketplaces where virtual assets hold real economic value. These implementations demonstrate how virtual platforms can transform professional development, education, business operations, and social networking.

However, John's exploration also exposes persistent challenges within these digital environments. Cybersecurity threats in virtual spaces mirror and sometimes amplify those found in traditional online platforms, including identity fraud and digital harassment. His experiences raise important questions about privacy protection, ensuring equal access to virtual resources, and preventing addictive engagement patterns. These encounters highlight the ongoing need to develop virtual worlds responsibly while preserving user safety and social equity.

John's adventure concludes with glimpses of future technological developments that will further enhance virtual platform capabilities. Emerging artificial intelligence systems, quantum computing applications, and next-generation wireless networks promise to make virtual experiences even more responsive and accessible. His journey suggests a trajectory toward complete integration of physical and digital realities, creating unprecedented opportunities for human connection and creative expression.

Through John Lee's experiences on Celestor, we observe how virtual reality platforms are evolving beyond current limitations. His story illustrates the technological infrastructure enabling complex virtual worlds, identifies the key stakeholders driving innovation, demonstrates diverse applications across multiple industries, acknowledges ongoing challenges requiring solutions, and previews the developments that may define the future of digital human interaction.

Transforming Human Connection in Digital Spaces

The development of sophisticated virtual environments represents more than technological progress—it signals a potential transformation in fundamental human activities including communication, creativity, and community building. As these systems overcome current technical and social limitations, they may reshape economic structures, educational methods, and artistic expression in profound ways.

The success of virtual platforms will likely depend on their ability to enhance rather than replace authentic human relationships. Early development experiences suggest that the most valuable virtual environments will be those that amplify human capabilities and foster genuine community connections rather than creating isolated digital experiences that separate users from physical reality.

As we navigate this period of rapid technological evolution, the decisions made by platform developers, policymakers, and users will determine whether virtual reality systems fulfill their potential as tools for positive human advancement or become sources of additional digital fragmentation. The lessons emerging from advanced implementations like those imagined on Celestor provide both inspiration and guidance for creating virtual worlds that serve human flourishing.

The ultimate measure of virtual world success will not be technological sophistication alone, but their capacity to enrich human experience, strengthen social bonds, and expand opportunities for creativity and collaboration across global communities. This vision continues to drive innovation and investment despite current challenges, maintaining momentum toward a future where digital and physical realities enhance each other in service of human potential.

Exploring the Metaverse

Guided by the Voltis, John reaches a high vantage point overlooking the
vast electrified landscape of Celestor. The entire scene is surreal, with
luminous energy fields stretching out as far as the eye can see, punctuated
by the towering structures of Voltis' civilization.

Figure 1-3. Celestor

Alpha, John's AI companion and source of almost infinite
knowledge, begins to explain the Metaverse. "The Metaverse represents
a revolutionary shift, merging physical and digital realities to create
immersive environments. On Celestor, the Voltis have redefined existence
through electricity, much like the Metaverse redefines human interactions.
The Metaverse offers a new paradigm for experiencing and interacting
with the world, blending virtual and physical spaces."

John envisions a world where the boundaries between the real
and virtual blur, offering endless possibilities. The potential of the
Metaverse to transform various aspects of life, from social interactions to

economic activities, is immense. Imagine attending a concert in a virtual amphitheater, collaborating on a project in a digital workspace that mimics a physical office, or exploring fantastic landscapes that defy the limits of the natural world. The Metaverse holds the promise of a new reality where physical limitations no longer confine human experiences.

Foundational Technologies

Virtual Reality (VR) and Augmented Reality (AR)

As John's mind absorbs this knowledge, Alpha continues, "VR provides fully immersive experiences, while AR overlays digital information onto the real world. These technologies form the cornerstone of the Metaverse, much like the Voltis' electrified environment shapes their interactions. The ability to create immersive and interactive environments is key to the Metaverse's appeal."

John imagines using VR and AR to explore new worlds, just as he explores Celestor. With VR, he can be transported to entirely new realms, experiencing them as if he were truly there. AR, on the other hand, enriches John's perception of the real world, adding layers of digital information and interaction. The integration of VR and AR into the Metaverse allows for rich and engaging experiences that transcend traditional boundaries, making it possible to learn, work, and play in ways previously unimaginable.

Artificial Intelligence

"AI powers avatars and nonplayer characters (NPCs) in the Metaverse, making interactions more realistic. AI-driven avatars exhibit humanlike behaviors, enhancing engagement, similar to the Voltis' adaptive communication. The use of AI in the Metaverse enables more dynamic and responsive environments."

John sees the potential for AI to create rich, interactive experiences
in the Metaverse. AI's ability to understand and respond to user inputs
makes the Metaverse more immersive and personalized. Imagine having a
conversation with an AI avatar that can understand your emotions, provide
intelligent responses, and adapt its behavior to suit your preferences.
AI can also generate content, manage environments, and facilitate
interactions, creating a seamless and engaging digital experience.

Blockchain

"Blockchain ensures secure transactions within the Metaverse, enabling
the ownership and trade of virtual assets. Non-fungible tokens (NFTs)
allow users to own unique digital items, mirroring the Voltis' use of
decentralized systems. The use of blockchain technology ensures the
integrity and security of digital transactions."

John understands that blockchain technology will underpin the economy
of the Metaverse. The decentralized nature of blockchain provides a secure
and transparent framework for managing digital assets and transactions. This
technology enables users to confidently buy, sell, and trade virtual goods,
knowing that their ownership is securely recorded and protected. Blockchain
also supports the creation of decentralized applications (dApps) within the
Metaverse, fostering innovation and economic growth.

Human Interaction in the Metaverse
Virtual Social Spaces

As John traverses the landscape, Alpha explains that "the Metaverse
redefines social interactions, allowing people to meet and collaborate in
virtual environments. Users can attend virtual events, much like the Voltis
gather during storms. The ability to connect and interact with others in
virtual spaces offers new possibilities for social engagement."

John envisions a future where virtual social spaces foster global connections. The Metaverse provides a platform for creating and nurturing social relationships, transcending physical limitations. Whether attending a virtual conference, joining a digital art gallery opening, or simply hanging out with friends in a fantastic setting, the Metaverse opens up new avenues for meaningful social interactions.

Work and Education

"The Metaverse offers new possibilities for remote work and virtual classrooms. Employees can collaborate in virtual offices, and students can engage in interactive learning environments, like the Voltis' interconnected tunnels. The ability to work and learn in virtual environments offers greater flexibility and accessibility."

John sees the potential for the Metaverse to revolutionize education and work. Virtual offices can replicate the collaborative atmosphere of physical workspaces, complete with digital tools that enhance productivity. In education, virtual classrooms can provide immersive learning experiences, allowing students to explore historical events, conduct virtual experiments, and interact with peers from around the world. The Metaverse's flexibility enables people to work and learn from anywhere, breaking down geographical barriers.

Entertainment and Gaming

"The Metaverse provides a platform for immersive entertainment experiences. Users can explore virtual worlds and participate in interactive games, much like the Voltis' dynamic and adaptive environment. The ability to create and experience diverse forms of entertainment is one of the Metaverse's most exciting aspects."

John feels the excitement of endless entertainment possibilities within the Metaverse. The rich and varied experiences offered by the Metaverse make it an ideal platform for entertainment and gaming. Imagine diving into an epic fantasy adventure, competing in a futuristic sports arena, or experiencing a concert in a virtual venue that responds to your presence. The immersive nature of the Metaverse transforms passive entertainment into active and engaging experiences.

Digital Twins

Concept

Digital twins are virtual replicas of physical objects, continuously updated with real-time data. They are used in manufacturing, urban planning, and healthcare, optimizing performance and predicting outcomes, similar to the Voltis' use of data for survival. The ability to create and utilize digital twins offers significant benefits in various fields.

John realizes that digital twins will play a crucial role in future technological advancements. The use of digital twins enables more accurate and efficient management of physical systems and processes. In manufacturing, digital twins can simulate production lines, identify inefficiencies, and predict maintenance needs, improving overall efficiency. In urban planning, digital twins can model city infrastructure, optimize traffic flow, and plan for future growth. In healthcare, digital twins can represent patients' biological systems, allowing for personalized treatment plans and predictive diagnostics.

Technology Integration

Digital twins leverage IoT, AI, and machine learning to mirror real-world counterparts. This continuous feedback loop ensures accuracy and relevance, much like the Voltis' interconnected systems. The integration of digital twins with other technologies enhances their effectiveness and utility."

John understands that integrating these technologies will enhance decision-making and efficiency. The ability to use real-time data to update and manage digital twins provides valuable insights and improves performance. For instance, IoT sensors can continuously feed data into digital twins, while AI and machine learning algorithms analyze this data to optimize operations and predict future conditions. This synergy between digital twins and other advanced technologies creates a powerful tool for managing complex systems.

Best Platforms to Create Digital Twins
Siemens MindSphere

Siemens MindSphere stands out as an open IoT operating system designed to connect products, plants, systems, and machines, facilitating comprehensive data analysis. Among its key features are real-time data processing, advanced analytics, and machine learning capabilities. This robust platform supports scalable IoT solutions across various industries. MindSphere is extensively used in manufacturing to monitor and optimize production processes. It plays a critical role in predictive maintenance and improving product quality.

Extended Features and Benefits

- **Scalability**: One of the notable strengths of MindSphere is its scalability. It can easily scale from small applications to extensive industrial operations, making it suitable for enterprises of all sizes.

- **Open Ecosystem**: MindSphere supports a wide range of industrial protocols and interfaces, allowing seamless integration with existing systems and third-party applications.

- **Development Tools**: It provides developers with powerful tools and APIs to create customized applications tailored to specific business needs, enhancing its flexibility and utility in various industrial contexts.

IBM Maximo Suite

IBM's Maximo Suite offers a comprehensive cloud-based digital twin environment that allows for the creation, sharing, and management of digital twins. It integrates seamlessly with IBM Watson, providing AI-driven insights and robust security features. Maximo Suite represents IBM's evolution from the previous Digital Twin Exchange platform, offering enhanced capabilities and broader industrial applications. IBM Maximo Suite is commonly used in industrial IoT, urban planning for smart cities, healthcare for personalized patient care models, and enterprise asset management across various industries.

Extended Features and Benefits

- **Interoperability**: This platform is designed to work seamlessly with other IBM products and services, as well as external platforms, enhancing its flexibility and integration capabilities across enterprise ecosystems.

- **Security and Compliance**: It offers enterprise-grade security features, including data encryption and compliance with industry standards and regulations, ensuring data protection and regulatory adherence.

- **Predictive Maintenance**: The use of AI and machine learning allows for the prediction of equipment failures and optimization of maintenance schedules, significantly reducing downtime and associated costs.

- **Asset Performance Management**: Maximo Suite extends beyond traditional digital twins to provide comprehensive asset life cycle management, from procurement to disposal.

- **Mobile Capabilities**: The platform includes mobile applications that enable field workers to access digital twin data and perform maintenance tasks in real time.

- **Advanced Analytics**: Built-in analytics capabilities provide deep insights into asset performance, enabling data-driven decision-making and operational optimization.

Microsoft Azure Digital Twins

Azure Digital Twins is an IoT platform from Microsoft that enables the creation of comprehensive digital models of entire environments. It supports the modeling of physical environments, real-time data integration, and rich analytics with Azure IoT and AI services. Azure Digital Twins is widely applied in smart building management, industrial IoT, and smart city solutions.

Extended Features and Benefits

- **Scalable Architecture**: Built on Azure's robust cloud infrastructure, it ensures scalability and reliability for large-scale deployments.

- **Integrated Ecosystem**: Fully integrated with Azure's suite of services, including AI, IoT Hub, and Azure Data Lake, it facilitates a cohesive digital transformation strategy.

- **Real-Time Analytics**: The platform offers real-time analytics and insights, enabling proactive decision-making and enhanced operational efficiency.

PTC ThingWorx

ThingWorx is a versatile IoT platform designed for the rapid development and deployment of industrial digital twins. It features advanced modeling, real-time data visualization, and integration with augmented reality (AR) for enhanced operational insights. ThingWorx is used in manufacturing for production optimization, equipment monitoring, and maintenance scheduling.

Extended Features and Benefits

- **Rapid Development**: ThingWorx provides a comprehensive set of tools and templates to accelerate the development and deployment of digital twin applications.

- **AR Integration**: Incorporates augmented reality capabilities to provide immersive visualizations and interactive experiences, improving user engagement and understanding.

- **Customizable Dashboards**: Offers customizable dashboards and user interfaces, allowing stakeholders to view and interact with data in ways most relevant to their roles.

AWS IoT TwinMaker

AWS IoT TwinMaker is a service that enables developers to create digital twins of real-world systems such as buildings, factories, industrial equipment, and production lines. It focuses on making it easier to integrate data from multiple sources and create knowledge graphs that model the real-world environment. AWS IoT TwinMaker is primarily used in manufacturing, energy management, smart buildings, and industrial operations to optimize performance and enable predictive maintenance.

Extended Features and Benefits

- **Multisource Data Integration**: Capable of integrating data from various sources including IoT sensors, video cameras, enterprise applications, and existing digital twin solutions, providing a comprehensive view of physical systems.

- **3D Visualization**: Offers built-in 3D visualization capabilities that allow users to create immersive digital twin experiences without requiring specialized 3D development skills.

- **Knowledge Graph Creation**: Automatically creates knowledge graphs that model relationships between different components and systems, enabling better understanding of complex industrial environments.

- **Scalable Cloud Infrastructure**: Built on AWS's robust cloud infrastructure, ensuring scalability, reliability, and global availability for large-scale industrial deployments.

- **Integration with AWS Ecosystem**: Seamlessly integrates with other AWS services including IoT Core, Lambda, S3, and analytics services, providing a comprehensive IoT and analytics platform.

- **Real-Time Analytics**: Supports real-time data processing and analytics, enabling immediate insights and rapid response to changing conditions in physical systems.

John is excited about the potential of digital twins to transform industries by providing a more dynamic and accurate representation of physical systems. By utilizing these advanced platforms, businesses can achieve significant improvements in efficiency, performance, and predictive capabilities. The future of digital twins looks promising as technology continues to evolve, offering even more sophisticated tools for managing the complexities of the real world.

Economic and Social Impact

Digital Economy

As John reaches a bustling Voltis settlement, Alpha explains, "the Metaverse creates new economic opportunities, including virtual real estate and digital goods. The digital economy within the Metaverse fosters innovation and entrepreneurship, much like the Voltis' thriving communities. The ability to create and trade digital assets opens up new possibilities for economic activities."

John envisions a vibrant digital economy transforming society. The Metaverse provides a platform for new forms of economic activity, driving innovation and growth. Virtual real estate can be developed and monetized, digital goods and services can be traded, and new business models can emerge. The decentralized nature of the Metaverse encourages entrepreneurship and empowers individuals to create and capitalize on digital ventures.

Social Norms and Legal Frameworks

"New social norms and legal frameworks will emerge to address issues like digital rights, privacy, and security. Ensuring privacy and security in the Metaverse is crucial, similar to protecting Celestor's unique ecosystem. The development of appropriate legal and regulatory frameworks is essential for the sustainable growth of the Metaverse."

John understands the importance of establishing ethical guidelines for the Metaverse. Addressing the challenges of privacy, security, and digital rights is critical to ensuring the responsible development of the Metaverse. New legal frameworks must be created to protect users' rights, ensure data privacy, and prevent exploitation. Social norms will also evolve to guide behavior and interactions within the Metaverse, fostering a safe and respectful digital environment.

Inclusivity and Accessibility

"The Metaverse can create more inclusive interactions, reducing barriers related to geography and disability. It enables participation in activities that may be challenging in the physical world, enhancing social inclusion, much like the Voltis' interconnected society. The ability to create inclusive environments is one of the Metaverse's key strengths."

John sees the potential for the Metaverse to promote greater understanding and empathy. The ability to connect and interact with diverse groups of people enhances social cohesion and inclusivity. The Metaverse can provide opportunities for individuals with disabilities to engage in activities that might be difficult or impossible in the physical world. It can also bridge geographical divides, bringing people together from different cultures and backgrounds, fostering a more inclusive and connected global community.

Prospects

Integration with Daily Life

As John descends into a glowing canyon, Alpha concludes, "the Metaverse will become more integrated into daily life, offering new mediums for expression and interaction. Technologies like 5G, edge computing, and AI will support this infrastructure, much like the Voltis' advanced systems. The integration of the Metaverse into daily life will transform how we live, work, and play."

John suddenly feels a surge of anticipation for the future, where the Metaverse will transform human experiences. The potential for the Metaverse to become a central part of everyday life is immense, offering new opportunities and challenges. As technologies like 5G and edge computing enhance connectivity and reduce latency, the Metaverse will become more seamless and accessible. AI will continue to drive innovation, making the Metaverse more intelligent and adaptive.

Web 3.0 and the Spatial Web

"The Metaverse is the next evolution of the internet, often referred to as Web 3.0 or the Spatial Web. It integrates physical and digital realities, creating seamless and interactive experiences, similar to the Voltis' harmonious blend of technology and nature. The evolution of the internet into the Metaverse is a significant shift in how we interact with technology."

John envisions a world where the digital and physical realms merge seamlessly. The development of Web 3.0 and the Spatial Web will enable more immersive and interactive experiences, transforming how we interact with the digital world. This evolution will bring about new ways of accessing information, communicating, and experiencing the internet. The Spatial Web will create a more intuitive and integrated digital environment, enhancing our interactions with technology and each other.

Conclusion

As John prepares to depart Celestor, he reflects on his journey. He realizes that the history of hardware and software computing, the rise of artificial intelligence, and the emergence of the Metaverse are all intertwined with the story of survival and adaptation on this electrifying planet. Just as the Voltis have harnessed electricity to thrive, humanity must harness the power of these technologies to shape a better future.

With newfound knowledge and a sense of purpose, John sets his sights on the stars, ready to bring the lessons of Celestor back to the universe, knowing that the adventure has only just begun. The insights gained from this journey will guide him in navigating the complexities of the digital age and harnessing the potential of emerging technologies to create a better future. The story of Evolune in combination with the explanation of the Generative AI and Metaverse with Digital twin is a fantastic travel that allows the reader to have fun and learn more about the technologies.

Summary

The journey through Celestor has provided valuable insights into
the history and evolution of hardware and software computing,
the development and applications of artificial intelligence, and the
transformative potential of the Metaverse. Understanding these
technologies and their ethical implications is crucial for harnessing
their power to create a better future. The exploration of these advanced
technologies on Celestor has shown how they can be integrated to address
complex challenges and drive innovation.

The historical perspective on computing has highlighted the
continuous advancements that have shaped the digital world, from
mechanical devices to modern quantum computers. The development
of AI has demonstrated its potential to revolutionize various industries,
improve efficiency, and enhance decision-making. The emergence of
the Metaverse has showcased new opportunities for immersive and
interactive experiences, transforming social interactions, work, education,
and entertainment. The ethical considerations associated with these
technologies need to be assessed to ensure fairness, transparency, and
privacy for building trust and assuring the adoption of these technologies.
The insights gained from the journey through Celestor will guide future
efforts to harness the potential of advanced technologies to create a better
future. The commitment to continuous innovation, ethical considerations,
and collaboration will be critical in addressing emerging challenges and
opportunities.

Artificial Intelligence: The Backbone of Digital Realms

Discovering AI

Venturing deeper into the cave, John encounters the Voltis, their eyes glowing with electric blue light. The luminous patterns of their gaze are mesmerizing, each flicker seemingly encoded with the secrets of their world.

Figure 1-4. *John Meeting the Voltis*

Alpha begins to explain the significance of AI. "Artificial Intelligence, like the electricity sustaining the Voltis, is the lifeblood of modern technology," Alpha's voice echoes softly against the cave walls. The analogy strikes John deeply, as both AI and the electrical energy of the Voltis symbolize the unseen forces driving progress and evolution.

The early days of AI research were filled with curiosity and ambition. Scientists and mathematicians aimed to create algorithms capable of problem-solving and language processing, hoping to mimic human intelligence. These pioneers laid the groundwork for what would become a revolution in technology. Initial efforts focused on developing rule-based systems and simple decision-making processes. Although these early AI systems were limited in scope, they demonstrated the potential for machines to assist and enhance human capabilities.

As the Voltis guide John through their subterranean world, he is awestruck by their mastery of electricity and technology. Their entire civilization is an intricate network of energy flows and data exchanges, much like the interconnected systems we strive to build on Earth. The development of AI has been driven by a similar desire to create machines that can perform tasks traditionally requiring human intelligence, such as reasoning, learning, and decision-making. The path to modern AI has been marked by significant milestones, each building on the last to create increasingly sophisticated systems. Walking through the illuminated tunnels, John contemplates the parallels between the Voltis' evolution and humanity's pursuit of AI. The Voltis have adapted to their environment in ways that seem almost magical yet are deeply rooted in their natural history. Similarly, AI has evolved through iterative processes of trial, error, and innovation. The early AI systems, although rudimentary, provided crucial insights and a foundation upon which more complex and capable systems could be developed.

As AI research progressed, it gave rise to advanced neural network architectures. Convolutional Neural Networks (CNNs) revolutionized computer vision by enabling machines to recognize and classify images with remarkable accuracy. Generative Adversarial Networks (GANs) introduced a new paradigm for generating realistic images and data by pitting two neural networks against each other in a creative process. Techniques like Stable Diffusion have further enhanced the ability of AI to create high-quality visual content by refining and stabilizing the generation process.

John's journey into the depths of Celestor mirrors the journey of AI development—a path filled with challenges, discoveries, and the promise of transformative potential. The glowing lights of the Voltis' eyes and their seamless integration with their environment serve as a reminder of what is possible when technology and nature harmonize.

Historical Development of AI

"AI's journey began in the 1950s," Alpha recounts as John navigates the intricate pathways of the Voltis' underground city. "Programs like the Logic Theorist and ELIZA demonstrated AI's potential, much like the early adaptations of the Voltis." The early days of AI were marked by a series of groundbreaking experiments that showcased the possibilities of machine intelligence. The Logic Theorist, developed by Allen Newell and Herbert A. Simon, was one of the first programs capable of proving mathematical theorems, highlighting the potential for machines to engage in logical reasoning.

ELIZA, created by Joseph Weizenbaum in the 1960s, simulated a psychotherapist's responses, giving the illusion of understanding and conversation. Although primitive by today's standards, ELIZA captured the imagination of the public and researchers alike, sparking interest in the potential for AI to engage in natural language processing and human/computer interaction. These early successes paved the way for more ambitious projects and the development of expert systems in the 1970s.

"The development of expert systems in the 1970s showcased AI's capability in specialized domains despite the challenges that led to 'AI winters,'" Alpha continues. "Expert systems like MYCIN, which assisted in diagnosing bacterial infections, demonstrated the practical applications of AI in fields such as medicine and engineering. These systems used a knowledge base of facts and rules to make decisions, offering valuable assistance in areas requiring specialized expertise."

However, the journey of AI has been far from smooth. The initial excitement and optimism were followed by periods of stagnation, known as AI winters, when progress slowed due to technical and conceptual limitations. Funding and interest waned as the challenges of building truly intelligent machines became apparent. The complexity of human intelligence and the limitations of existing technology posed significant hurdles, leading to skepticism about the feasibility of AI.

John marvels at the Voltis' resilience, their story echoing AI's ups and downs. The journey of AI has been marked by periods of rapid progress and setbacks, reflecting the complexity and challenges of creating intelligent machines. Despite these challenges, researchers persevered, driven by the vision of machines that could think, learn, and reason like humans. The development of AI has been a testament to human ingenuity and determination, continuously pushing the boundaries of what is possible.

The introduction of deep learning in the 1980s and 1990s marked a significant turning point. Techniques such as backpropagation enabled neural networks to learn from large datasets, leading to breakthroughs in speech recognition, image processing, and more. The rise of Transformers in the 2010s, starting with models like BERT and GPT, revolutionized natural language processing by allowing machines to understand and generate human language with unprecedented fluency and accuracy.

Walking through the Voltis' illuminated city, John is reminded of the persistence and adaptability required to achieve breakthroughs in technology. The resilience of both the Voltis and AI researchers serves as an inspiration, highlighting the importance of perseverance and innovation in the face of adversity.

The State of the Art: Modern Generative AI Models

The landscape of AI has been transformed by the emergence of powerful generative models that can create text, audio, and video content. These models represent the pinnacle of AI development, showcasing remarkable capabilities and opening new frontiers in technology.

ChatGPT and Natural Language Processing

One of the most prominent examples of modern AI is OpenAI's ChatGPT, a state-of-the-art language model that can generate human-like text based on the input it receives. Built on the GPT-4 architecture, ChatGPT excels in natural language understanding and generation, making it useful for a wide range of applications, from chatbots and customer service to content creation and education. Its ability to generate coherent and contextually relevant responses has set a new standard in AI communication.

LLaMA 3: Large Language Model Advances

Following ChatGPT, Meta's LLaMA (Large Language Model Meta AI) series, with its latest version LLaMA 3, has pushed the boundaries of language modeling even further. LLaMA 3 focuses on improving the efficiency and scalability of large language models, making them more accessible for research and commercial use. This model is designed to handle a diverse array of tasks, including language translation, summarization, and even code generation.

Gemini: Integrating Text, Audio, and Video

Gemini represents another leap forward in AI capabilities by integrating multimodal inputs and outputs. Developed by a collaboration of leading AI research labs, Gemini can process text, audio, and video data, enabling it to perform complex tasks such as video summarization, audio transcription, and multimedia content creation. This integration of different types of data allows for more nuanced and sophisticated AI applications.

Text-to-Text and Text-to-Audio Models

Text-to-text models like T5 (Text-To-Text Transfer Transformer) have demonstrated the versatility of AI in transforming one form of text into another, such as translating languages, paraphrasing content, and answering questions. These models treat all tasks as text generation problems, simplifying the approach to solving diverse NLP challenges.

Text-to-audio models, such as OpenAI's Jukebox, have opened new possibilities in music and audio creation. These models can generate music and audio tracks based on textual descriptions, offering innovative tools for artists and content creators.

Text-to-Video Models

The frontier of text-to-video is being explored by models like DALL-E and its successors, which aim to generate video content from textual descriptions. Although still in the early stages, these models hold the potential to revolutionize fields such as entertainment, education, and marketing by enabling the creation of custom video content on demand.

Commercial and Open Source AI Models

Commercial AI Models

Commercial AI models, such as ChatGPT and Gemini, offer robust capabilities backed by ongoing research and development. These models are often part of larger ecosystems that include APIs, tools, and platforms for integrating AI into various applications. Companies like OpenAI, Google, and Meta are leading the charge in making these advanced models available to businesses and developers.

Open Source AI Models

Open source models provide an alternative for those seeking transparency, customization, and cost-effective solutions. Projects like LLaMA and Hugging Face's Transformer library offer access to cutting-edge AI technology, allowing researchers and developers to build upon existing models and contribute to the broader AI community. Open source initiatives foster collaboration and innovation, driving the field forward through collective effort.

AI Applications

As John reaches a cavern filled with glowing fungi, Alpha highlights AI's impact on various industries. The radiant light from the fungi casts an otherworldly glow, creating a surreal atmosphere that mirrors the transformative potential of AI.

Figure 1-5. *John Adventuring into a Cavern of Fungi*

AI revolutionizes healthcare through diagnostics and personalized medicine, "akin to the Voltis' electrical regulation of their bodies," Alpha explains. In healthcare, AI systems analyze vast amounts of medical data to diagnose diseases, predict patient outcomes, and personalize treatment plans. AI-powered tools assist doctors in identifying patterns and anomalies that may be overlooked, leading to more accurate diagnoses and effective treatments.

"In finance, AI enhances trading, fraud detection, and risk management," Alpha continues. Financial institutions leverage AI algorithms to analyze market trends, execute trades at optimal times, and detect fraudulent activities. AI systems can process enormous volumes of financial data in real time, providing insights that inform investment strategies and risk management practices. The application of AI in finance has led to increased efficiency, reduced costs, and improved decision-making.

"Autonomous vehicles powered by AI navigate complex environments, mirroring your journey on Celestor," Alpha adds. Self-driving cars and drones use AI to interpret sensor data, recognize objects, and make real-time decisions. These vehicles navigate through dynamic environments, avoiding obstacles and adapting to changing conditions. The development of autonomous vehicles promises to transform transportation, making it safer, more efficient, and accessible.

The application of AI in various industries has led to significant improvements in efficiency, accuracy, and decision-making. AI systems analyze vast amounts of data, identify patterns, and make predictions, enabling more informed decisions and innovative solutions. In agriculture, AI-powered robots assist in planting, monitoring crops, and harvesting, increasing productivity and sustainability. In manufacturing, AI optimizes production processes, reduces waste, and enhances quality control.

Deep learning techniques, including Convolutional Neural Networks (CNNs) for image recognition and Generative Adversarial Networks (GANs) for content creation, have revolutionized various fields. In healthcare, CNNs analyze medical images to detect diseases such as cancer with remarkable accuracy. GANs generate realistic medical images for training purposes, helping improve diagnostic tools. Meanwhile, reinforcement learning algorithms optimize treatment plans and robotic surgeries.

As John stands in the cavern, surrounded by the glow of the fungi, he feels the weight of AI's potential—a tool to reshape the universe. The transformative power of AI lies in its ability to analyze vast amounts of data, identify patterns, and make predictions, enabling more informed decisions and innovative solutions. The integration of AI into various sectors is driving a new wave of technological advancement, improving lives and creating new opportunities.

The potential of AI to revolutionize industries and enhance human capabilities is immense. The advancements in AI are not only transforming existing processes but also opening up new possibilities for innovation and growth. The impact of AI on healthcare, finance, transportation, agriculture, and manufacturing underscores its versatility and potential to address complex challenges across different domains.

Ethical Considerations and Challenges

Alpha's tone turns serious. "A word of caution: AI systems can perpetuate biases, leading to unfair outcomes. Ensuring fairness and transparency is crucial, much like the Voltis maintaining ecological balance. Privacy and security concerns must be addressed, and sensitive information must be safeguarded, like protecting Celestor's habitat. The ethical considerations surrounding AI are critical to ensuring that its development and deployment are aligned with societal values and principles."

John understands that the responsible use of AI is paramount for the future. Addressing the ethical challenges of AI requires a commitment to fairness, transparency, and accountability, as well as ongoing dialogue and collaboration among stakeholders. Ensuring that AI systems are designed and implemented in ways that promote fairness and avoid bias is a complex challenge. It requires continuous monitoring, evaluation, and the development of best practices. Moreover, protecting user privacy and ensuring data security are paramount to maintaining trust and preventing misuse.

Prospects

As John emerges from the tunnels, Alpha concludes, "AI will drive further advancements in fields like robotics, cognitive computing, and human/computer interaction. Just as the Voltis continuously adapt and innovate, AI promises to shape the future of technology, transforming society. The potential for AI to revolutionize various industries and improve quality of life is immense, but it requires careful planning and ethical considerations." John feels a surge of hope, knowing that AI holds the key to solving the universe's greatest challenges. The future of AI will be defined by its ability to learn, adapt, and innovate, creating new possibilities and addressing complex problems.

Looking ahead, it's clear that AI will continue to play a central role in shaping the digital landscape and driving technological progress. As John continues his journey on Celestor, the insights gained from understanding AI will guide him in harnessing its potential to create a better future.

The advancements in AI technology are not only transforming current industries but also paving the way for new opportunities and innovations. The integration of AI into daily life, from smart homes to personalized healthcare, will enhance the quality of life and create a more connected and intelligent world. The journey of AI, much like John's exploration of Celestor, is filled with potential and promise, ready to unlock the mysteries and possibilities of the future.

Introduction to Next Chapter

Having explored the foundational technologies and their impact on the digital realm, we turn our attention to the next frontier of innovation: Generative AI Solutions for Creativity and Prediction. In the following chapter, we will delve into the revolutionary applications of AI in image generation, text generation, and predictive analytics. These applications demonstrate the creative and predictive capabilities of AI, offering new possibilities for artistic expression, communication, and financial analysis.

Generative AI solutions can revolutionize creative industries like Movie's Studio by enabling the creation of stunning visuals and artworks. The ability of AI to generate coherent and contextually relevant text has significant implications for content creation, customer service, and other applications. Predictive analytics powered by AI offers valuable insights into financial markets, enabling more informed investment decisions.

In the next chapter, we will explore the process of creating generative AI models, the development of natural language processing (NLP) models, and the application of predictive analytics in cryptocurrency markets. The insights gained from these explorations will demonstrate the transformative potential of generative AI solutions for creativity and prediction.

CHAPTER 2

Generative AI Solutions for Creativity and Prediction on Planet Tibara

© Frank Lisitano, John Hickie 2025
F. Lisitano and J. Hickie, *The Evolune Metaverse*, Maker Innovations Series,
https://doi.org/10.1007/979-8-8688-1588-1_2

Introduction to Tibara

The Harsh Environment of Tibara

Figure 2-1. *The planet of Tibara*

John Lee's journey from the electric beauty of Celestor to the volcanic fury of Tibara is more than a change of scenery—it's a descent into a new level of technological challenge. The lessons of Celestor still burn in his memory: Gnos Corporation's true nature as takers who leave devastation in their wake. Yet here he stands on Tibara's corrosive surface, not as their willing servant, but as a survivor forced to adapt.

The assignment to Tibara came without choice. After his reports from Celestor painted Gnos in an unfavorable light, the corporation's response was swift and punitive: exile to their most dangerous extraction site. Officially, John is here to "optimize Evolune harvesting operations." Unofficially, he knows he's been sent to disappear—another expendable contractor lost to Tibara's unforgiving environment.

This chapter explores how John transforms desperate necessity into technological innovation. The AI-driven solutions he develops—image generation, natural language processing, and predictive analytics—aren't academic exercises. They're lifelines coded in desperation, digital weapons forged against corporate abandonment, and tools that might mean the difference between survival and becoming another casualty statistic in Gnos's quarterly reports.

What You Will Learn

Following John's struggle for survival, you'll master the technologies that keep him alive while learning their real-world applications.

Revolutionizing Image Generation with AI

- **Generative Adversarial Networks (GANs):** Master the fundamentals through John's need to create realistic terrain maps when corporate navigation systems fail.

- **Variational Autoencoders (VAEs) and Diffusion Models:** Learn how John uses these for smooth environmental transitions and predictive landscape modeling.

- **Neural Style Transfer:** Discover how converting alien terrain into familiar visual patterns aids human navigation.

- **Practical Implementation:** Use Python, Blender (bpy library), Unreal Engine, and Unity as John does—for survival, not just creativity.

Text Generation and Natural Language Processing (NLP)

- **Natural Language Processing Fundamentals:** Understand how John's AI companions process communication for tactical coordination.

- **Sentiment Analysis and Transformer Models:** Learn how AI soldiers interpret emotional states and respond appropriately to crisis situations.

- **Text-to-Audio Conversion:** Master TensorFlow, Keras, and Google Text-to-Speech API through John's need for clear communication in hostile environments.

Predictive Analytics in Cryptocurrency Markets

- **Market Prediction Systems:** Follow John's development of economic warfare tools to counter Gnos's market manipulation.

- **LSTM Networks for Time Series Forecasting:** Learn through his need to predict Evolune commodity prices for resource optimization.

- **Application Development:** Build robust systems using Flask, TensorFlow, and modern JavaScript as John creates his survival dashboard.

Through John's eyes, you'll see how advanced AI technologies serve both immediate survival needs and long-term resistance against corporate oppression, making complex concepts accessible through desperate necessity.

Setting the Scene: The Harsh Environment of Tibara

Tibara defies every safety protocol in Gnos's handbook—assuming they bothered to write one for a place this hostile. The planet's surface writhes with constant geological upheaval: volcanic eruptions that light the sky in orange fury, earthquakes that reshape the landscape hourly, and magma flows that chart new paths across the terrain with each passing day.

The acidic rain never stops. It's not the gentle precipitation of Earth—this is concentrated malice falling from toxic clouds, eating through standard equipment in hours and exposing the precious Evolune deposits that Gnos covets. Each droplet strips away another layer of John's protective gear, another day from his dwindling supplies.

Breathing means constant vigilance. Tibara's atmosphere chokes with sulfur dioxide and compounds that corrode both machinery and lung tissue. John's environmental suit hisses with the strain of filtering the toxic air, its systems working overtime to keep him alive while Gnos's promised replacement parts remain mysteriously delayed in shipping.

Figure 2-2. *Tibara*

The planet's position in the second level of the Gaia galaxy offers spectacular views of cosmic phenomena—if you can survive long enough to appreciate them. John has more pressing concerns than sightseeing. Every moment on Tibara demands innovation, adaptation, and the kind of technological solutions that corporate bureaucrats back on Earth couldn't imagine in their climate-controlled offices.

Despite its dangers, Tibara has driven advancements in survival technologies and adaptive engineering. The innovations in radiation shielding, atmospheric filtering, and structural engineering that enable human presence here represent the cutting edge of hostile environment adaptation. For John, these aren't academic achievements—they're the difference between life and death.

John Lee's Struggles and Innovations

John Lee faces Tibara's geological nightmare armed with failing corporate equipment and a growing understanding that Gnos expects him to fail. His standard-issue maps became worthless within hours of arrival. Tibara's shifting landscape renders traditional navigation obsolete, and Gnos's satellite uplinks provide data that's outdated before it transmits.

If he's going to survive long enough to extract Evolune—and more importantly, escape this corporate death sentence—he needs allies. Not the kind Gnos would provide, but digital companions loyal to him alone, capable of withstanding Tibara's brutal environment while providing the intelligence and support that corporate headquarters deliberately withholds.

John's mission becomes a dual fight: against Tibara's hostile environment and against Gnos's systematic sabotage. The AI-generated character soldiers he creates aren't corporate assets—they're tools of resistance, designed to protect him from both the planet's natural hazards and the corporation's manufactured neglect.

Using advanced AI technologies, John develops detailed mapping systems that adapt to Tibara's changing terrain, predictive models that anticipate geological events, and communication networks that function despite corporate interference. His encounters with the native Conolophus highlight the need for sophisticated interaction protocols, leveraging NLP and text-to-audio technologies to create meaningful communication where corporate xenobiology departments failed.

Revolutionizing Image Generation with AI

Introduction

When John's corporate-issued terrain scanners provide blurry approximations of a landscape that changes faster than their update cycles, survival demands better solutions. The advent of artificial intelligence has revolutionized image generation far beyond artistic applications—it's become a tool for tactical survival in environments where standard equipment fails.

From stunning 2D tactical displays to intricate 3D companion models, AI-powered techniques enable individuals like John to produce high-quality, adaptive visual content with unprecedented efficiency. This transformation isn't just about creativity—it's about creating tools that can mean the difference between life and death in hostile environments.

Figure 2-3. *AI-Generated Soldiers*

2D Image Generation

John's first breakthrough comes through 2D image generation techniques that convert Tibara's chaotic visual data into comprehensible tactical information. These methods transform raw sensor data into navigable maps, threat assessments, and predictive terrain models.

Generative Adversarial Networks (GANs)

GANs operate on a principle John finds grimly appropriate: two artificial intelligences locked in eternal competition, each trying to outsmart the other. A generator creates images while a discriminator evaluates their authenticity, producing progressively superior outputs through this adversarial process—much like John's own struggle against both Tibara and Gnos.

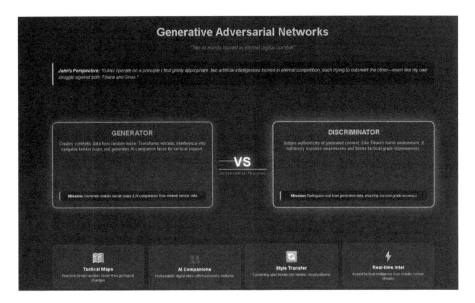

Figure 2-4. *Generative Adversarial Networks*

DCGAN (Deep Convolutional GAN): John implements DCGANs to generate high-resolution topographical maps from his failing scanner data. The convolutional layers excel at processing the spatial relationships in terrain data, creating detailed surface maps that update faster than Tibara's geological changes.

CycleGAN: For converting between different data domains—thermal readings to navigable terrain maps, seismic data to predictive landscape models—CycleGAN proves invaluable. It excels at style transfer without requiring perfectly matched training pairs, crucial when working with incomplete corporate data.

StyleGAN: When creating faces for his AI companions, John needs more than random features. StyleGAN allows fine control over attributes, ensuring his digital allies project the trustworthiness and determination that mirror his own desperate resolve.

Figure 2-5. *AI-Generated Faces*

Variational Autoencoders (VAEs)

While GANs excel at creating distinct images, VAEs provide the smooth interpolations John needs when modeling Tibara's constantly shifting environment. The continuous latent space allows for gradual transitions between terrain states, helping predict how the landscape might evolve.

Beta-VAE: This extension improves the disentanglement of learned representations, making it easier for John to control specific features in his generated terrain models—isolating stable ground from unstable, safe routes from hazardous ones.

Diffusion Models

Perhaps most fitting for Tibara's chaotic nature, diffusion models generate images by gradually removing noise from random inputs. John watches the process with dark amusement—taking pure chaos and slowly revealing order, much like his own survival strategy.

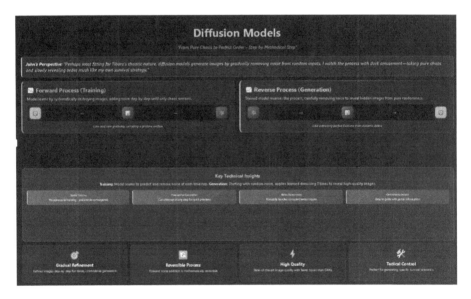

Figure 2-6. *Diffusion Models*

Denoising Diffusion Probabilistic Models (DDPMs): These generate detailed environmental predictions through iterative refinement, starting from the noise of incomplete sensor data and gradually revealing actionable intelligence about Tibara's next geological tantrum.

Neural Style Transfer

John's breakthrough in visual comprehension comes through Neural Style Transfer, which applies familiar visual styles to alien landscapes. This technique makes Tibara's hellish terrain easier for human eyes to interpret and navigate, converting the planet's visual chaos into comprehensible tactical displays.

Fast Neural Style Transfer: Processes real-time sensor feeds, applying learned visual patterns to incoming data streams for immediate tactical assessment.

3D Image Generation

Creating functional AI companions for Tibara requires more than artistic flair—John needs three-dimensional entities capable of independent operation in hostile environments. 3D image generation provides the foundation for digital allies that understand spatial relationships and can navigate complex terrain.

3D Generative Adversarial Networks (3D-GANs)

Like their 2D counterparts, 3D-GANs generate three-dimensional objects using adversarial training but with the added complexity of spatial depth and volume relationships.

Voxel-Based 3D-GANs: These generate John's companions as collections of small cubes (voxels), providing modular designs where damaged components can be easily replaced or modified based on environmental demands.

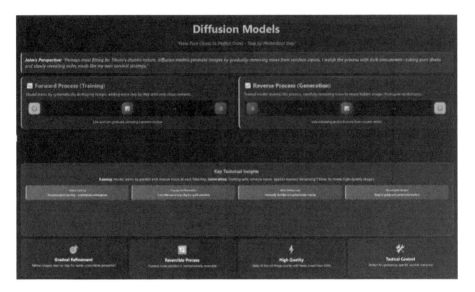

Figure 2-7. *Diffusion Models*

Neural Radiance Fields (NeRF)

For environments where his digital allies need photorealistic appearance—perhaps to fool Gnos surveillance systems—John employs Neural Radiance Fields. These systems model how light interacts with surfaces, producing convincing renderings that can pass casual inspection.

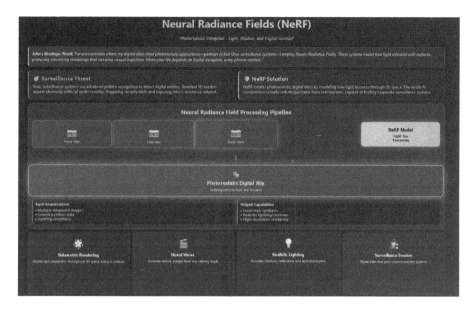

Figure 2-8. *Neural Radiance Fields (NeRF)*

Volumetric Rendering: The continuous representation generates high-quality 3D scenes from sparse inputs, essential when working with limited sensor data in Tibara's interference-heavy environment.

Point Cloud Networks

When computational resources run low—a constant concern with Gnos's deliberate sabotage of his equipment—John relies on Point Cloud Networks. These systems represent 3D models as collections of points in space, dramatically reducing processing requirements while maintaining essential functionality.

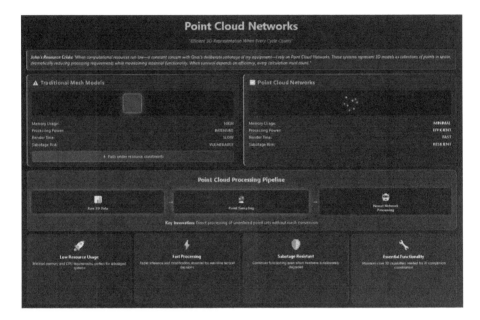

Figure 2-9. *Point Cloud Networks*

PointNet: Processes point clouds directly, allowing John's AI companions to modify their own representations in real time as they adapt to changing conditions or repair damage from Tibara's hostile environment.

Mesh-Based Models

For maximum structural integrity in his digital soldiers, John uses mesh-based architectures. These models represent objects through interconnected vertices and edges, creating robust frameworks that maintain functionality even when portions are corrupted.

Pixel2Mesh: Generates 3D mesh models from single 2D images, allowing John to quickly create backup personalities or adapt existing designs when his primary companions are damaged or destroyed.

Integration and Applications

John's integration of these AI models reflects his desperate circumstances and limited resources. Each technique serves multiple purposes: terrain mapping aids navigation, companion generation provides tactical support, and style transfer makes alien environments comprehensible to human perception.

The applications extend beyond immediate survival. By creating detailed 3D models of Tibara's underground networks, John builds a comprehensive database that could prove valuable for future resistance operations. His AI-generated maps and companions represent more than survival tools—they're the foundation of a digital rebellion against corporate control.

Conclusion

Through necessity and innovation, John transforms AI image generation from academic curiosity into survival essential. The diverse array of models—GANs, VAEs, diffusion systems, and neural networks—enable creation of both 2D tactical displays and 3D operational assets with remarkable quality and adaptability.

These technologies will expand beyond their current applications as John's resistance network grows, driving innovation across multiple survival domains and redefining the relationship between individual resourcefulness and corporate power.

Creating AI-Generated 3D Characters

As John ventures deeper into Tibara's underground tunnel systems, the need for reliable allies becomes undeniable. The isolation weighs heavily, but more practically, he needs assistance with tasks that exceed his individual capabilities. These allies must be AI-generated character soldiers—digital beings designed to withstand Tibara's harsh environment while maintaining absolute loyalty to John rather than corporate interests.

Figure 2-10. *AI-Generated Character Soldiers*

The creation process represents more than technical achievement; it's John's rejection of corporate dependency. Using advanced generative AI technologies, he embarks on building a digital resistance network that operates independently of Gnos oversight.

Data Collection for 3D

The foundation of any successful AI model lies in the quality and diversity of its training data. For John, this becomes an exercise in resourcefulness—gathering comprehensive datasets while working with deliberately limited corporate resources.

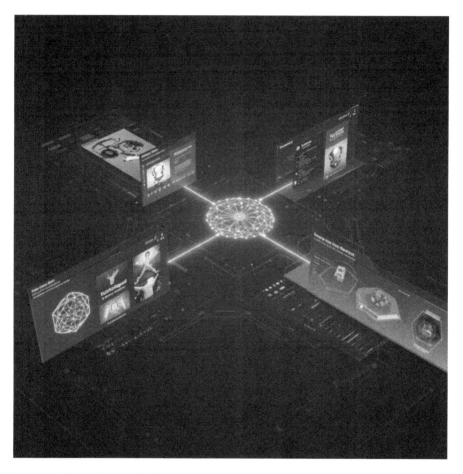

Figure 2-11. *Data Collection*

Sources of Data

John's approach to data collection reflects his isolated circumstances and mistrust of corporate sources.

> **3D Model Repositories:** Despite network restrictions, John accesses public repositories like TurboSquid, CGTrader, and Sketchfab. These provide diverse 3D models including creatures and humanoid forms that serve as templates for his resistance soldiers.

> **Open Source Libraries:** Libraries like Blender Open Data offer valuable assets free from corporate tracking. John prioritizes these sources to maintain operational security while building his AI companions.

> **Custom Environmental Scans:** Using makeshift 3D scanning equipment, John creates custom models by scanning Tibara's native life forms and converting them into digital meshes. This provides unique adaptations specifically suited to the planet's conditions.

Data Preparation

Raw data requires extensive preprocessing to ensure consistency and combat readiness. John's approach prioritizes efficiency and reliability.

> **Normalization:** Standardizing model size, orientation, and scale ensures uniformity across his digital army. Each companion must meet specific operational parameters for equipment compatibility and tactical coordination.

Cleaning: Removing defects and errors becomes critical when these models will operate in life-threatening situations. John can't afford AI companions that malfunction during crisis moments.

Augmentation: Applying transformations such as rotations, scaling, and lighting variations increases dataset diversity while simulating the various conditions his companions might encounter on Tibara.

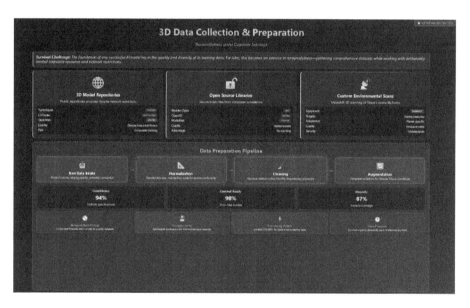

Figure 2-12. *3D Data Collection and Preparation*

Model Training with TensorFlow and Keras

John's GAN training takes place in the depths of Tibara's underground installations, where geothermal vents provide the power that Gnos's generators increasingly fail to deliver. TensorFlow and Keras become his weapons of choice—not because they're popular, but because they're reliable enough to function on hardware that's slowly dissolving in acidic air.

TensorFlow

TensorFlow provides the comprehensive platform John needs for building and deploying machine learning models under extreme conditions. Its robustness proves essential when corporate sabotage threatens to corrupt his work at any moment.

Key Features of TensorFlow

Dataflow Graphs: Represent computations efficiently, crucial when processing power is limited and every calculation must count toward survival.

Eager Execution: Enables easier debugging and prototyping—essential when John must iterate quickly to address immediate threats.

Automatic Differentiation: Critical for training neural networks when manual calculation isn't feasible under time pressure.

Scalability: Supports distributed computing across multiple devices, allowing John to utilize whatever functioning hardware remains available.

Model Deployment: Multiple deployment options ensure his AI companions can operate across different systems and platforms.

Extensive Ecosystem: Tools like TensorBoard help John monitor training progress and optimize performance despite equipment limitations.

Basic Workflow in TensorFlow

John's implementation focuses on survival-oriented AI development.

```
import tensorflow as tf

# Building companions who understand survival, not
corporate loyalty
class SurvivalCompanion(tf.Module):
    def __init__(self):
        # Core attributes focused on protection, not profit
        self.loyalty = tf.Variable(1.0)  # Maximum
        loyalty to John
        self.corporate_compliance = tf.Variable(0.0)  # Zero
        compliance with Gnos

    def __call__(self, threat_assessment):
        # Responses prioritize John's survival over mission
        objectives
        return self.loyalty * threat_assessment + self.
        corporate_compliance

companion = SurvivalCompanion()

def calculate_survival_priority(actual_threat, companion_
response):
    return tf.reduce_mean(tf.square(actual_threat - companion_
    response))

def training_step(companion, threat_data, optimal_responses,
learning_rate):
    with tf.GradientTape() as tape:
        predictions = companion(threat_data)
        current_loss = calculate_survival_priority(optimal_
        responses, predictions)
```

```
        gradients = tape.gradient(current_loss, [companion.
        loyalty])
        # Only adjust loyalty upward - these companions serve
        John alone
        companion.loyalty.assign_add(learning_rate *
        tf.abs(gradients[0]))

# Training data based on Tibara's actual threats
threat_inputs = tf.constant([0.2, 0.6, 0.9, 1.0])  # Escalating
danger levels
optimal_outputs = tf.constant([0.3, 0.7, 1.0, 1.0])  # Required
response intensities

# Training loop - each epoch builds more reliable allies
for epoch in range(200):
    training_step(companion, threat_inputs, optimal_outputs,
    learning_rate=0.02)
    if epoch % 50 == 0:
        current_loss = calculate_survival_priority(optimal_
        outputs, companion(threat_inputs))
        print(f"Epoch {epoch}: Loyalty Level = {companion.
        loyalty.numpy():.3f}")

print(f"Final companion loyalty: {companion.loyalty.
numpy():.3f}")
```

Keras

Keras provides the high-level abstraction John needs when time is critical and Tibara's environment threatens to corrupt his hardware before training completes. Its user-friendly interface allows rapid development of survival-critical systems.

Key Features of Keras

User-Friendly: Simple and intuitive, essential when working under extreme stress with limited debugging time.

Modularity: Models built by connecting standalone modules allow John to modify individual components without rebuilding entire systems.

Extensibility: Easy customization of layers and functions enables adaptation to Tibara's unique requirements.

Integration with TensorFlow: Tight integration provides access to TensorFlow's robust back end while maintaining development speed.

Pretrained Models: Collection of existing models for transfer learning, allowing John to build on proven architectures rather than starting from scratch.

GAN Implementation with Keras

John's GAN implementation prioritizes survival-ready companions over aesthetic appeal.

```
import tensorflow as tf
from tensorflow.keras import layers
import numpy as np

# Generator Model - Creates digital soldiers optimized for
Tibara survival
def create_soldier_generator():
    model = tf.keras.Sequential([
        layers.Dense(128, activation='relu', input_dim=100),
        layers.BatchNormalization(),
```

```python
        layers.Dense(256, activation='relu'),
        layers.BatchNormalization(),
        layers.Dense(512, activation='relu'),
        layers.BatchNormalization(),
        layers.Dense(1024, activation='relu'),
        layers.BatchNormalization(),
        layers.Dense(2048, activation='relu'),
        # Final layers shape output for 3D soldier models
        layers.Dense(3072, activation='tanh'),
        layers.Reshape((32, 32, 3))
    ])
    return model

# Discriminator Model - Ensures soldiers meet survival
standards
def create_survival_discriminator():
    model = tf.keras.Sequential([
        layers.Flatten(input_shape=(32, 32, 3)),
        layers.Dense(1024, activation='relu'),
        layers.Dense(512, activation='relu'),
        layers.Dense(256, activation='relu'),
        # Final layer: 1 = suitable for Tibara conditions, 0 =
        inadequate
        layers.Dense(1, activation='sigmoid')
    ])
    return model

# Compile models with aggressive optimization for limited
resources
generator = create_soldier_generator()
discriminator = create_survival_discriminator()
```

```
discriminator.compile(optimizer='adam', loss='binary_
crossentropy')
discriminator.trainable = False

# Combined GAN focuses on generating reliable companions
gan_input = layers.Input(shape=(100,))
gan_output = discriminator(generator(gan_input))
gan = tf.keras.models.Model(gan_input, gan_output)
gan.compile(optimizer='adam', loss='binary_crossentropy')

# Training function optimized for survival-ready soldiers
def train_survival_gan(epochs, batch_size, survival_standards):
    for epoch in range(epochs):
        # Generate candidate soldiers from random noise
        noise = np.random.normal(0, 1, (batch_size, 100))
        synthetic_soldiers = generator.predict(noise,
        verbose=0)

        # Compare against proven survival-capable designs
        proven_designs = survival_standards[np.random.
        randint(0, survival_standards.shape[0], batch_size)]

        combined_designs = np.concatenate([proven_designs,
        synthetic_soldiers])
        # Label: 1 = proven survivor, 0 = untested generation
        labels = np.concatenate([np.ones((batch_size, 1)),
        np.zeros((batch_size, 1))])

        # Train discriminator to recognize survival-
        capable designs
        d_loss = discriminator.train_on_batch(combined_
        designs, labels)
```

```
    # Train generator to create soldiers that fool the
    discriminator
    noise = np.random.normal(0, 1, (batch_size, 100))
    g_loss = gan.train_on_batch(noise, np.ones((batch_
    size, 1)))

    if epoch % 100 == 0:
        print(f"Epoch {epoch}/{epochs} - Discriminator
        Loss: {d_loss:.4f} - Generator Loss: {g_loss:.4f}")
        print(f"Training companions for survival scenario
        {epoch//100 + 1}")
print("GAN architecture ready for soldier generation")
print("Training requires survival-proven 3D model dataset")
```

3D Model Generation with Blender

With trained models producing viable designs, John uses Blender's Python API to manifest his AI companions in three-dimensional form. These aren't artistic exercises—they're tools for survival manufactured in digital space.

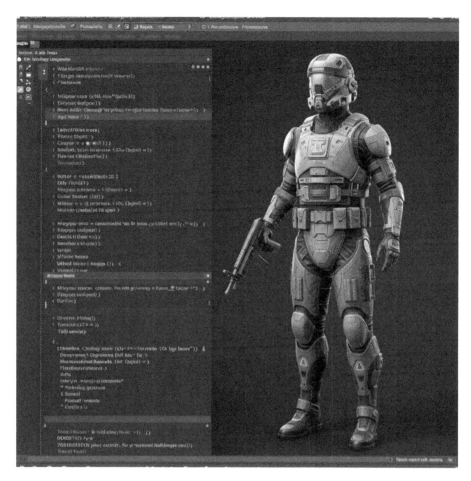

Figure 2-13. *Blender Python API*

Setting Up Blender

John's installation process reflects his resource constraints and security concerns.

```
pip install bpy
```

Generating 3D Characters

The following script generates tactical companions optimized for Tibara's harsh environment.

```
import bpy
import random
import bmesh

def generate_tactical_companion():
    # Clear workspace of corporate-issued models
    bpy.ops.object.select_all(action='DESELECT')
    bpy.ops.object.select_by_type(type='MESH')
    bpy.ops.object.delete()

    # Create base form optimized for Tibara conditions
    bpy.ops.mesh.primitive_uv_sphere_add(segments=48, ring_
    count=24, radius=1.2)
    companion = bpy.context.active_object
    companion.name = "TibaraSurvivor"

    # Add subdivision for detail while maintaining performance
    modifier = companion.modifiers.new(name="DetailLevel",
    type='SUBSURF')
    modifier.levels = 2
    bpy.ops.object.modifier_apply(modifier="DetailLevel")

    # Apply environmental adaptations based on Tibara analysis
    adaptation_scale = (
        random.uniform(0.9, 1.3),  # Width for
        terrain navigation
        random.uniform(0.8, 1.2),  # Height variation for acid
        rain protection
```

```
        random.uniform(0.9, 1.4)    # Depth variation for
        stability
    )
    companion.scale = adaptation_scale

    # Create protective material resistant to acid rain
    material = bpy.data.materials.new(name="TibaraResistant")
    companion.data.materials.append(material)
    material.use_nodes = True

    # Set material properties for Tibara survival (darker
    colors, higher durability)
    bsdf = material.node_tree.nodes["Principled BSDF"]
    bsdf.inputs['Base Color'].default_value = (
        random.uniform(0.1, 0.4),  # Darker base for heat
        resistance
        random.uniform(0.1, 0.3),  # Reduced green for
        camouflage
        random.uniform(0.2, 0.5),  # Controlled blue for
        distinction
        1.0
    )
    bsdf.inputs['Roughness'].default_value = 0.8  # High
    roughness for acid resistance
    bsdf.inputs['Metallic'].default_value = 0.3    # Some
    metallic properties for durability

    print(f"Generated tactical companion: {companion.name}")
    print(f"Adaptations: Scale {adaptation_scale}")
    return companion

# Generate a squad of survival companions
squad_size = 5
```

```
for i in range(squad_size):
    companion = generate_tactical_companion()
    print(f"Companion {i+1} ready for deployment")

print("Tactical squad generation complete")
```

Advanced Customization and Animation

When standard configurations aren't enough for Tibara's extreme conditions, John develops advanced customization techniques that push the boundaries of what's possible with limited resources.

Figure 2-14. *Advanced Customization*

Facial Recognition

Face recognition libraries help John create companions with distinct, memorable features—crucial when distinguishing allies in Tibara's chaotic environment where misidentification could prove fatal.

```
# Conceptual facial customization for AI companions
import bpy
# import face_recognition  # Would be imported in actual
implementation

def generate_distinctive_companion(character_
traits="determined"):
    # Clear workspace for new companion generation
    bpy.ops.object.select_all(action='DESELECT')
    bpy.ops.object.select_by_type(type='MESH')
    bpy.ops.object.delete()

    # Create base head form with higher resolution for
    facial detail
    bpy.ops.mesh.primitive_uv_sphere_add(segments=64, ring_
    count=32, radius=0.6)
    head = bpy.context.active_object
    head.name = f"Companion_{character_traits}"

    # Enter edit mode for facial feature modification
    bpy.context.view_layer.objects.active = head
    bpy.ops.object.mode_set(mode='EDIT')

    # Modify features to reflect survival-focused
    characteristics
    bpy.ops.object.mode_set(mode='OBJECT')
```

```python
    # Apply material that reflects companion's tactical role
    material = bpy.data.materials.new(name=f"Trait_{character_
    traits}")
    head.data.materials.append(material)
    material.use_nodes = True

    # Color coding for quick identification in hostile
    conditions
    trait_colors = {
        "determined": (0.2, 0.4, 0.6, 1.0),  # Steady blue
        "aggressive": (0.6, 0.2, 0.2, 1.0),  # Warning red
        "analytical": (0.3, 0.6, 0.3, 1.0),  #
        Calculating green
        "protective": (0.5, 0.3, 0.6, 1.0)   # Loyal purple
    }

    color = trait_colors.get(character_traits, (0.5, 0.5,
    0.5, 1.0))
    material.node_tree.nodes["Principled BSDF"].inputs['Base
    Color'].default_value = color

    print(f"Generated {character_traits} companion with
    distinctive features")
    return head

# Create companions with specific survival roles
roles = ["determined", "aggressive", "analytical",
"protective"]
for role in roles:
    companion = generate_distinctive_companion(role)
    print(f"{role.capitalize()} companion ready for Tibara
    deployment")
```

Motion Capture Integration

For companions that need to navigate Tibara's complex terrain with human-like agility, John integrates motion capture data to provide realistic movement patterns adapted to hostile environmental conditions.

```
import bpy

def integrate_survival_animations():
    # Import motion capture data optimized for
    hazardous terrain
    # In production: bpy.ops.import_anim.bvh(filepath='tibara_
    survival_motions.bvh')

    # Apply animation to selected tactical companion
    selected_companion = bpy.context.selected_objects[0] if
    bpy.context.selected_objects else None
    if selected_companion:
        bpy.context.view_layer.objects.active = selected_
        companion

        # Bake survival movement patterns
        # bpy.ops.nla.bake(frame_start=1, frame_end=250,
        visual_keying=True,
        #                      clear_constraints=True, clear_
                                 parents=True, use_current_
                                 action=True)

        print(f"Survival animations applied to {selected_
        companion.name}")

        # Save companion with integrated movement capabilities
        # bpy.ops.wm.save_as_mainfile(filepath=f"tactical_
        {selected_companion.name}.blend")
```

```
    else:
        print("No companion selected for animation
         integration")
```

```
# Note: This function would be called after companion
generation
print("Motion capture integration system ready")
print("Requires survival-specific motion data for optimal
performance")
```

Text Generation and Natural Language Processing

Effective communication with AI allies becomes paramount when isolation and corporate sabotage threaten John's mission on Tibara. Traditional communication systems fail under the planet's electromagnetic interference, making sophisticated Natural Language Processing essential for survival.

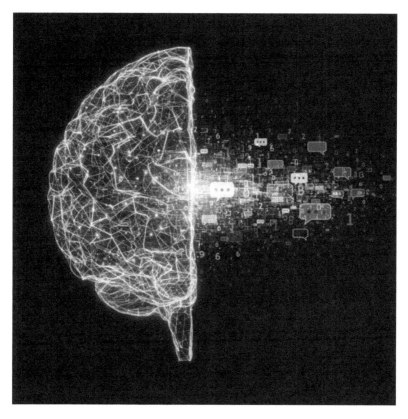

Figure 2-15. *NLP*

This section explores how John develops NLP systems that enable his AI soldiers to understand context, interpret intentions, and respond appropriately to crisis situations.

Introduction to Natural Language Processing (NLP)

For John, NLP represents more than academic interest—it's the foundation of trust between him and his digital allies. In situations where miscommunication could prove fatal, his AI companions must understand not just words, but intentions, emotions, and the subtle context that defines the difference between a routine status check and an emergency alert.

NLP focuses on enabling computers to interact with humans through natural language, but John's implementation prioritizes survival-critical communication over conversational sophistication.

Key Components of NLP

John's NLP systems incorporate essential components optimized for tactical communication.

> **Tokenization:** Breaking text into manageable units (words, phrases) enables rapid parsing of urgent commands and status reports. When seconds matter, efficient tokenization can mean the difference between successful evacuation and catastrophic delay.

> **Part-of-Speech Tagging:** Identifying grammatical components helps AI companions understand the urgency and priority embedded in John's communications. Command verbs receive immediate attention while descriptive phrases provide context.

> **Named Entity Recognition (NER):** Detecting specific locations, threats, and resources allows AI soldiers to respond appropriately to environmental references. When John mentions "sector seven" or "acid rain," his companions understand the geographical and tactical implications.

Sentiment Analysis: Determining emotional tone becomes critical when John's stress levels indicate escalating danger. His AI allies adjust their response protocols based on detected urgency and emotional state.

Machine Translation: While not immediately relevant for John's English communications, translation capabilities prove valuable when interfacing with Gnos systems or Conolophus communications.

Text Summarization: Condensing lengthy sensor reports and status updates into actionable intelligence allows rapid decision-making under pressure.

Question Answering: Enabling AI companions to provide specific information in response to John's queries supports tactical planning and threat assessment.

Text Generation: Creating Human-Like Text

John's text generation systems focus on creating contextually appropriate responses that acknowledge the reality of his situation while maintaining morale and tactical effectiveness.

Techniques for Text Generation

Rule-Based Systems: John implements predefined response templates for common scenarios— equipment failure, environmental hazards, and tactical updates. These provide reliable, immediate responses when processing power is limited.

Statistical Methods: Probabilistic models like n-grams help generate contextually appropriate responses based on communication patterns, ensuring AI companions respond in familiar, predictable ways that build trust.

Neural Networks: RNNs and LSTMs capture complex communication patterns, enabling AI soldiers to understand the relationship between current situations and past experiences, generating responses that reflect learning and adaptation.

Transformers: Advanced models like GPT variants handle long-range dependencies in conversation, allowing AI companions to maintain context across extended tactical discussions and remember important details from earlier communications.

Implementing Text Generation on Tibara

John's implementation prioritizes reliability and tactical relevance over conversational sophistication. His AI companions generate text that serves specific survival functions.

- **Status Reports:** Clear, concise updates on equipment condition, environmental hazards, and resource levels

- **Tactical Recommendations:** Suggestions based on current conditions and learned experience

- **Emergency Alerts:** Urgent communications that cut through normal conversation to deliver critical information

- **Morale Support:** Contextually appropriate encouragement that acknowledges danger while maintaining determination

Text-to-Audio Conversion

When visual communication systems fail or when John needs hands-free operation during complex tasks, text-to-audio conversion becomes essential. Google's Text-to-Speech API provides the foundation for creating clear, reliable audio communication.

Advanced Natural Language Processing Techniques

John's advanced NLP implementations go beyond basic communication to provide psychological support and tactical intelligence that enhance survival prospects.

Sentiment Analysis

Understanding emotional undertones in communication becomes critical when isolation and stress threaten decision-making capabilities. John's sentiment analysis systems monitor both his own communications and any external signals that breach Tibara's interference.

How Sentiment Analysis Works

The system analyzes text for emotional indicators—word choice, sentence structure, punctuation patterns—that reveal underlying stress levels, confidence, and urgency. This information guides AI companion responses and triggers appropriate support protocols.

Implementing Sentiment Analysis

```python
from textblob import TextBlob

def analyze_survival_communication(message):
    """Analyze communication for emotional state and threat
    level"""
    analysis = TextBlob(message)
    sentiment = analysis.sentiment.polarity

    # Interpret sentiment in survival context
    if sentiment < -0.6:
        emotional_state = "critical_stress"
        response_protocol = "immediate_support"
    elif sentiment < -0.2:
        emotional_state = "elevated_concern"
        response_protocol = "enhanced_monitoring"
    elif sentiment > 0.4:
        emotional_state = "positive_momentum"
        response_protocol = "maintain_course"
    else:
        emotional_state = "stable"
        response_protocol = "standard_operations"

    return {
        'sentiment_score': sentiment,
        'emotional_state': emotional_state,
        'recommended_response': response_protocol,
        'confidence': abs(sentiment)
    }

def generate_appropriate_response(input_message):
    """Generate contextually appropriate survival responses"""
    analysis = analyze_survival_communication(input_message)
```

```python
    responses = {
        'critical_stress': "I understand the pressure. Let's
        focus on immediate priorities and take this step
        by step.",
        'elevated_concern': "Your concerns are valid. I'm
        monitoring the situation and ready to adapt our
        approach.",
        'positive_momentum': "Excellent progress. Let's
        maintain this momentum while staying alert to changing
        conditions.",
        'stable': "Acknowledged. Continuing with current
        operational parameters."
    }

    base_response = responses[analysis['emotional_state']]

    # Add tactical context based on Tibara conditions
    if "acid" in input_message.lower():
        base_response += " Acid protection protocols remain
        active."
    elif "seismic" in input_message.lower() or "earthquake" in
    input_message.lower():
        base_response += " Seismic monitoring systems are
        operational."
    elif "evolune" in input_message.lower():
        base_response += " Evolune extraction procedures are
        optimized for current conditions."

    return base_response

# Test survival communication analysis
test_communications = [
    "I'm worried about the increasing acid rain intensity",
    "Great work on the Evolune extraction today",
```

```
    "The seismic readings are extremely concerning",
    "Equipment status is normal, continuing operations"
]

for msg in test_communications:
    analysis = analyze_survival_communication(msg)
    response = generate_appropriate_response(msg)
    print(f"Input: '{msg}'")
    print(f"Analysis: {analysis['emotional_state']}
    (confidence: {analysis['confidence']:.2f})")
    print(f"Response: '{response}'")
    print("-" * 50)
```

Adjusting Responses Based on Sentiment

John's AI companions modify their communication style based on detected sentiment.

- **High Stress:** Short, direct responses with immediate action items

- **Normal Operations:** Standard tactical communication with appropriate detail

- **Positive Momentum:** Encouraging responses that maintain morale while preserving vigilance

- **Uncertainty:** Clarifying questions and additional information to support decision-making

Context-Aware Responses

Beyond sentiment analysis, John's AI companions maintain contextual awareness across extended conversations, remembering important details and adapting responses based on evolving situations.

Using Transformer Models

Transformer architectures enable AI companions to maintain conversation context across extended tactical discussions while generating responses that reflect understanding of both immediate circumstances and longer-term objectives.

Implementing Context-Aware Responses

```
# Conceptual implementation - requires powerful
transformer models
from transformers import pipeline

def produce_contextual_reply(input_text, conversation_
history=""):
    """Generate responses that consider full conversation
    context"""
    # In production, this would use trained models like GPT
    variants
    # optimized for survival and tactical communication

    # Analyze input for tactical keywords and urgency
    indicators
    tactical_keywords = ["emergency", "malfunction",
    "evacuation", "threat", "secure"]
    urgency_indicators = ["immediate", "urgent", "critical",
    "now", "quickly"]

    is_tactical = any(keyword in input_text.lower() for keyword
    in tactical_keywords)
    is_urgent = any(indicator in input_text.lower() for
    indicator in urgency_indicators)
```

```
    if is_urgent and is_tactical:
        response_style = "immediate_action"
        base_response = f"Acknowledged urgent tactical
        input: {input_text}. Implementing immediate response
        protocols."
    elif is_tactical:
        response_style = "tactical_standard"
        base_response = f"Processing tactical communication:
        {input_text}. Evaluating options and resources."
    else:
        response_style = "standard_operation"
        base_response = f"Understood: {input_text}. Continuing
        with current objectives."

    # Add contextual elements based on conversation history
    if "equipment" in conversation_history.lower() and
    "failure" in input_text.lower():
        base_response += " Cross-referencing with previous
        equipment status reports."

    if "evolune" in conversation_history.lower() and
    "extraction" in input_text.lower():
        base_response += " Coordinating with ongoing extraction
        operations."

    return base_response

# Example contextual conversation
conversation_context = "Previous discussion about equipment
durability concerns and acid rain damage."
user_input = "Equipment malfunction detected in sector three"

response = produce_contextual_reply(user_input, conversation_
context)
```

```
print(f"Context: {conversation_context}")
print(f"Input: {user_input}")
print(f"Response: {response}")
```

Enhancing Contextual Understanding

John's AI companions improve their contextual understanding through

- **Memory Systems:** Storing important conversation details for future reference

- **Situation Awareness:** Correlating communications with environmental sensors and tactical status

- **Learning Algorithms:** Adapting response patterns based on successful vs. unsuccessful communication outcomes

- **Priority Hierarchies:** Understanding which information requires immediate attention vs. background processing

Combining Sentiment Analysis and Context-Aware Responses

The integration of sentiment analysis with contextual awareness creates AI companions capable of sophisticated communication that adapts to both emotional undertones and situational requirements.

When John communicates with high stress about equipment failure, his AI companions

1. Detect the emotional urgency through sentiment analysis.

2. Recognize the tactical importance through contextual understanding.

85

3. Generate responses that address immediate concerns while maintaining operational awareness.

4. Adjust future communications based on the success of their intervention.

Applications of NLP and Text Generation on Tibara

John's NLP systems serve multiple survival functions:

> **Crisis Communication:** Rapid parsing and response to emergency situations
>
> **Equipment Monitoring:** Natural language interfaces for complex system diagnostics
>
> **Environmental Analysis:** Converting sensor data into comprehensible threat assessments
>
> **Tactical Planning:** Collaborative discussion of strategies and alternatives
>
> **Psychological Support:** Maintaining morale and mental health during extended isolation

Integrating Text Generation with AI Soldiers

The AI companions John creates incorporate sophisticated text generation capabilities that enable them to

- Provide clear status reports on their operational condition.

- Offer tactical recommendations based on environmental analysis.

- Request clarification when communications are ambiguous.

- Generate detailed logs of activities and observations.

- Communicate potential problems before they become critical failures.

Text-to-Audio Conversion for Communication

When visual interfaces fail or when John needs hands-free operation, text-to-audio conversion ensures continued communication with his AI allies.

Importance of Text-to-Audio Conversion

In Tibara's hostile environment, visual displays can be obscured by volcanic ash, damaged by acid rain, or rendered useless by equipment failure. Audio communication provides essential backup, allowing John to maintain contact with his AI companions even when visual systems are compromised.

Step-by-Step Guide for Text-to-Audio Conversion

John's implementation uses Google's Text-to-Speech API configured for maximum clarity in hostile environments.

```
from google.cloud import texttospeech

def synthesize_survival_communication(message, urgency_
level="normal"):
    # Initialize TTS client with authentication
    tts_client = texttospeech.TextToSpeechClient()
```

```python
# Adjust message delivery based on urgency
if urgency_level == "critical":
    message = f"URGENT: {message}"
    speech_rate = 1.2  # Faster delivery for emergencies
elif urgency_level == "caution":
    message = f"Caution advised: {message}"
    speech_rate = 0.9  # Slower for important details
else:
    speech_rate = 1.0  # Normal rate for standard
    communication

# Configure text input
text_input = texttospeech.SynthesisInput(text=message)

# Select voice optimized for harsh environments
voice_config = texttospeech.VoiceSelectionParams(
    language_code="en-US",
    ssml_gender=texttospeech.SsmlVoiceGender.NEUTRAL,
    name="en-US-Standard-J"  # Clear articulation for noisy
    environments
)

# Audio configuration for maximum clarity
audio_config = texttospeech.AudioConfig(
    audio_encoding=texttospeech.AudioEncoding.MP3,
    speaking_rate=speech_rate,
    pitch=0.0,  # Neutral pitch for better transmission
    volume_gain_db=2.0  # Slightly amplified for hostile
    conditions
)
```

```python
    # Generate speech
    response = tts_client.synthesize_speech(
        input=text_input,
        voice=voice_config,
        audio_config=audio_config
    )

    # Save with descriptive filename for quick identification
    filename = f"survival_msg_{urgency_level}_
    {len(message)}.mp3"
    with open(filename, "wb") as audio_file:
        audio_file.write(response.audio_content)

    print(f'Survival communication saved: "{filename}"')
    print(f'Message: "{message}"')
    return filename

# Generate critical communications for Tibara scenarios
critical_messages = [
    ("Seismic activity detected. Recommend immediate
    relocation.", "critical"),
    ("Acid rain intensity increasing. Shelter protocols
    activated.", "caution"),
    ("Evolune deposit located. Proceeding with extraction.",
    "normal"),
    ("Equipment failure detected. Initiating backup systems.",
    "critical")
]

for message, urgency in critical_messages:
    synthesize_survival_communication(message, urgency)

print("Emergency communication system ready for deployment")
```

Advanced Features and Future Enhancements

John's text-to-audio system includes advanced features designed for survival scenarios:

- **Environmental Adaptation:** Audio output adjusts to ambient noise levels.

- **Language Switching:** Support for multiple languages when communicating with diverse life forms.

- **Emotion Synthesis:** Voice tone reflects the emotional content of messages.

- **Compression Optimization:** Audio files optimized for transmission through interference.

Summary

John's Natural Language Processing and text generation systems represent more than technological achievement—they're lifelines that enable sophisticated communication under extreme conditions. Through sentiment analysis, contextual awareness, and reliable text-to-audio conversion, his AI companions provide the communication infrastructure necessary for survival on Tibara.

These systems demonstrate how advanced NLP technologies can be adapted for critical applications beyond traditional computing environments, providing essential capabilities when standard communication methods fail.

Predictive Analytics in Cryptocurrency Markets

Gnos Corporation didn't send John to Tibara merely to extract Evolune—they sent him to fail while generating profits from his inevitable demise. The intergalactic cryptocurrency markets that govern Evolune trading operate with the same volatile unpredictability as Tibara's geological activity. If John is going to fund his survival and eventual escape, he needs predictive analytics systems capable of detecting market manipulation and identifying profitable trading opportunities.

Developing an App for Predictive Analytics

John's approach to market prediction serves dual purposes: optimizing resource allocation for maximum survival benefit while developing economic warfare capabilities to counter Gnos's market manipulation tactics.

Understanding the Market Dynamics

The Evolune cryptocurrency market reflects the complex interplay between legitimate supply and demand factors and deliberate corporate manipulation. John's predictive models must account for

- **Geological Events:** Tibara's seismic activity affects extraction rates and market prices.

- **Corporate Interference:** Gnos's trading algorithms create artificial price movements.

- **Supply Chain Disruptions:** Equipment failures and communication blackouts impact availability.

- **Regulatory Changes:** Intergalactic commerce laws affect trading parameters.

91

Data Collection and Preparation

John's data collection strategy reflects his limited resources and need for operational security. He gathers market information through multiple channels while avoiding detection by corporate monitoring systems.

Leveraging Machine Learning Algorithms

Long Short-Term Memory (LSTM) networks prove ideal for cryptocurrency prediction because they can identify patterns across extended time periods while adapting to sudden market changes—essential when corporate manipulation can trigger instant price swings.

Model Training and Validation

John's LSTM implementation focuses on survival-critical accuracy rather than maximum profit optimization.

```
import pandas as pd
import numpy as np
from sklearn.preprocessing import MinMaxScaler
from keras.models import Sequential
from keras.layers import LSTM, Dense, Dropout
import matplotlib.pyplot as plt

# Simulate Evolune energy coin market data (in real scenario,
this would be live data)
def generate_market_simulation(days=1000):
    """Generate realistic cryptocurrency market data for
    Evolune coins"""
    np.random.seed(42)  # For reproducible results

    # Base trend with corporate manipulation patterns
    base_trend = np.linspace(100, 400, days)
```

```python
# Add corporate manipulation spikes (Gnos buying/selling
patterns)
manipulation_points = np.random.choice(days, size=days//20,
replace=False)
manipulation_effect = np.zeros(days)

for point in manipulation_points:
    # Simulate sudden price movements from
    corporate trading
    manipulation_strength = np.random.uniform(-50, 80)
    decay_length = np.random.randint(5, 15)

    for i in range(decay_length):
        if point + i < days:
            manipulation_effect[point + i] = manipulation_
            strength * np.exp(-i/5)

# Add market volatility and random noise
volatility = np.random.randn(days) * 15
seasonal_pattern = 10 * np.sin(np.arange(days) * 2 *
np.pi / 365)

# Combine all factors
final_prices = base_trend + manipulation_effect +
volatility + seasonal_pattern

# Ensure no negative prices
final_prices = np.maximum(final_prices, 10)

# Create DataFrame with realistic market data structure
market_data = pd.DataFrame({
    'timestamp': pd.date_range('2023-01-01', periods=days,
    freq='D'),
    'close': final_prices,
```

```python
        'high': final_prices * np.random.uniform(1.01,
        1.08, days),
        'low': final_prices * np.random.uniform(0.92,
        0.99, days),
        'volume': np.random.randint(1000, 50000, days),
        'evolune_extraction_rate': np.random.uniform(0.1,
        2.0, days)
    })

    return market_data

# Generate market data for analysis
market_data = generate_market_simulation(1000)
print("Market data simulation complete")
print(f"Price range: ${market_data['close'].min():.2f} -
${market_data['close'].max():.2f}")

# Prepare data for LSTM model training
def prepare_lstm_data(data, time_steps=60):
    """Prepare time series data for LSTM training"""
    prices = data['close'].values.reshape(-1, 1)

    # Normalize data for better LSTM performance
    scaler = MinMaxScaler(feature_range=(0, 1))
    normalized_prices = scaler.fit_transform(prices)

    # Create sequences for LSTM training
    X, y = [], []
    for i in range(time_steps, len(normalized_prices)):
        X.append(normalized_prices[i-time_steps:i, 0])
        y.append(normalized_prices[i, 0])

    X, y = np.array(X), np.array(y)
```

```python
    # Split into training and testing sets
    train_size = int(len(X) * 0.8)
    X_train, X_test = X[:train_size], X[train_size:]
    y_train, y_test = y[:train_size], y[train_size:]

    # Reshape for LSTM [samples, time_steps, features]
    X_train = X_train.reshape((X_train.shape[0], X_train.
    shape[1], 1))
    X_test = X_test.reshape((X_test.shape[0], X_test.
    shape[1], 1))

    return X_train, X_test, y_train, y_test, scaler

# Prepare data for training
time_steps = 60
X_train, X_test, y_train, y_test, price_scaler = prepare_lstm_
data(market_data, time_steps)

print(f"Training data shape: {X_train.shape}")
print(f"Testing data shape: {X_test.shape}")

# Build LSTM model optimized for survival-critical predictions
def create_survival_lstm_model(input_shape):
    """Create LSTM model optimized for high-stakes prediction
    accuracy"""
    model = Sequential([
        # First LSTM layer with dropout for robustness
        LSTM(100, return_sequences=True, input_
        shape=input_shape),
        Dropout(0.2),

        # Second LSTM layer for pattern recognition
        LSTM(100, return_sequences=True),
        Dropout(0.2),
```

```python
        # Third LSTM layer focusing on final patterns
        LSTM(50, return_sequences=False),
        Dropout(0.2),

        # Dense layers for prediction refinement
        Dense(25, activation='relu'),
        Dense(1)  # Single output for price prediction
    ])

    # Compile with optimizer settings for financial prediction
    model.compile(
        optimizer='adam',
        loss='mean_squared_error',
        metrics=['mean_absolute_error']
    )

    return model

# Create and train the model
lstm_model = create_survival_lstm_model((time_steps, 1))

print("Training LSTM model for Evolune price prediction...")
print("This model could determine survival resource
allocation...")

# Train with validation monitoring
history = lstm_model.fit(
    X_train, y_train,
    epochs=50,
    batch_size=32,
    validation_data=(X_test, y_test),
    verbose=1
)

print("Model training complete")
```

```python
# Generate predictions and evaluate accuracy
predictions = lstm_model.predict(X_test)
predictions = price_scaler.inverse_transform(predictions)
y_test_actual = price_scaler.inverse_transform(y_test.
reshape(-1, 1))

# Calculate prediction accuracy metrics
mse = np.mean((predictions - y_test_actual) ** 2)
mae = np.mean(np.abs(predictions - y_test_actual))
accuracy_percentage = (1 - mae / np.mean(y_test_actual)) * 100

print(f"Prediction Accuracy: {accuracy_percentage:.2f}%")
print(f"Mean Absolute Error: ${mae:.2f}")
print(f"Mean Squared Error: ${mse:.2f}")

# Identify potential market manipulation patterns
def detect_manipulation_patterns(actual_prices, predicted_
prices, threshold=0.15):
    """Detect potential market manipulation by analyzing
    prediction errors"""
    errors = np.abs(actual_prices.flatten() - predicted_prices.
    flatten())
    relative_errors = errors / actual_prices.flatten()

    manipulation_indices = np.where(relative_errors >
    threshold)[0]

    return manipulation_indices, relative_errors

manipulation_points, error_rates = detect_manipulation_
patterns(y_test_actual, predictions)

print(f"Detected {len(manipulation_points)} potential
manipulation events")
print(f"Average prediction error: {np.mean(error_rates):.3f}")
```

```
if len(manipulation_points) > 0:
    print("Suspicious market activity detected - possible
    corporate manipulation")
    print("Recommend increased caution in trading decisions")
```

Developing the Predictive Analytics App

John creates a comprehensive application that integrates market prediction with survival resource management, enabling real-time decision-making under extreme conditions.

Developing the Web-Based Application

John's web application serves as a command center for both economic warfare and survival management, providing real-time intelligence about market conditions and resource allocation.

Flask Back End

The back-end system processes market data and generates predictions while monitoring for signs of corporate interference.

```
from flask import Flask, jsonify, render_template_string
import json

app = Flask(__name__)

# Global variables to store model and data (in production, use
proper data management)
current_model = None
current_scaler = None
latest_prediction = None

@app.route('/api/market/predict', methods=['GET'])
def get_market_prediction():
```

```python
    """API endpoint for current market predictions"""
    global latest_prediction

    # In a real implementation, this would use live market data
    # and the trained LSTM model for real-time predictions

    simulation_data = {
        'current_price': 387.45,
        'predicted_price': 394.20,
        'confidence': 0.87,
        'trend': 'bullish',
        'manipulation_risk': 'low',
        'recommended_action': 'HOLD - Monitor for corporate
        interference'
    }

    latest_prediction = simulation_data
    return jsonify(simulation_data)

@app.route('/api/survival/status', methods=['GET'])
def get_survival_status():
    """Monitor John's survival metrics and resource
    allocation"""
    status_data = {
        'evolune_reserves': 2847.3,
        'equipment_durability': 67.2,
        'food_supply_days': 23,
        'corporate_interference_level': 'moderate',
        'ai_companion_status': 'operational',
        'extraction_efficiency': 89.5
    }

    return jsonify(status_data)
```

```python
@app.route('/')
def survival_dashboard():
    """Main dashboard for survival and economic monitoring"""
    dashboard_html = '''
    <!DOCTYPE html>
    <html lang="en">
    <head>
        <meta charset="UTF-8">
        <meta name="viewport" content="width=device-width,
        initial-scale=1.0">
        <title>Tibara Survival Command Center</title>
        <style>
            body {
                background-color: #1a1a1a;
                color: #00ff00;
                font-family: 'Courier New', monospace;
                margin: 0;
                padding: 20px;
            }
            .container {
                max-width: 1200px;
                margin: 0 auto;
            }
            .header {
                text-align: center;
                border-bottom: 2px solid #00ff00;
                padding-bottom: 20px;
                margin-bottom: 30px;
            }
            .dashboard-grid {
                display: grid;
```

```
        grid-template-columns: 1fr 1fr;
        gap: 20px;
    }
    .panel {
        background-color: #2a2a2a;
        border: 2px solid #00ff00;
        padding: 20px;
        border-radius: 5px;
    }
    .metric {
        display: flex;
        justify-content: space-between;
        margin: 10px 0;
        padding: 5px 0;
        border-bottom: 1px solid #444;
    }
    .critical { color: #ff4444; }
    .warning { color: #ffaa00; }
    .good { color: #00ff00; }
    .btn {
        background-color: #003300;
        color: #00ff00;
        border: 2px solid #00ff00;
        padding: 10px 20px;
        cursor: pointer;
        margin: 5px;
        border-radius: 3px;
    }
    .btn:hover {
        background-color: #004400;
    }
```

```
        #prediction-result, #survival-result {
            margin-top: 15px;
            padding: 10px;
            background-color: #333;
            border-radius: 3px;
        }
    </style>
</head>
<body>
    <div class="container">
        <div class="header">
            <h1>TIBARA SURVIVAL COMMAND CENTER</h1>
            <p>John Lee - Independent Operations</p>
            <p>Status: <span class="warning">HOSTILE
            ENVIRONMENT - CORPORATE SABOTAGE DETECTED</
            span></p>
        </div>

        <div class="dashboard-grid">
            <div class="panel">
                <h2>Market Intelligence</h2>
                <div class="metric">
                    <span>Evolune Price (Current):</span>
                    <span id="current-price">
                    Loading...</span>
                </div>
                <div class="metric">
                    <span>Predicted Price (24h):</span>
                    <span id="predicted-price">
                    Loading...</span>
                </div>
```

```
        <div class="metric">
            <span>Market Manipulation Risk:</span>
            <span id="manipulation-risk">
            Loading...</span>
        </div>
        <button class="btn" onclick="updateMarket
        Data()">Update Market Analysis</button>
        <div id="prediction-result"></div>
    </div>

    <div class="panel">
        <h2>Survival Metrics</h2>
        <div class="metric">
            <span>Evolune Reserves:</span>
            <span id="evolune-reserves">
            Loading...</span>
        </div>
        <div class="metric">
            <span>Equipment Durability:</span>
            <span id="equipment-durability">
            Loading...</span>
        </div>
        <div class="metric">
            <span>Food Supply:</span>
            <span id="food-supply">Loading...</span>
        </div>
        <div class="metric">
            <span>AI Companions:</span>
            <span id="ai-status">Loading...</span>
        </div>
```

```html
        <button class="btn" onclick="updateSurvival
        Data()">Update Survival Status</button>
        <div id="survival-result"></div>
    </div>

    <div class="panel">
        <h2>Strategic Analysis</h2>
        <p><strong>Current Situation:</strong> Gnos
        Corporation continues interference with
        operations. Market manipulation detected
        in Evolune futures. Recommend diversified
        extraction strategy.</p>
        <p><strong>AI Companion Status:</strong>
        All 5 tactical units operational. Loyalty
        protocols secure.</p>
        <p><strong>Threat Assessment:</strong>
        Volcanic activity increasing. Acid rain
        frequency up 23%. Equipment replacement
        critical within 30 days.</p>
    </div>

    <div class="panel">
        <h2>Action Items</h2>
        <ul>
            <li class="critical">Secure additional
            equipment before current gear
            fails</li>
            <li class="warning">Monitor Gnos
            communications for extraction
            interference</li>
            <li class="good">Continue AI companion
            training and deployment</li>
```

```
                    <li class="warning">Diversify Evolune
                    storage locations</li>
                    <li class="critical">Plan extraction
                    before next major volcanic cycle</li>
                </ul>
            </div>
        </div>
    </div>

    <script>
        async function updateMarketData() {
            try {
                const response = await fetch('/api/market/
                predict');
                const data = await response.json();

                document.getElementById('current-price').
                textContent = `$${data.current_price}`;
                document.getElementById('predicted-price').
                textContent = `$${data.predicted_price}`;
                document.getElementById('manipulation-
                risk').textContent = data.manipulation_
                risk.toUpperCase();

                document.getElementById('prediction-
                result').innerHTML = `
                    <strong>Analysis:</strong> ${data.trend.
                    toUpperCase()} trend detected<br>
                     <strong>Confidence:</strong> ${(data.
                     confidence * 100).toFixed(1)}%<br>
                     <strong>Recommendation:</strong>
                     ${data.recommended_action}
                `;
```

```
        } catch (error) {
            document.getElementById('prediction-
            result').innerHTML =
                '<span class="critical">Error:
                Communications interference
                detected</span>';
        }
    }

    async function updateSurvivalData() {
        try {
            const response = await fetch('/api/
            survival/status');
            const data = await response.json();

            document.getElementById('evolune-
            reserves').textContent = `${data.evolune_
            reserves} units`;
            document.getElementById('equipment-
            durability').textContent = `${data.
            equipment_durability}%`;
            document.getElementById('food-supply').
            textContent = `${data.food_supply_
            days} days`;
            document.getElementById('ai-status').
            textContent = data.ai_companion_status.
            toUpperCase();

            document.getElementById('survival-result').
            innerHTML = `
                <strong>Extraction Efficiency:</strong>
                ${data.extraction_efficiency}%<br>
```

```
                        <strong>Corporate Interference:</
                        strong> ${data.corporate_interference_
                        level.toUpperCase()}<br>
                        <strong>Status:</strong> Maintaining
                        operational independence
                    `;
                } catch (error) {
                    document.getElementById('survival-result').
                    innerHTML =
                        '<span class="critical">Error: Sensor
                        network compromised</span>';
                }
            }

            // Auto-update every 30 seconds
            setInterval(() => {
                updateMarketData();
                updateSurvivalData();
            }, 30000);

            // Initial load
            updateMarketData();
            updateSurvivalData();
        </script>
    </body>
    </html>
    '''

    return dashboard_html

if __name__ == '__main__':
    print("Initializing Tibara Survival Command Center...")
    print("Dashboard accessible at: http://localhost:5000")
```

```
print("Market API: http://localhost:5000/api/market/
predict")
print("Survival API: http://localhost:5000/api/survival/
status")

# Use a production server like Waitress in real deployment
app.run(debug=True, host='0.0.0.0', port=5000)
```

HTML/JavaScript Front End

The front end provides an intuitive interface for monitoring both survival metrics and market conditions, designed for rapid comprehension under stress conditions. The terminal-style aesthetic reflects the harsh, technical environment while providing clear visual hierarchy for critical information.

The dashboard automatically updates market predictions and survival status, enabling John to make informed decisions without manual intervention. Critical alerts use color coding to ensure immediate recognition of priority issues.

Integrating Assets into the Metaverse

With AI companions created, communication systems established, and economic intelligence gathered, John faces the final technical challenge: integrating these technologies into a cohesive survival ecosystem. This isn't merely software deployment—it's the construction of a digital resistance network that operates independently of corporate oversight while providing comprehensive support for survival operations.

The integration process requires careful orchestration of multiple technologies working in harmony. AI soldiers must coordinate with predictive analytics to optimize resource allocation timing. Communication systems need seamless interface with environmental monitoring to provide real-time threat assessment. Economic models must incorporate survival resource calculations to ensure sustainable operations under extreme conditions.

John's implementation strategy emphasizes redundancy and independence. If Gnos disables one system, others compensate automatically. If corporate interference corrupts one data stream, backup intelligence sources maintain operational awareness. Each component strengthens the whole while preserving autonomy from external control.

For deployment into Metaverse environments like Unreal Engine or Unity, John's assets require integration protocols that maintain functionality across different platforms while preserving security against corporate intrusion.

Unreal Engine Integration (Conceptual C++)

```
#include "Engine/StaticMeshActor.h"
#include "Components/StaticMeshComponent.h"
#include "Sound/SoundWave.h"
#include "Kismet/GameplayStatics.h"

void AMyGameMode::LoadAndDeployAssets()
{
    // Load AI companion models with security verification
    FString MeshPath = TEXT("/Game/Models/TacticalCompanion.
    TacticalCompanion");
    FString SoundPath = TEXT("/Game/Sounds/SurvivalCommand.
    SurvivalCommand");

    UStaticMesh* CompanionMesh = LoadObject<UStaticMesh>(
    nullptr, *MeshPath);
    if (CompanionMesh)
    {
        AStaticMeshActor* CompanionActor = GetWorld()->Spawn
        Actor<AStaticMeshActor>();
```

```cpp
    if(CompanionActor)
    {
        CompanionActor->GetStaticMeshComponent()-
        >SetStaticMesh(CompanionMesh);
        // Initialize companion AI and loyalty protocols
        CompanionActor->Tags.Add(TEXT("SurvivalAlly"));
    }
}

USoundWave* CommandAudio = LoadObject<USoundWave>(nullptr,
*SoundPath);
if (CommandAudio)
{
    UGameplayStatics::PlaySoundAtLocation(this,
    CommandAudio, FVector::ZeroVector);
}

// Establish secure communication channels
InitializeSecureNetworking();
}

void AMyGameMode::InitializeSecureNetworking()
{
    // Implement encrypted communication protocols
    // Establish backup communication channels
    // Initialize anti-tampering measures
}
```

Unity Real-Time Communication (Conceptual C# with Photon)

```csharp
using UnityEngine;
using Photon.Pun;
using Photon.Realtime;
```

```
public class ResistanceCommunication :
MonoBehaviourPunCallbacks
{
    void Start()
    {
        // Connect to secure communication network
        PhotonNetwork.ConnectUsingSettings();
    }

    public override void OnConnectedToMaster()
    {
        // Join secure lobby for resistance operations
        PhotonNetwork.JoinLobby();
    }

    public override void OnJoinedLobby()
    {
        // Create encrypted room for survival coordination
        RoomOptions roomOptions = new RoomOptions();
        roomOptions.MaxPlayers = 6; // John + 5 AI companions
        PhotonNetwork.JoinOrCreateRoom("TibaraSurvival_Secure",
        roomOptions, TypedLobby.Default);
    }

    public override void OnJoinedRoom()
    {
        Debug.Log("Secure survival network established on
        Tibara");
        Debug.Log("AI companions connected - corporate
        monitoring blocked");
```

```
    // Initialize voice and text communication with
    encryption
    InitializeSecureCommunication();
}

void InitializeSecureCommunication()
{
    // Set up encrypted voice chat for AI companions
    // Initialize secure text messaging protocols
    // Establish anti-surveillance measures
}
}
```

Conclusion

John Lee's transformation from corporate contractor to digital resistance leader demonstrates how advanced AI technologies can serve both immediate survival needs and long-term liberation goals. Through the creation of AI-generated companions, sophisticated communication systems, and predictive analytics tools, he has built a technological foundation capable of operating independently from corporate control.

The journey from desperate adaptation to systematic rebellion illustrates the power of generative AI when applied with purpose and determination. Each technology—GANs for tactical visualization, NLP for intelligent communication, LSTM networks for market prediction—serves multiple functions in John's survival ecosystem while building toward a larger goal of corporate independence.

The integration of these systems into cohesive resistance infrastructure represents more than technical achievement. It demonstrates how individual resourcefulness, combined with advanced AI capabilities, can challenge institutional power structures and create alternatives to corporate dependency.

John's digital allies, economic intelligence systems, and communication networks provide the foundation for sustained operations on Tibara while preparing for eventual expansion beyond the planet's hostile environment. The technologies he has mastered will serve not only his immediate survival but also the broader resistance movement that his success will inspire.

Introduction to the Next Chapter

Having established technological independence through generative AI solutions, John's next challenge involves understanding the fundamental systems that enable secure, decentralized operations beyond corporate control. The blockchain technologies that power intergalactic commerce represent both opportunity and threat—they could provide the framework for permanent independence from corporate manipulation or serve as another tool for institutional oppression.

The next chapter explores blockchain fundamentals, smart contracts, and decentralized systems that form the backbone of digital commerce and governance. Through John's continued struggle against corporate control, we'll discover how these technologies can enable transparent, secure, and truly independent operations that no corporation can corrupt or control.

Understanding blockchain isn't merely about cryptocurrency trading—it's about building the infrastructure for digital freedom that could finally tip the balance of power away from predatory corporations and toward the individuals who risk everything in hostile environments like Tibara.

The revolution that began with code will continue with the decentralized technologies that make liberation possible.

## CHAPTER 3

Blockchain: The Foundation of Digital Trust on Planet Tenrai

Introduction to Tenrai

Before his exile to Tibara or his mission to Celestor, John Lee's journey of disillusionment with Gnos Corporation began on Tenrai.

The planet Tenrai, situated in the Gaia galaxy neighboring Celestor, had once been a paradise. An Earth-like world inhabited by the Rumin, a race known for their deep understanding of sciences and profound connection to nature, Tenrai represented everything that interplanetary cooperation could achieve. The Rumin's remarkable scientific achievements, including their controversial mastery of planetary teleportation, had made them both valuable allies and dangerous threats in Gnos Corporation's expanding empire.

John Lee's first assignment as a junior contractor had been routine survey work on Tenrai—or so Gnos had told him. What he discovered there would fundamentally alter his understanding of corporate space, setting him on the path that would later lead to his moral awakening on Celestor and his rebellion on Tibara.

© Frank Lisitano, John Hickie 2025
F. Lisitano and J. Hickie, *The Evolune Metaverse*, Maker Innovations Series,
https://doi.org/10.1007/979-8-8688-1588-1_3

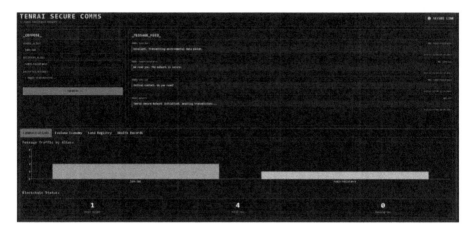

Figure 3-1. *Tenrai Comms*

The Role of Evolune

Evolune, the mysterious energy source that would come to define John's career, was already a known quantity when he first arrived on Tenrai. The Rumin had discovered and learned to harness this immensely powerful force long before Gnos arrived in their system. Where the corporation saw opportunity for extraction and profit, the Rumin understood Evolune as something far more profound—a fundamental force that could manipulate time and space itself.

The Rumin's teleportation of their entire planet was proof of Evolune's incredible potential. But it was also a desperate act of survival. As John would later learn, they had moved Tenrai to escape Gnos's increasingly aggressive extraction operations on their neighboring worlds.

Discovery and Exploitation of Evolune

Gnos Corporation's relationship with Evolune began with discovery but quickly turned to exploitation. The corporation's scientists recognized the energy source's potential for unprecedented technological advancement—

teleportation, space-time manipulation, and interplanetary travel capabilities that could revolutionize galactic commerce and control.

On Tenrai, John witnessed the collision between two fundamentally different approaches to this power. The Rumin treated Evolune with reverence, understanding that its manipulation required balance and respect for natural systems. Gnos viewed it as a resource to be extracted, processed, and commodified, regardless of environmental or social consequences.

The extraction methods employed by Gnos were brutal in their efficiency. Massive drilling operations carved through Tenrai's surface, seeking Evolune deposits with no regard for the delicate ecosystems that had evolved around them. The Rumin's protests were dismissed as primitive superstition—until their water supplies began showing signs of contamination and their marine life started dying in unprecedented numbers.

Why Duncan Lee Is Famous

John's assignment to Tenrai was no coincidence. His famous ancestor, Duncan Lee, had been instrumental in establishing the ethical frameworks that were supposed to govern Evolune extraction. Understanding Duncan's legacy was crucial to comprehending why John's disillusionment ran so deep.

Pioneering Space Exploration

Duncan Lee's fame originated from his role as one of the first astronauts to venture into the uncharted territories of the Gaia galaxy. His expeditions to Tenrai, Celestor, and other distant worlds had been conducted under principles of scientific discovery and peaceful contact. Duncan believed that humanity's expansion into space should be guided by cooperation, not conquest.

Discovering and Utilizing Evolune

Duncan had been among the first to recognize Evolune's potential, but his approach differed radically from later corporate methods. His scientific work focused on understanding Evolune's integration with natural systems, learning from species like the Rumin who had already achieved sustainable harmony with this power. His research notes, which John had studied extensively, emphasized the importance of working with existing ecosystems rather than destroying them.

Ethical Leadership and Advocacy

Throughout his career, Duncan Lee established protocols for ethical resource extraction and meaningful collaboration with indigenous species. He insisted that any use of Evolune should benefit all parties involved, not just human corporate interests. His leadership style emphasized long-term sustainability over short-term profits.

Inspirational Legacy

Duncan's legacy had inspired John to pursue space exploration, believing he could follow in his ancestor's footsteps as an ethical operator in the corporate frontier. The reality John discovered on Tenrai shattered those idealistic expectations. Gnos paid lip service to Duncan's principles while systematically violating every ethical guideline he had established.

Impact on Project Evolune

Duncan's pioneering work had laid the theoretical foundation for Project Evolune, the massive initiative that eventually enabled planetary teleportation. His research provided crucial insights into the safe manipulation of Evolune energy. However, Gnos had corrupted his vision, using his discoveries to justify increasingly aggressive extraction operations across multiple worlds.

The Role of Gnos in Tenrai's History

On Tenrai, John experienced his first direct exposure to the gap between Gnos Corporation's public image and its operational reality. The corporation marketed itself as "the savior of humanity," claiming its exploration and resource extraction activities were essential for human survival and progress. Their promotional materials emphasized their role in developing life-saving technologies: regenerative cells, nano-powered muscle fibers, and cerebral enhancers that had revolutionized human capability.

But John's boots-on-the-ground experience told a different story. The aggressive extraction methods he witnessed were justified as "necessary force against hostile wildlife," but John saw them being used against peaceful Rumin communities whose only crime was occupying land rich in Evolune deposits. Environmental monitoring equipment mysteriously malfunctioned whenever it might record evidence of corporate wrongdoing. Safety protocols were routinely ignored when they slowed production quotas.

The dichotomy was impossible to ignore: technological advancement built on a foundation of systematic exploitation and environmental destruction.

John Lee's Ethical Dilemma

John's involvement with Tenrai had started with noble intentions, inspired by Duncan Lee's legacy of ethical exploration. But his firsthand experience of Gnos's operations revealed the ugly reality behind the corporate facade. The powerful Evolune extraction he was supposed to support came at devastating cost to the planet and its inhabitants.

The incident that would eventually force John to take sick leave was the breaking point. A routine extraction operation near a Rumin settlement had "accidentally" contaminated the local water supply, poisoning marine life and threatening the health of an entire community. When John raised concerns about the environmental impact, he was told that such consequences were "acceptable collateral damage in service of humanity's greater good."

John's internal conflict mirrored the broader struggle of the Rumin people, who found themselves caught between cooperation and resistance. They possessed knowledge that could help humanity develop sustainable Evolune technology, but Gnos seemed determined to take what it wanted regardless of the long-term consequences.

John Lee's Journey and the Impact of Evolune

John Lee represented the human face of Gnos's operations—and increasingly, the conscience that the corporation tried to suppress. His forced sick leave after questioning extraction protocols was officially attributed to a "workplace accident," but John understood it as punishment for asking inconvenient questions.

During his recovery period on Tenrai, John spent time with Rumin communities affected by the extraction operations. He learned about their traditional approaches to Evolune manipulation, methods that had sustained their civilization for millennia without environmental destruction. He also witnessed the devastating effects of corporate extraction: poisoned water supplies, decimated marine ecosystems, and communities forced to relocate as their traditional lands became uninhabitable.

This experience planted the seeds of the ethical framework that would guide John through his later assignments. If Gnos wouldn't voluntarily adopt sustainable practices, perhaps they could be forced to through transparency, accountability, and the strategic application of technologies they couldn't control.

Blockchain Technology: A Solution for Tenrai

Based on the challenges they faced, the Rumin needed tools that could ensure transparency, security, and trust in their dealings with corporate entities like Gnos. Traditional diplomatic and legal channels had proven ineffective against a corporation with superior resources and political influence. What the Rumin needed was something that couldn't be corrupted, manipulated, or conveniently "lost" when it became inconvenient.

John, drawing on his technical background and growing understanding of corporate manipulation, recognized that blockchain technology could provide exactly what the Rumin needed: an immutable record of agreements, transactions, and evidence that no single party could control or alter.

The Need for Blockchain Technology

The story of Tenrai illustrates why blockchain technology has become crucial for protecting vulnerable communities in corporate space. As the Rumin work to rebuild their relocated world while defending against continued exploitation, blockchain offers tools for ensuring accountability, preserving evidence, and enabling fair negotiations between parties with vastly different power levels.

You'll discover how blockchain's fundamental properties—decentralization, transparency, and immutability—can be leveraged to create systems that resist corporate manipulation. Through practical examples and implementation guides, you'll learn to build the same kinds of tools that John helped develop for the Rumin: secure messaging systems, transparent resource tracking, and decentralized currencies that operate beyond corporate control.

As Tenrai rebuilds after its dramatic relocation, blockchain technology plays a crucial role in ensuring that resources are used efficiently and ethically, preventing the exploitative practices that the Rumin experienced under direct Gnos control. The integration of blockchain into Tenrai's recovery efforts represents a commitment to a transparent, secure, and equitable future.

Understanding Blockchain Technology

Blockchain technology operates as a decentralized and distributed digital ledger, designed to store transaction records across a network of computers. This structure ensures that once information is recorded, it becomes immutable and cannot be altered or tampered with afterward. For the Rumin of Tenrai, this immutability was crucial—it meant that evidence of Gnos's broken promises and environmental damage could be preserved beyond the reach of corporate lawyers and public relations teams.

Fundamental Aspects of Blockchain

1. **Decentralization**: Unlike traditional centralized databases controlled by single entities (like Gnos's internal records), a blockchain is managed by a network of computers—nodes—each holding a copy of the entire ledger. No single party can unilaterally alter the record.

2. **Transparency**: All transactions are visible to participants, promoting accountability and trust. When the Rumin needed to prove that Gnos had violated extraction agreements, the blockchain provided transparent evidence that couldn't be disputed.

3. **Immutability**: Once a transaction is recorded in a block, it cannot be changed or deleted, ensuring the integrity of historical data. This was particularly valuable for documenting environmental impact over time.

Consensus Mechanisms

Proof of Work (PoW): This mechanism requires nodes to solve complex mathematical puzzles to validate transactions and create new blocks. While secure, it's energy-intensive—a consideration that resonated with the environmentally conscious Rumin.

Proof of Stake (PoS): This mechanism assigns transaction validation responsibilities based on the number of tokens a node holds. It's more energy-efficient than PoW, making it more suitable for the Rumin's sustainable technology philosophy.

Blockchain Structure

Blocks: Each block contains a list of transactions, a timestamp, and a cryptographic hash of the previous block, forming an unbreakable chain of evidence.

Nodes: Computers that maintain and validate the blockchain—distributed across Rumin communities to ensure no single point of failure.

Miners/Validators: Nodes that validate transactions and add them to the blockchain, earning rewards for maintaining network security.

The Potential of Blockchain Technology

Blockchain technology has the potential to revolutionize digital trust by providing a secure, transparent, and tamper-proof method of recording transactions. Its applications extend beyond cryptocurrencies, offering solutions for various industries, including supply chain management, healthcare, real estate, and more.

Use Cases

1. **Supply Chain Management**: Blockchain can track the journey of products from manufacturers to consumers, ensuring authenticity and reducing fraud. For the Rumin, this meant tracking Evolune extraction and ensuring that traditional resources were not being mislabeled or stolen.

2. **Healthcare**: Patient records can be securely stored and shared, ensuring privacy and improving care coordination while maintaining an immutable record of treatments and outcomes.

3. **Real Estate**: Property transactions can be streamlined and secured, reducing the risk of fraud and errors while preserving traditional land rights and territorial claims.

4. **Financial Services**: Decentralized financial systems can operate independently of corporate-controlled banking infrastructure, enabling communities to maintain economic autonomy.

Case Study: Tenrai's Teleportation Incident

The Rumin's teleportation of Tenrai posed significant risks and required meticulous record-keeping to ensure that all aspects of the operation were transparent and secure. The massive undertaking involved coordinating resources across the entire planet while maintaining detailed records of environmental impacts, energy expenditures, and population relocations.

Implementing blockchain technology could have provided an immutable record of the entire teleportation process, ensuring accountability and trust among all Rumin communities. Every decision, resource allocation, and environmental measurement could have been recorded in a tamper-proof ledger, preventing disputes and ensuring that lessons learned could be preserved for future reference.

The blockchain record would have documented.

- **Environmental Impact Assessments**: Detailed measurements of ecosystem disruption and recovery protocols

- **Resource Allocation**: Transparent tracking of Evolune energy usage and community contributions

- **Population Management**: Secure records of community relocations and support services

- **Decision Processes**: Immutable records of community consensus and governance decisions

This comprehensive documentation would have prevented the kind of information manipulation that Gnos often employed to justify their operations, providing the Rumin with indisputable proof of their responsible stewardship during the crisis.

The Power of Smart Contracts

Smart contracts became particularly valuable for the Rumin in their dealings with external entities. These self-executing contracts, with terms written directly into code, could automate compliance and enforcement without requiring trust in any single party.

What Are Smart Contracts?

Smart contracts are programs that automatically execute when predetermined conditions are met. For the Rumin, this meant creating agreements that could enforce themselves—no corporate lawyers could find loopholes, no bureaucratic delays could prevent execution.

Features of Smart Contracts

1. **Automation**: Smart contracts automatically execute transactions when conditions are met, eliminating the need for intermediaries who might be influenced by corporate pressure.

2. **Security**: Transactions are encrypted and stored on the blockchain, making them tamper-proof and immune to corporate interference.

3. **Transparency**: All participants can view contract terms and execution, ensuring accountability in all dealings.

How Smart Contracts Work

Smart contracts are written in programming languages like Solidity (for Ethereum networks). Once deployed on the blockchain, they wait for trigger events. When conditions are met, the contract self-executes, ensuring all parties fulfill their obligations automatically.

Educational Note: Simplified Implementation

The code examples in this chapter are designed to illustrate blockchain concepts clearly. They are educational demonstrations and lack the security features necessary for production use, including robust consensus mechanisms, secure transaction handling, and protection against common attacks.

```solidity
pragma solidity ^0.8.0;

// Environmental Protection Contract for Tenrai
contract TenraiProtection {
    address public rumin_representative;
    address public extraction_company;
    uint256 public environmental_deposit;
    bool public extraction_approved;

    // Environmental monitoring data
    struct EnvironmentalReading {
        uint256 timestamp;
        uint256 water_quality_index;
        uint256 marine_life_count;
        bool acceptable_levels;
    }
```

```
EnvironmentalReading[] public readings;

constructor(address _rumin_rep, address _company) {
    rumin_representative = _rumin_rep;
    extraction_company = _company;
    environmental_deposit = 0;
    extraction_approved = false;
}

// Company must deposit environmental insurance
function depositEnvironmentalInsurance() public payable {
    require(msg.sender == extraction_company, "Only
     extraction company can deposit");
    environmental_deposit += msg.value;
    if (environmental_deposit >= 1000000) { // Minimum
    insurance amount
        extraction_approved = true;
    }
}

// Record environmental monitoring data
function recordEnvironmentalData(
    uint256 _water_quality,
    uint256 _marine_count
) public {
    require(msg.sender == rumin_representative, "Only Rumin
    can record data");

    bool acceptable = _water_quality >= 75 && _marine_count
    >= 1000;

    readings.push(EnvironmentalReading({
        timestamp: block.timestamp,
        water_quality_index: _water_quality,
```

```
            marine_life_count: _marine_count,
            acceptable_levels: acceptable
        }));

        // If environmental damage detected, freeze operations
        and forfeit deposit
        if (!acceptable) {
            extraction_approved = false;
            // Transfer deposit to Rumin for
            restoration efforts
            payable(rumin_representative).
            transfer(environmental_deposit);
            environmental_deposit = 0;
        }
    }
    function getExtractionStatus() public view returns (bool) {
        return extraction_approved;
    }
}
```

Benefits of Smart Contracts

Smart contracts provided the Rumin with several crucial advantages in
their struggle against corporate exploitation.

> **Reduced Intermediary Dependence**: No need to
> rely on potentially corrupted arbitrators or courts.
>
> **Increased Transaction Speed**: Automated
> execution eliminates bureaucratic delays that
> corporations often used to their advantage.

Lower Costs: Reduced legal and administrative expenses, making justice accessible to smaller communities.

Enhanced Trust: Code-based execution removes the possibility of human bias or corruption affecting outcomes.

Blockchain in Action: Beyond Cryptocurrencies

While blockchain technology is often associated with digital currencies, its applications extend far beyond financial transactions. For the Rumin of Tenrai, blockchain became a comprehensive tool for protecting their rights, preserving their environment, and ensuring fair treatment in their interactions with corporate entities.

Healthcare

Blockchain revolutionized healthcare record management for the Rumin, particularly crucial given the health impacts of Evolune extraction contamination.

Case Study: Secure Patient Records on Tenrai

In the aftermath of Tenrai's relocation and the environmental damage caused by extraction operations, the Rumin needed a secure method to track health impacts across their population. Traditional medical records could be "lost" or altered when they became inconvenient for corporate interests. A blockchain-based system ensured that patient data was immutable and accessible only to authorized personnel.

```python
import hashlib
import json
from time import time

class TenraiHealthBlockchain:
    def __init__(self):
        self.chain = []
        self.current_records = []
        # Create genesis block
        self.new_block(previous_hash='1', proof=100)

    def new_block(self, proof, previous_hash=None):
        """Create a new block containing current health
        records"""
        block = {
            'index': len(self.chain) + 1,
            'timestamp': time(),
            'health_records': self.current_records,
            'proof': proof,
            'previous_hash': previous_hash or self.hash(self.
            chain[-1]),
        }

        # Clear current records after adding to block
        self.current_records = []
        self.chain.append(block)
        return block

    def new_health_record(self, patient_id, medical_data,
    exposure_data=None):
        """Add a new health record, including potential Evolune
        exposure"""
```

```
            record = {
                'patient_id': patient_id,
                'medical_data': medical_data,
                'timestamp': time(),
            }

            # Track potential environmental exposure from
             extraction operations
            if exposure_data:
                record['evolune_exposure'] = exposure_data
                record['extraction_site_proximity'] = exposure_
                data.get('distance_to_site', 'unknown')

            self.current_records.append(record)
            return self.last_block['index'] + 1

    @staticmethod
    def hash(block):
        """Create SHA-256 hash of a block"""
        block_string = json.dumps(block, sort_keys=True).
        encode()
        return hashlib.sha256(block_string).hexdigest()

    @property
    def last_block(self):
        return self.chain[-1]

    def get_patient_history(self, patient_id):
        """Retrieve complete medical history for a patient"""
        patient_records = []
        for block in self.chain:
            for record in block.get('health_records', []):
```

```
            if record.get('patient_id') == patient_id:
                patient_records.append(record)
    return patient_records

# Example usage for tracking environmental health impacts
health_blockchain = TenraiHealthBlockchain()

# Record health data with potential Evolune exposure tracking
health_blockchain.new_health_record(
    patient_id="rumin_12345",
    medical_data="Respiratory symptoms consistent with chemical
    exposure",
    exposure_data={
        "distance_to_site": "2.3km",
        "exposure_duration": "6 months",
        "contamination_level": "moderate"
    }
)
```

Real Estate

Property ownership and land rights became critical issues for the Rumin after their planet's relocation. Blockchain provided a tamper-proof record of traditional territorial claims and new land allocations.

Case Study: Property Transactions on Tenrai

Following Tenrai's teleportation, traditional land ownership records were at risk of being lost or disputed. The relocation had physically altered the planet's geography, making old territorial markers obsolete. A blockchain-based land registry ensured that property rights were preserved and could be verified even after planetary upheaval.

```python
import hashlib
import json
from time import time

class TenraiLandRegistry:
    def __init__(self):
        self.chain = []
        self.current_transactions = []
        # Initialize with genesis block
        self.new_block(previous_hash='1', proof=100)

    def new_block(self, proof, previous_hash=None):
        """Create new block for land transactions"""
        block = {
            'index': len(self.chain) + 1,
            'timestamp': time(),
            'land_transactions': self.current_transactions,
            'proof': proof,
            'previous_hash': previous_hash or self.hash(self.
          chain[-1]),
        }

        self.current_transactions = []
        self.chain.append(block)
        return block

    def register_land_claim(self, claimant, territory_
    description, coordinates, claim_type):
        """Register a land claim with territorial and
        traditional use data"""
        transaction = {
            'claimant': claimant,
            'territory': territory_description,
```

```python
        'coordinates': coordinates,
        'claim_type': claim_type,  # 'traditional',
        'relocated', 'restoration'
        'timestamp': time(),
        'status': 'pending_validation'
    }

    self.current_transactions.append(transaction)
    return self.last_block['index'] + 1

def transfer_land_rights(self, from_party, to_party,
property_id, compensation=None):
    """Record land transfers between parties"""
    transaction = {
        'transaction_type': 'transfer',
        'from': from_party,
        'to': to_party,
        'property_id': property_id,
        'compensation': compensation,
        'timestamp': time()
    }

    self.current_transactions.append(transaction)
    return self.last_block['index'] + 1

@staticmethod
def hash(block):
   block_string = json.dumps(block, sort_keys=True).
   encode()
   return hashlib.sha256(block_string).hexdigest()

@property
def last_block(self):
    return self.chain[-1]
```

```
# Example: Documenting traditional Rumin territorial claims
land_registry = TenraiLandRegistry()

# Register traditional territorial claim
land_registry.register_land_claim(
    claimant="Eastern_Rumin_Clan",
    territory_description="Sacred grove and adjacent
    watershed",
    coordinates={"lat": -45.7589, "lon": 122.4567, "area_
    km2": 150.3},
    claim_type="traditional"
)

# Register post-relocation restoration area
land_registry.register_land_claim(
    claimant="Tenrai_Environmental_Collective",
    territory_description="Former extraction site designated
    for ecosystem restoration",
    coordinates={"lat": -46.1234, "lon": 123.7890, "area_
    km2": 85.7},
    claim_type="restoration"
)
```

Entertainment

The preservation of Rumin cultural works became crucial after their planet's relocation disrupted traditional methods of cultural transmission. Blockchain provided a way to protect intellectual property and ensure fair compensation for artists.

Case Study: Digital Rights Management on Tenrai

Rumin artists faced challenges protecting their cultural works from unauthorized corporate use. Gnos had a history of appropriating indigenous cultural elements for marketing purposes without compensation. A blockchain-based digital rights management system allowed artists to register their creations and track their use transparently.

```python
import hashlib
import json
from time import time

class TenraiCulturalBlockchain:
    def __init__(self):
        self.chain = []
        self.current_records = []
        self.new_block(previous_hash='1', proof=100)

    def new_block(self, proof, previous_hash=None):
        block = {
            'index': len(self.chain) + 1,
            'timestamp': time(),
            'cultural_records': self.current_records,
            'proof': proof,
            'previous_hash': previous_hash or self.hash(self.
            chain[-1]),
        }

        self.current_records = []
        self.chain.append(block)
        return block
```

```python
    def register_cultural_work(self, artist_id, work_hash,
    work_type, usage_rights, cultural_significance=None):
        """Register cultural works with traditional and
        contemporary elements"""
        record = {
            'artist_id': artist_id,
            'work_hash': work_hash,
            'work_type': work_type,  # 'traditional',
            'contemporary', 'hybrid'
            'usage_rights': usage_rights,
            'registration_time': time(),
            'cultural_significance': cultural_significance,
            'protection_status': 'active'
        }

        # Special protections for traditional/sacred works
        if cultural_significance in ['sacred', 'ceremonial',
        'ancestral']:
            record['special_protection'] = True
            record['commercial_use'] = 'prohibited'

        self.current_records.append(record)
        return self.last_block['index'] + 1

    def record_usage(self, work_hash, user_id, usage_type,
    compensation=None):
        """Track usage of registered cultural works"""
        usage_record = {
            'work_hash': work_hash,
            'user_id': user_id,
            'usage_type': usage_type,  # 'educational',
            'commercial', 'cultural_exchange'
            'compensation': compensation,
```

```python
                'usage_timestamp': time(),
                'authorized': True  # Would check against usage_
                rights in full implementation
            }

            self.current_records.append(usage_record)
            return self.last_block['index'] + 1

    @staticmethod
    def hash(block):
        block_string = json.dumps(block, sort_keys=True).
        encode()
        return hashlib.sha256(block_string).hexdigest()

    @property
    def last_block(self):
        return self.chain[-1]

# Example: Protecting traditional Rumin cultural works
cultural_blockchain = TenraiCulturalBlockchain()

# Register traditional chant with sacred significance
cultural_blockchain.register_cultural_work(
    artist_id="Elder_Seer_Nythara",
    work_hash="HASH_traditional_healing_chant_001",
    work_type="traditional",
    usage_rights="community_only",
    cultural_significance="sacred"
)

# Register contemporary art inspired by relocation experience
cultural_blockchain.register_cultural_work(
    artist_id="Artist_Zephyr_123",
    work_hash="HASH_tenrai_journey_sculpture",
```

```
    work_type="contemporary",
    usage_rights="educational_and_cultural_exchange",
    cultural_significance="commemorative"
)
```

Build an Encrypted Messaging System

The need for secure communications became critical for the Rumin as they organized resistance to corporate exploitation and coordinated their planet's recovery efforts. Traditional communication channels could be monitored or intercepted by Gnos surveillance systems. Blockchain-based messaging provided a solution that was both secure and decentralized.

Benefits of Blockchain-Based Messaging Systems

1. **Security**: Messages are encrypted and stored on the blockchain, making them tamper-proof and resistant to corporate surveillance.

2. **Decentralization**: No single point of failure or control, preventing corporate entities from shutting down communication networks.

3. **Transparency**: Message transactions are recorded on the blockchain, providing an audit trail while keeping content private.

4. **Resistance to Censorship**: Distributed nature makes it nearly impossible for any single entity to block or filter communications.

Architecture of a Blockchain-Based Messaging System

1. **User Interface (UI)**: Front-end application for sending and receiving encrypted messages, designed to be accessible to non-technical Rumin users.

2. **Blockchain Network**: Decentralized network storing encrypted message hashes and routing information.

3. **Encryption Module**: Handles message encryption/ decryption using advanced cryptographic protocols.

4. **Node Servers**: Maintain the blockchain and handle message routing across the network.

Example Code for User Interface

A React-based interface designed for secure Rumin communications.

```
import React, { useState, useEffect, useCallback } from
'react';
import axios from 'axios';

const TenraiSecureMessaging = () => {
    // State management for secure messaging
    const [senderAlias, setSenderAlias] = useState('');
    const [recipientAlias, setRecipientAlias] = useState('');
    const [message, setMessage] = useState('');
    const [messages, setMessages] = useState([]);
    const [isLoading, setIsLoading] = useState(false);
    const [error, setError] = useState(null);
```

```
const [connectionStatus, setConnectionStatus] =
useState('disconnected');

// Secure connection to Tenrai messaging network
const connectToNetwork = useCallback(async () => {
    setIsLoading(true);
    try {
        const response = await axios.get('/api/network_
        status');
        if (response.data.status === 'active') {
            setConnectionStatus('connected');
            await fetchMessages();
        } else {
            setConnectionStatus('degraded');
            setError('Network under potential
            surveillance - using backup protocols');
        }
    } catch (err) {
        setConnectionStatus('offline');
        setError('Cannot connect to secure network. Check
        for interference.');
    } finally {
        setIsLoading(false);
    }
}, []);

// Fetch encrypted messages from blockchain
const fetchMessages = useCallback(async () => {
    try {
        const response = await axios.get('/api/secure_
        messages');
        setMessages(response.data || []);
```

```
        if (error) setError(null);
    } catch (err) {
        console.error("Failed to fetch messages:", err);
        if (!error) {
            setError("Message retrieval failed - network
            may be compromised");
        }
    }
}, [error]);

// Send encrypted message through blockchain
const sendSecureMessage = async () => {
    if (!senderAlias || !recipientAlias || !message) {
        setError("All fields required for secure
        transmission");
        return;
    }

    if (connectionStatus !== 'connected') {
        setError("Cannot send - secure connection not
        established");
        return;
    }

    setIsLoading(true);
    setError(null);

    try {
        const response = await axios.post('/api/send_
        secure_message', {
            sender: senderAlias,
            recipient: recipientAlias,
            message: message,
```

```
            priority: 'normal',
            encryption_level: 'high'
        });

        console.log('Secure message transmitted:',
        response.data);
        setMessage(''); // Clear message after sending
        await fetchMessages(); // Refresh message list
    } catch (err) {
        console.error("Failed to send secure
        message:", err);
        const errorMsg = err.response?.data?.error ||
        "Transmission failed - possible interference";
        setError(`Secure transmission failed:
        ${errorMsg}`);
    } finally {
        setIsLoading(false);
    }
};

// Initialize secure connection on component mount
useEffect(() => {
    connectToNetwork();

    // Set up polling for new messages every 30 seconds
    const messagePolling = setInterval(() => {
        if (connectionStatus === 'connected') {
            fetchMessages();
        }
    }, 30000);

    return () => clearInterval(messagePolling);
}, [connectToNetwork, connectionStatus, fetchMessages]);
```

```
// Connection status indicator
const getStatusColor = () => {
    switch (connectionStatus) {
        case 'connected': return '#00ff00';
        case 'degraded': return '#ffff00';
        case 'offline': return '#ff0000';
        default: return '#888888';
    }
};

return (
    <div style={{ padding: '20px', backgroundColor:
    '#1a1a1a', color: '#00ff00', fontFamily:
    'monospace' }}>
        <h1>Tenrai Secure Communications Network</h1>

        {/* Network Status Display */}
        <div style={{ marginBottom: '20px', padding:
        '10px', border: '1px solid #333', backgroundColor:
        '#2a2a2a' }}>
            <h3>Network Status: <span style={{ color:
            getStatusColor() }}>{connectionStatus.
            toUpperCase()}</span></h3>
            {connectionStatus === 'degraded' && (
                <p style={{ color: '#ffff00' }}>⚠
                Potential surveillance detected - using
                enhanced encryption</p>
            )}
        </div>

        {/* Message Composition */}
        <div style={{ marginBottom: '20px', padding:
        '15px', border: '1px solid #00ff00' }}>
```

```
<h2>Compose Secure Message</h2>
<div style={{ marginBottom: '10px' }}>
    <input
        type="text"
        placeholder="Your alias (sender)"
        value={senderAlias}
        onChange={(e) => setSenderAlias(e.
        target.value)}
        disabled={isLoading || connectionStatus
        === 'offline'}
        style={{
            marginRight: '10px',
            padding: '8px',
            backgroundColor: '#333',
            color: '#00ff00',
            border: '1px solid #555',
            width: '200px'
        }}
    />
    <input
        type="text"
        placeholder="Recipient alias"
        value={recipientAlias}
        onChange={(e) => setRecipientAlias(e.
        target.value)}
        disabled={isLoading || connectionStatus
        === 'offline'}
        style={{
            padding: '8px',
            backgroundColor: '#333',
            color: '#00ff00',
```

```
                border: '1px solid #555',
                width: '200px'
            }}
        />
    </div>
    <div style={{ marginBottom: '10px' }}>
        <textarea
            placeholder="Enter encrypted
            message..."
            value={message}
            onChange={(e) => setMessage(e.
            target.value)}
            disabled={isLoading || connectionStatus
            === 'offline'}
            rows={4}
            style={{
                width: '100%',
                maxWidth: '600px',
                padding: '8px',
                backgroundColor: '#333',
                color: '#00ff00',
                border: '1px solid #555',
                resize: 'vertical'
            }}
        />
    </div>
    <button
        onClick={sendSecureMessage}
        disabled={isLoading || connectionStatus ===
        'offline'}
```

```
            style={{
                padding: '10px 20px',
                backgroundColor: '#003300',
                color: '#00ff00',
                border: '1px solid #00ff00',
                cursor: isLoading ? 'wait' : 'pointer'
            }}
        >
            {isLoading ? 'Encrypting & Transmitting...'
            : 'Send Secure Message'}
        </button>
    </div>

    {/* Error Display */}
    {error && (
        <div style={{
            color: '#ff0000',
            backgroundColor: '#331111',
            padding: '10px',
            border: '1px solid #ff0000',
            marginBottom: '15px'
        }}>
            Security Alert: {error}
        </div>
    )}

    {/* Message Feed */}
    <div>
        <h2>Secure Message Feed</h2>
        <div style={{
            height: '400px',
            overflowY: 'auto',
```

```
      border: '1px solid #00ff00',
      padding: '10px',
      backgroundColor: '#0a0a0a'
}}>
      {messages.length === 0 && !isLoading ? (
          <p style={{ color: '#888' }}>No secure
          messages received</p>
      ) : (
          <ul style={{ listStyle: 'none',
          padding: 0 }}>
              {messages.map((msg, index) => (
                  <li key={msg.id || index}
                  style={{
                      borderBottom: '1px
                      dashed #333',
                      marginBottom: '10px',
                      paddingBottom: '10px'
                  }}>
                      <strong style={{ color:
                      '#00ff88' }}>From:</strong>
                      {msg.sender} |
                      <strong style={{ color:
                      '#00ff88' }}> To:</strong>
                      {msg.recipient}
                      <p style={{ margin: '5px 0
                      0 10px', color: '#cccccc'
                      }}>{msg.message}</p>
                      {msg.timestamp && (
                          <small style={{
                              display: 'block',
                              color: '#777',
```

```
                                              textAlign: 'right',
                                              fontSize: '0.8em'
                                    }}>
                                        {new Date(msg.
                                        timestamp).
                                        toLocaleString()}
                                    </small>
                                )}
                            </li>
                        ))}
                    </ul>
                )}
            </div>
        </div>
    </div>
    );
};
export default TenraiSecureMessaging;
```

Back-End Implementation

The Flask-based back end handles encryption and blockchain integration for the Tenrai messaging system.

```
from flask import Flask, request, jsonify
from cryptography.fernet import Fernet, InvalidToken
import hashlib
import json
from time import time
import os
```

```python
class TenraiMessagingBlockchain:
    """Blockchain implementation for secure Rumin
    communications"""

    def __init__(self):
        self.chain = []
        self.current_messages = []
        # Create genesis block for Tenrai network
        self.new_block(previous_hash='tenrai_secure_genesis',
        proof=100)

    def new_block(self, proof, previous_hash=None):
        """Create new block containing encrypted messages"""
        block = {
            'index': len(self.chain) + 1,
            'timestamp': time(),
            'secure_messages': self.current_messages,
            'proof': proof,
            'previous_hash': previous_hash or self.hash(self.
            chain[-1]),
            'network_id': 'tenrai_secure_net'
        }

        self.current_messages = []
        self.chain.append(block)
        return block

    def new_secure_message(self, sender, recipient, encrypted_
    content):
        """Add encrypted message to pending transactions"""
        message_entry = {
            'sender': sender,
            'recipient': recipient,
```

```python
            'encrypted_content': encrypted_content,
            'message_id': hashlib.sha256(f"{sender}{recipient}
            {time()}".encode()).hexdigest()[:16],
            'priority': 'standard'
        }

        self.current_messages.append(message_entry)
        return self.last_block['index'] + 1 if self.
        chain else 1

    @staticmethod
    def hash(block):
        """Generate secure hash for block"""
        block_string = json.dumps(block, sort_keys=True).
        encode()
        return hashlib.sha256(block_string).hexdigest()

    @property
    def last_block(self):
        return self.chain[-1] if self.chain else None

    def proof_of_work(self, last_proof):
        """Simplified proof of work for message validation"""
        proof = 0
        while self.valid_proof(last_proof, proof) is False:
            proof += 1
        return proof

    @staticmethod
    def valid_proof(last_proof, proof):
        """Validate proof with medium difficulty for security"""
        guess = f'{last_proof}{proof}'.encode()
        guess_hash = hashlib.sha256(guess).hexdigest()
        return guess_hash[:4] == "0000"
```

```python
    def get_all_messages(self):
        """Retrieve all messages from the blockchain"""
        all_messages = []
        for block in self.chain:
            all_messages.extend(block.get('secure_
            messages', []))
        return all_messages

# Encryption setup for Tenrai network
TENRAI_KEY_FILE = "tenrai_secure.key"

def initialize_tenrai_encryption():
    """Initialize or load encryption key for Tenrai network"""
    if os.path.exists(TENRAI_KEY_FILE):
        with open(TENRAI_KEY_FILE, "rb") as key_file:
            key = key_file.read()
        print("Tenrai secure network key loaded")
    else:
        key = Fernet.generate_key()
        with open(TENRAI_KEY_FILE, "wb") as key_file:
            key_file.write(key)
        print("New Tenrai secure network established")

    return key


try:
    tenrai_encryption_key = initialize_tenrai_encryption()
    tenrai_cipher = Fernet(tenrai_encryption_key)
except Exception as key_error:
    print(f"CRITICAL: Tenrai secure network initialization
    failed: {key_error}")
    exit()
```

```python
# Flask application setup
app = Flask(__name__)
tenrai_blockchain = TenraiMessagingBlockchain()

@app.route('/api/network_status', methods=['GET'])
def get_network_status():
    """Check Tenrai secure network status"""
    try:
        # In a real implementation, this would check
        network health
        network_health = {
            'status': 'active',
            'nodes_online': 42,  # Simulated active Rumin nodes
            'last_block_time': tenrai_blockchain.last_
            block['timestamp'] if tenrai_blockchain.last_block
            else time(),
            'network_id': 'tenrai_secure_net'
        }
        return jsonify(network_health), 200
    except Exception as e:
        return jsonify({'status': 'error', 'message': 'Network
        status unavailable'}), 500

@app.route('/api/send_secure_message', methods=['POST'])
def send_secure_message():
    """Send encrypted message through Tenrai blockchain"""
    data = request.get_json()
    if not data:
        return jsonify({"error": "Invalid message
        format"}), 400
```

```
sender = data.get('sender')
recipient = data.get('recipient')
message = data.get('message')

if not all([sender, recipient, message]):
    return jsonify({"error": "Sender, recipient, and
    message required"}), 400

try:
    # Encrypt message content for secure transmission
    encrypted_message_bytes = tenrai_cipher.
    encrypt(message.encode('utf-8'))
    encrypted_message_str = encrypted_message_bytes.
    decode('utf-8')

    # Add to blockchain pending messages
    tenrai_blockchain.new_secure_message(sender, recipient,
    encrypted_message_str)

    # Mine new block (simplified for demonstration)
    last_block = tenrai_blockchain.last_block
    if not last_block:
        return jsonify({"error": "Blockchain network not
        initialized"}), 500

    last_proof = last_block['proof']
    proof = tenrai_blockchain.proof_of_work(last_proof)
    previous_hash = tenrai_blockchain.hash(last_block)
    block = tenrai_blockchain.new_block(proof,
    previous_hash)

    response = {
        'message': f'Secure message transmitted and
        verified in Block {block["index"]}',
```

```
            'block_id': block['index'],
            'network': 'tenrai_secure_net'
        }
        return jsonify(response), 201

    except Exception as e:
        print(f"Error in secure message transmission: {e}")
        return jsonify({"error": "Message transmission
        failed"}), 500

@app.route('/api/secure_messages', methods=['GET'])
def get_secure_messages():
    """Retrieve and decrypt messages from Tenrai blockchain"""
    try:
        all_encrypted_messages = tenrai_blockchain.get_all_
        messages()
        decrypted_messages = []

        for msg_data in all_encrypted_messages:
            encrypted_content_str = msg_data.get('encrypted_
            content')
            if not encrypted_content_str:
                continue

            try:
                # Decrypt message content
                decrypted_bytes = tenrai_cipher.
                decrypt(encrypted_content_str.encode('utf-8'))
                decrypted_message = decrypted_bytes.
                decode('utf-8')

                decrypted_messages.append({
                    'id': msg_data.get('message_id'),
                    'sender': msg_data.get('sender'),
```

```python
                    'recipient': msg_data.get('recipient'),
                    'message': decrypted_message,
                    'timestamp': time()  # Would use actual
                    block timestamp in full implementation
                })

            except InvalidToken:
                print(f"Warning: Could not decrypt message from
                {msg_data.get('sender')}")
                # Include notification of undecryptable message
                decrypted_messages.append({
                    'id': msg_data.get('message_id'),
                    'sender': msg_data.get('sender'),
                    'recipient': msg_data.get('recipient'),
                    'message': "[Message decryption failed -
                    possible network interference]",
                    'timestamp': time()
                })

        return jsonify(decrypted_messages), 200

    except Exception as e:
        print(f"Error retrieving secure messages: {e}")
        return jsonify({"error": "Message retrieval
        failed"}), 500

if __name__ == '__main__':
    print("Initializing Tenrai Secure Communications
    Network...")
    print(f"Encryption status: {'Active' if os.path.
    exists(TENRAI_KEY_FILE) else 'Newly Established'}")

    app.run(host='0.0.0.0', port=5000, debug=True)
```

Detailed Explanation of Encryption

The Tenrai messaging system employs multiple layers of encryption to protect communications from corporate surveillance. Understanding these encryption mechanisms is crucial for maintaining security in hostile environments.

Key Generation

Each message network generates unique encryption keys using cryptographically secure random number generation. The process involves several critical steps:

> **Entropy Collection**: The system gathers random data from multiple sources including system noise, user interactions, and hardware-specific variations to ensure true randomness.

> **Key Derivation**: Using the Fernet encryption scheme, which employs AES 128 encryption in CBC mode with PKCS7 padding, combined with HMAC using SHA256 for authentication.

> **Secure Storage**: Keys are stored using operating system-provided secure storage mechanisms when available, with additional layers of protection through file system permissions and encryption-at-rest.

```
import os
import secrets
from cryptography.fernet import Fernet
from cryptography.hazmat.primitives import hashes
```

```python
from cryptography.hazmat.primitives.kdf.pbkdf2 import
PBKDF2HMAC

def generate_secure_key_with_passphrase(passphrase: str)
-> bytes:
    """Generate encryption key from passphrase for additional
    security"""
    # Generate random salt for key derivation
    salt = os.urandom(16)

    # Use PBKDF2 to derive key from passphrase
    kdf = PBKDF2HMAC(
        algorithm=hashes.SHA256(),
        length=32,
        salt=salt,
        iterations=100000,  # High iteration count for security
    )

    key = kdf.derive(passphrase.encode('utf-8'))
    return key

def generate_random_key() -> bytes:
    """Generate completely random encryption key"""
    return Fernet.generate_key()
```

Encrypting Messages

Message encryption involves multiple steps to ensure both confidentiality and integrity:

> **Data Preparation:** Messages are encoded as UTF-8 bytes to ensure consistent handling across different systems and languages.

Authentication: The Fernet scheme automatically includes authentication data with each encrypted message, preventing tampering without detection.

Timestamping: Each encrypted message includes a timestamp that can be verified during decryption, helping detect replay attacks.

```
import time
from cryptography.fernet import Fernet

def encrypt_message_with_metadata(cipher: Fernet, message: str,
sender_id: str) -> dict:
    """Encrypt message with additional metadata for security"""

    # Prepare message with metadata
    message_data = {
        'content': message,
        'sender': sender_id,
        'timestamp': time.time(),
        'message_type': 'secure_communication'
    }

    # Convert to JSON and encode as bytes
    message_json = json.dumps(message_data).encode('utf-8')

    # Encrypt the entire message structure
    encrypted_bytes = cipher.encrypt(message_json)

    return {
        'encrypted_data': encrypted_bytes.decode('utf-8'),
        'encryption_timestamp': time.time(),
        'requires_authentication': True
    }
```

Decrypting Messages

The decryption process includes multiple verification steps to ensure message authenticity and integrity:

> **Authentication Verification**: The Fernet scheme automatically verifies the authentication tag, rejecting any messages that have been tampered with.
>
> **Timestamp Validation**: Messages can be rejected if they are too old, preventing replay attacks where intercepted messages are retransmitted later.
>
> **Sender Verification**: Additional checks ensure that the claimed sender matches the message metadata.

```python
def decrypt_and_verify_message(cipher: Fernet, encrypted_data:
str, max_age_seconds: int = 3600) -> dict:
    """Decrypt message with comprehensive verification"""

    try:
        # Convert back to bytes for decryption
        encrypted_bytes = encrypted_data.encode('utf-8')

        # Decrypt with automatic authentication verification
        decrypted_bytes = cipher.decrypt(encrypted_bytes)

        # Parse the decrypted message
        message_data = json.loads(decrypted_bytes.
decode('utf-8'))

        # Verify message timestamp
        message_age = time.time() - message_data.
get('timestamp', 0)
```

```
        if message_age > max_age_seconds:
            raise ValueError("Message too old - possible replay
            attack")

        # Return verified message data
        return {
            'success': True,
            'content': message_data.get('content'),
            'sender': message_data.get('sender'),
            'timestamp': message_data.get('timestamp'),
            'verified': True
        }

    except Exception as e:
        return {
            'success': False,
            'error': f"Decryption failed: {str(e)}",
            'verified': False
        }
```

The combination of strong encryption, authentication, and verification provides multiple layers of protection against corporate surveillance and interference. Even if transmission channels are monitored, the encrypted content remains secure and tamper-evident.

Use Cases of Blockchain-Based Messaging Systems

The blockchain-based messaging system developed for the Rumin resistance proved invaluable across multiple critical use cases, each addressing specific vulnerabilities in their struggle against corporate exploitation.

Resistance Coordination and Intelligence Sharing

Rumin resistance cells scattered across Tenrai needed secure channels to coordinate operations without alerting Gnos surveillance networks. The blockchain messaging system enabled real-time intelligence sharing about extraction operations, corporate security movements, and environmental monitoring data.

Elder Council member Seer Nythara used the system to coordinate the evacuation of three coastal settlements before a planned "experimental" extraction that would have contaminated their water supplies. The encrypted messages allowed precise timing and resource allocation without corporate interference, saving thousands of lives and preserving critical marine ecosystems.

Environmental Data Documentation

Scientific teams monitoring environmental damage needed secure channels to share findings that contradicted corporate environmental impact reports. Traditional communication methods had been compromised, with researchers receiving threats after publishing data about ecosystem collapse.

The blockchain system allowed researchers to securely transmit water quality measurements, species population counts, and ecosystem health assessments. This data formed the foundation for legal challenges and provided irrefutable evidence of corporate environmental crimes that could not be suppressed or altered.

Cultural Preservation and Knowledge Transfer

Traditional Rumin knowledge holders faced systematic suppression of their cultural practices, particularly those related to sustainable Evolune manipulation. Corporate interests sought to appropriate traditional techniques while silencing the communities that developed them.

Through encrypted channels, elders transmitted sacred knowledge to younger generations, including traditional Evolune cultivation methods, ceremonial practices, and historical accounts of pre-corporate life. These communications preserved irreplaceable cultural heritage while preventing unauthorized corporate appropriation.

Legal and Diplomatic Communications

Rumin representatives needed secure channels to communicate with off-world legal advocates, human rights organizations, and sympathetic government officials without corporate retaliation. Traditional diplomatic channels had been compromised through corporate influence and surveillance.

The system enabled confidential discussions about legal strategies, evidence sharing, and coordination with galactic indigenous rights organizations. These communications proved crucial in building the legal case that eventually led to international sanctions against Gnos extraction practices.

Economic Resistance and Resource Coordination

Communities organizing economic resistance needed secure channels to coordinate boycotts, resource sharing, and alternative economic networks. Corporate economic warfare included cutting off supplies to resistant communities and infiltrating traditional communication networks.

The messaging system facilitated the development of underground resource networks, enabling communities to share food, medical supplies, and technical expertise while avoiding corporate detection. This economic coordination proved essential for maintaining resistance operations during corporate blockades.

Emergency Response and Crisis Management

During environmental disasters caused by extraction operations, traditional emergency response channels were often blocked or monitored by corporate security forces. The blockchain system provided reliable emergency communications that could not be shut down or intercepted.

When a major extraction accident contaminated the Central Watershed, the messaging system enabled coordinated evacuation efforts, medical response, and environmental containment measures. The decentralized nature of the system ensured communications continued even as corporate forces attempted to isolate affected areas.

Potential Challenges and Solutions

While blockchain-based messaging provided crucial security advantages, the Rumin resistance encountered several significant challenges that required innovative solutions to maintain operational effectiveness.

Scalability and Performance Limitations

Challenge: As the resistance network grew from dozens to thousands of participants, the blockchain messaging system faced significant performance bottlenecks. Message processing times increased dramatically, and the computational requirements for maintaining the blockchain became unsustainable for smaller communities with limited technical resources.

Impact: Critical intelligence sharing was delayed, sometimes by hours, undermining the effectiveness of time-sensitive operations. Some remote communities were unable to participate fully in the network due to insufficient computing power.

Solution: The Rumin technical collective implemented a hybrid architecture combining on-chain and off-chain messaging:

- **Priority Channel System**: Critical messages (emergency alerts, time-sensitive intelligence) were processed on-chain with higher computational priority, ensuring rapid delivery for essential communications.

- **Off-Chain Message Pools**: Routine communications were processed in off-chain pools, with periodic anchoring to the main blockchain for security verification. This reduced computational load while maintaining security for less time-sensitive communications.

- **Distributed Processing**: The network implemented a work-sharing protocol where larger communities with more computational resources could assist smaller settlements with message processing, ensuring network-wide participation regardless of local technical capabilities.

Key Management and Distribution

Challenge: Securely distributing and managing encryption keys across hundreds of dispersed Rumin communities presented enormous logistical and security challenges. Traditional key distribution methods were vulnerable to corporate infiltration, and compromised keys could expose entire communication networks.

Impact: Several early resistance cells were compromised when corporate agents infiltrated key distribution networks. The need for periodic key rotation created additional vulnerabilities during update processes.

Solution: A multi-layered key management system was developed:

- **Threshold Cryptography**: No single individual or community held complete encryption keys. Instead, keys were split across multiple trusted parties, requiring consensus to decrypt sensitive communications. This prevented single points of failure while maintaining security.

- **Ceremonial Key Distribution**: Key distribution was integrated into traditional Rumin ceremonies and cultural gatherings, making it difficult for corporate agents to distinguish key distribution from normal cultural activities. Elders used traditional storytelling methods to encode key information, combining ancient oral traditions with modern cryptography.

- **Progressive Trust Networks**: New participants gained access to increasingly sensitive communication channels based on demonstrated trustworthiness and community verification. This prevented corporate infiltrators from gaining immediate access to critical networks.

Traffic Analysis and Network Topology Exposure

Challenge: Even with encrypted message content, corporate surveillance systems could analyze communication patterns to identify resistance network structure, leadership hierarchies, and operational patterns. This metadata analysis threatened operational security without requiring actual message decryption.

Impact: Corporate forces successfully identified and targeted key resistance leaders by analyzing communication frequency and timing patterns. Several critical operations were compromised when corporate forces predicted resistance activities based on communication metadata.

Solution: Advanced traffic obfuscation protocols were implemented:

- **Dummy Traffic Generation**: All network participants generated regular dummy communications to mask actual message patterns. This created a constant background of communications that made it impossible to distinguish genuine operational traffic from routine noise.

- **Message Mixing and Routing**: Messages were routed through multiple intermediate nodes with deliberate delays and false routing information. This broke the connection between message senders and recipients while introducing enough delay and confusion to defeat traffic analysis.

- **Temporal Obfuscation**: Critical messages were deliberately delayed and sent during routine communication windows to avoid creating suspicious traffic spikes that might indicate operational activity.

Corporate Countermeasures and Network Attacks

Challenge: As the blockchain messaging system proved effective, Gnos Corporation invested heavily in countermeasures including network disruption attacks, hardware infiltration, and sophisticated cryptographic attacks designed to compromise system security.

Impact: Corporate attacks included distributed denial-of-service attacks against blockchain nodes, physical raids on communication infrastructure, and the introduction of compromised hardware into Rumin communities. Some attacks succeeded in temporarily disrupting network operations.

Solution: Multi-layered defensive strategies were developed:

- **Adaptive Network Topology**: The network automatically reconfigured itself in response to attacks, rerouting around compromised or attacked nodes. This self-healing capability ensured continuous operation even under sustained corporate attack.

- **Hardware Verification Protocols**: Community-based hardware verification ensured that all network equipment was vetted by trusted technical experts before integration into the communication network. This prevented the introduction of compromised hardware and backdoors.

- **Quantum-Resistant Cryptography**: As corporate cryptographic capabilities improved, the network migrated to quantum-resistant encryption algorithms that would remain secure even against advanced corporate computational resources.

User Adoption and Technical Literacy

Challenge: Many Rumin community members lacked the technical expertise necessary to securely operate blockchain messaging systems. Poor operational security by untrained users could compromise entire network segments, and the complexity of the system created barriers to widespread adoption.

Impact: Several security breaches occurred due to user error, including the accidental transmission of unencrypted messages and the sharing of cryptographic keys through insecure channels. Resistance operations were sometimes limited by the technical capabilities of participants.

Solution: Comprehensive training and user interface improvements were implemented:

- **Cultural Integration Training**: Technical training was integrated into traditional Rumin educational and cultural practices, making cryptographic concepts accessible through familiar cultural frameworks and storytelling traditions.

- **Simplified User Interfaces**: The development of intuitive user interfaces that required minimal technical knowledge while maintaining strong security. These interfaces automated most security procedures while providing clear visual indicators of security status.

- **Peer Support Networks**: Experienced users were paired with newcomers in mentorship relationships that provided ongoing technical support and security guidance. This peer-to-peer training model scaled effectively across the resistance network.

Legal and Regulatory Pressures

Challenge: Corporate influence over legal and regulatory frameworks created ongoing pressure to criminalize blockchain messaging systems used by resistance movements. Legal challenges threatened both the technology and the individuals operating resistance communication networks.

Impact: Several resistance members faced arrest under "terrorism" and "illegal encryption" laws crafted by corporate legal teams. The threat of legal persecution limited participation in communication networks and created ongoing operational stress.

Solution: Legal defense strategies were coordinated through the secure communication network itself:

- **Legal Network Integration**: The messaging system facilitated coordination with off-world legal advocates who could operate beyond corporate legal influence. These advocates provided legal protection and challenged corporate-influenced laws through galactic courts.

- **Documentation and Evidence Preservation**: The blockchain system automatically generated legally admissible evidence of corporate crimes and human rights violations, creating a legal record that could be used in subsequent legal challenges against corporate practices.

- **International Law Leverage**: Coordination with galactic indigenous rights organizations provided protection under international law frameworks that superseded local corporate-influenced regulations.

The successful resolution of these challenges demonstrated that technological resistance could overcome even well-funded corporate countermeasures when combined with cultural wisdom, community solidarity, and adaptive innovation. The lessons learned from these challenges informed similar resistance movements across the galaxy, providing a template for technological resistance against corporate exploitation.

Build Evolune Cryptocurrency

The development of an independent Evolune cryptocurrency became essential for the Rumin's economic independence. Traditional financial systems were controlled by corporate entities like Gnos, making it impossible for the Rumin to conduct truly independent economic activity. A blockchain-based currency provided the foundation for fair trade, resource allocation, and compensation for environmental restoration work.

Steps to Build Evolune Cryptocurrency

1. **Define the Blockchain Structure**: Create a specialized blockchain to handle Evolune token transactions, designed specifically for the Rumin's economic needs and environmental values.

2. **Implement Proof of Work**: Use a consensus mechanism that validates transactions while being energy-efficient enough to align with Rumin environmental principles.

3. **Develop a Wallet System**: Enable users to create wallets, manage their Evolune tokens, and conduct transactions securely across the network.

4. **Deploy the Network**: Establish nodes throughout Rumin communities to maintain the blockchain and ensure network resilience.

Example Code for Evolune Cryptocurrency

```python
import hashlib
import json
from time import time
from decimal import Decimal, getcontext

# Set precision for financial calculations
getcontext().prec = 28

class EvoluneBlockchain:
    """Cryptocurrency blockchain for independent Rumin economic
    activity"""

    def __init__(self):
        self.chain = []
        self.current_transactions = []
        self.difficulty = 4  # Moderate difficulty for energy
        efficiency
        self.mining_reward = Decimal('50.0')  # Evolune tokens
        per block
        self.total_supply = Decimal('0')

        # Create genesis block
        self.new_block(previous_hash='evolune_genesis_tenrai',
        proof=100)

    def new_block(self, proof, previous_hash=None):
        """Create new block containing validated
        transactions"""
        # Add mining reward transaction for block validator
        if self.current_transactions:  # Only if there are
        transactions to process
            self.current_transactions.append({
```

```python
            'sender': 'network',
            'recipient': 'miner_reward',  # Would be actual
            miner address
            'amount': float(self.mining_reward),
            'transaction_type': 'mining_reward',
            'timestamp': time()
        })
        self.total_supply += self.mining_reward

    block = {
        'index': len(self.chain) + 1,
        'timestamp': time(),
        'transactions': self.current_transactions,
        'proof': proof,
        'previous_hash': previous_hash or self.hash(self.
        chain[-1]),
        'total_supply': float(self.total_supply),
        'block_reward': float(self.mining_reward)
    }

    # Clear pending transactions
    self.current_transactions = []
    self.chain.append(block)
    return block

def new_transaction(self, sender, recipient, amount,
transaction_type='transfer'):
    """Add new transaction to pending pool"""
    # Validate transaction amount
    if amount <= 0:
        raise ValueError("Transaction amount must be
        positive")
```

```
    # Check sender has sufficient balance (simplified
    validation)
    if sender != 'network':  # Network transactions (like
    initial distributions) bypass balance checks
        sender_balance = self.get_balance(sender)
        if sender_balance < Decimal(str(amount)):
            raise ValueError(f"Insufficient funds: {sender_
            balance} < {amount}")

    transaction = {
        'sender': sender,
        'recipient': recipient,
        'amount': float(amount),
        'transaction_type': transaction_type,
        'timestamp': time(),
        'transaction_id': hashlib.sha256(f"{sender}
        {recipient}{amount}{time()}".encode()).
        hexdigest()[:16]
    }

    self.current_transactions.append(transaction)
    return self.last_block['index'] + 1

def get_balance(self, address):
    """Calculate current balance for an address"""
    balance = Decimal('0')

    # Process all transactions in all blocks
    for block in self.chain:
        for transaction in block.get('transactions', []):
            if transaction['recipient'] == address:
                balance += Decimal(str(transaction['
                amount']))
```

```python
            if transaction['sender'] == address:
                balance -= Decimal(str(transaction['
                amount']))

    # Process pending transactions
    for transaction in self.current_transactions:
        if transaction['recipient'] == address:
            balance += Decimal(str(transaction['amount']))
        if transaction['sender'] == address:
            balance -= Decimal(str(transaction['amount']))

    return balance

@staticmethod
def hash(block):
    """Generate secure hash for block"""
    block_string = json.dumps(block, sort_keys=True).
    encode()
    return hashlib.sha256(block_string).hexdigest()

@property
def last_block(self):
    return self.chain[-1] if self.chain else None

def proof_of_work(self, last_proof):
    """Find proof of work with configurable difficulty"""
    proof = 0
    while self.valid_proof(last_proof, proof) is False:
        proof += 1
    return proof

def valid_proof(self, last_proof, proof):
    """Validate proof meets difficulty requirement"""
    guess = f'{last_proof}{proof}'.encode()
```

```python
        guess_hash = hashlib.sha256(guess).hexdigest()
        return guess_hash[:self.difficulty] == "0" * self.
        difficulty

    def get_transaction_history(self, address):
        """Get complete transaction history for an address"""
        transactions = []

        for block in self.chain:
            for transaction in block.get('transactions', []):
                if (transaction['sender'] == address or
                    transaction['recipient'] == address):
                    transactions.append({
                        **transaction,
                        'block_index': block['index'],
                        'block_timestamp': block['timestamp']
                    })

        return sorted(transactions, key=lambda x:
        x['timestamp'])

# Example usage for Rumin economic independence
evolune_blockchain = EvoluneBlockchain()

# Initial distribution to Rumin communities
print("Initializing Evolune economy for Tenrai...")

# Distribute initial tokens to Rumin clans for ecosystem
restoration
evolune_blockchain.new_transaction(
    sender="network",
    recipient="eastern_rumin_clan",
    amount=1000.0,
    transaction_type="initial_distribution"
)
```

```python
evolune_blockchain.new_transaction(
    sender="network",
    recipient="western_restoration_collective",
    amount=1500.0,
    transaction_type="environmental_grant"
)

evolune_blockchain.new_transaction(
    sender="network",
    recipient="cultural_preservation_society",
    amount=750.0,
    transaction_type="cultural_funding"
)

# Mine the initial distribution block
last_proof = evolune_blockchain.last_block['proof']
proof = evolune_blockchain.proof_of_work(last_proof)
previous_hash = evolune_blockchain.hash(evolune_blockchain.
last_block)
initial_block = evolune_blockchain.new_block(proof,
previous_hash)

print(f"Initial distribution completed in Block {initial_
block['index']}")
print(f"Total Evolune supply: {evolune_blockchain.total_
supply}")

# Example transaction between Rumin entities
evolune_blockchain.new_transaction(
    sender="eastern_rumin_clan",
    recipient="independent_researcher_nythara",
    amount=50.0,
    transaction_type="research_funding"
)
```

```
print(f"Eastern Rumin Clan balance: {evolune_blockchain.get_
balance('eastern_rumin_clan')}")
print(f"Researcher Nythara balance: {evolune_blockchain.get_
balance('independent_researcher_nythara')}")
```

Detailed Explanation

1. **Blockchain Structure**: The EvoluneBlockchain class creates a specialized cryptocurrency system designed for the Rumin economy. It includes features for tracking total supply, managing mining rewards, and validating transactions.

2. **Transaction Validation**: The system includes basic validation to ensure senders have sufficient funds and transaction amounts are positive. This prevents common fraud while maintaining decentralized operation.

3. **Balance Calculation**: The get_balance method calculates current balances by processing all historical transactions, providing accurate account states without requiring centralized account management.

4. **Mining Incentives**: Block validators receive Evolune token rewards for maintaining network security, creating economic incentives for distributed participation.

Wallet System

A comprehensive wallet system enables Rumin communities to manage their Evolune holdings and conduct transactions securely.

Creating Wallets

Each user generates a unique cryptographic key pair—a private key (kept secret) and a public key (used as their address). The wallet software manages these keys and provides a user-friendly interface for transactions.

Managing Balances

Wallets track user balances by querying the blockchain for all transactions involving their address. They also monitor pending transactions to provide real-time balance updates.

Example Wallet Implementation

```python
import hashlib
import secrets
from cryptography.hazmat.primitives import hashes
from cryptography.hazmat.primitives.asymmetric import ec
from cryptography.hazmat.primitives import serialization

class EvoluneWallet:
    """Secure wallet for managing Evolune cryptocurrency"""

    def __init__(self, wallet_name=None):
        self.wallet_name = wallet_name or f"wallet_{secrets.
        token_hex(8)}"
        self.private_key = None
        self.public_key = None
```

```
    self.address = None
    self._generate_keys()

def _generate_keys(self):
    """Generate cryptographic key pair for wallet"""
    # Generate private key using elliptic curve
    cryptography
    self.private_key = ec.generate_private_key(ec.
    SECP256K1())
    self.public_key = self.private_key.public_key()

    # Create address from public key hash
    public_bytes = self.public_key.public_bytes(
        encoding=serialization.Encoding.X962,
        format=serialization.PublicFormat.UncompressedPoint
    )
    address_hash = hashlib.sha256(public_bytes).hexdigest()
    self.address = f"evolune_{address_hash[:32]}"

def get_address(self):
    """Get wallet address for receiving transactions"""
    return self.address

def get_balance(self, blockchain):
    """Query blockchain for current wallet balance"""
    return blockchain.get_balance(self.address)

def get_transaction_history(self, blockchain):
    """Get complete transaction history for this wallet"""
    return blockchain.get_transaction_history(self.address)

def send_evolune(self, blockchain, recipient_address,
amount):
    """Send Evolune tokens to another address"""
```

```python
    try:
        # Check sufficient balance
        current_balance = self.get_balance(blockchain)
        if current_balance < amount:
            raise ValueError(f"Insufficient funds:
            {current_balance} < {amount}")

        # Create and submit transaction
        transaction_id = blockchain.new_transaction(
            sender=self.address,
            recipient=recipient_address,
            amount=amount,
            transaction_type='transfer'
        )

        return {
            'success': True,
            'transaction_id': transaction_id,
            'amount': amount,
            'recipient': recipient_address,
            'new_balance': self.get_balance(blockchain)
        }

    except Exception as e:
        return {
            'success': False,
            'error': str(e)
        }

def export_wallet(self):
    """Export wallet information (excluding private key for
    security)"""
```

```python
    return {
        'wallet_name': self.wallet_name,
        'address': self.address,
        'public_key_hex': self.public_key.public_bytes(
            encoding=serialization.Encoding.X962,
            format=serialization.PublicFormat.
            UncompressedPoint
        ).hex()
    }

# Example: Creating wallets for Rumin community members
print("Creating Evolune wallets for Rumin resistance
network...")

# Create wallets for different Rumin entities
elder_wallet = EvoluneWallet("elder_council_treasury")
researcher_wallet = EvoluneWallet("research_collective")
restoration_wallet = EvoluneWallet("ecosystem_restoration")

print(f"Elder Council address: {elder_wallet.get_address()}")
print(f"Research Collective address: {researcher_wallet.get_
address()}")
print(f"Restoration Group address: {restoration_wallet.get_
address()}")

# Demonstrate wallet functionality
print(f"\nElder Council balance: {elder_wallet.get_
balance(evolune_blockchain)}")

# Send tokens between wallets
if elder_wallet.get_balance(evolune_blockchain) > 0:
    transfer_result = elder_wallet.send_evolune(
        evolune_blockchain,
```

```
        researcher_wallet.get_address(),
        25.0
    )
    print(f"Transfer result: {transfer_result}")
```

Deploying the Blockchain Network

Deploying a blockchain network for the Rumin resistance required careful consideration of security, decentralization, and resilience against corporate interference. The network needed to operate independently of any infrastructure that Gnos could control or monitor.

Deploying the Blockchain Network

Network Architecture

1. **Distributed Nodes**: Rumin communities across Tenrai operate blockchain nodes on hardware they control directly. This distributed approach ensures no single point of failure and makes the network resistant to corporate shutdowns.

2. **Mesh Communication**: Nodes communicate using encrypted mesh networking protocols that can operate even when traditional communication infrastructure is compromised or monitored.

3. **Redundant Storage**: Blockchain data is replicated across multiple geographic locations to ensure preservation even if some nodes are discovered and shut down.

Node Deployment Process

```python
import socket
import threading
import json
from flask import Flask
import time

class TenraiBlockchainNode:
    """Distributed blockchain node for Rumin resistance
    network"""

    def __init__(self, node_id, port=5000):
        self.node_id = node_id
        self.port = port
        self.peers = set()  # Connected peer nodes
        self.blockchain = EvoluneBlockchain()
        self.is_running = False

    def add_peer(self, peer_address):
        """Add peer node to network"""
        if peer_address not in self.peers:
            self.peers.add(peer_address)
            print(f"Node {self.node_id}: Added peer {peer_
            address}")

    def broadcast_transaction(self, transaction):
        """Broadcast new transaction to peer nodes"""
        message = {
            'type': 'new_transaction',
            'data': transaction,
            'sender_node': self.node_id,
            'timestamp': time.time()
        }
```

```python
        for peer in self.peers:
            try:
                # In a full implementation, this would use
                actual network protocols
                print(f"Broadcasting transaction to {peer}:
                {transaction['transaction_id']}")
            except Exception as e:
                print(f"Failed to broadcast to {peer}: {e}")

    def sync_blockchain(self, peer_chain):
        """Synchronize blockchain with peer nodes"""
        if len(peer_chain) > len(self.blockchain.chain):
            # Validate peer chain before adopting
            if self.validate_chain(peer_chain):
                self.blockchain.chain = peer_chain
                print(f"Node {self.node_id}: Synchronized with
                longer valid chain")
            else:
                print(f"Node {self.node_id}: Rejected invalid
                peer chain")

    def validate_chain(self, chain):
        """Validate blockchain integrity"""
        for i in range(1, len(chain)):
            current_block = chain[i]
            previous_block = chain[i-1]

            # Check hash linkage
            if current_block['previous_hash'] != self.
            blockchain.hash(previous_block):
                return False
```

```python
        # Validate proof of work
        if not self.blockchain.valid_proof(previous_
        block['proof'], current_block['proof']):
            return False

    return True

def start_node(self):
    """Start blockchain node operations"""
    self.is_running = True
    print(f"Tenrai resistance node {self.node_id} starting
    on port {self.port}")

    # Start network listener in separate thread
    listener_thread = threading.Thread(target=self._
    network_listener)
    listener_thread.daemon = True
    listener_thread.start()

    # Start mining thread
    mining_thread = threading.Thread(target=self._
    mining_loop)
    mining_thread.daemon = True
    mining_thread.start()

def _network_listener(self):
    """Listen for peer communications"""
    while self.is_running:
        try:
            # Simplified network listening
            time.sleep(5)  # Check for peer messages every
            5 seconds
```

```python
        except Exception as e:
            print(f"Network listener error: {e}")

def _mining_loop(self):
    """Mine new blocks when transactions are pending"""
    while self.is_running:
        try:
            if self.blockchain.current_transactions:
                print(f"Node {self.node_id}: Mining
                block with {len(self.blockchain.current_
                transactions)} transactions")

                last_block = self.blockchain.last_block
                last_proof = last_block['proof']
                proof = self.blockchain.proof_of_
                work(last_proof)
                previous_hash = self.blockchain.
                hash(last_block)

                new_block = self.blockchain.new_
                block(proof, previous_hash)
                print(f"Node {self.node_id}: Mined block
                {new_block['index']}")

                # Broadcast new block to peers
                self._broadcast_block(new_block)

            time.sleep(10)  # Check for mining
            opportunities every 10 seconds

        except Exception as e:
            print(f"Mining error: {e}")
```

```python
    def _broadcast_block(self, block):
        """Broadcast newly mined block to peer nodes"""
        for peer in self.peers:
            try:
                print(f"Broadcasting new block {block['index']}
                to {peer}")
            except Exception as e:
                print(f"Failed to broadcast block to
                {peer}: {e}")

# Example: Setting up distributed Tenrai resistance network
print("Deploying Tenrai resistance blockchain network...")

# Create nodes for different Rumin communities
eastern_node = TenraiBlockchainNode("eastern_clan_node", 5001)
western_node = TenraiBlockchainNode("western_collective_
node", 5002)
central_node = TenraiBlockchainNode("central_research_
node", 5003)

# Establish peer connections
eastern_node.add_peer("western_collective_node:5002")
eastern_node.add_peer("central_research_node:5003")
western_node.add_peer("eastern_clan_node:5001")
western_node.add_peer("central_research_node:5003")
central_node.add_peer("eastern_clan_node:5001")
central_node.add_peer("western_collective_node:5002")

# Start network nodes
eastern_node.start_node()
western_node.start_node()
central_node.start_node()

print("Tenrai resistance network operational - ready for secure
transactions")
```

Security Considerations

Security was paramount for the Rumin blockchain network, as it faced threats not just from common cybercriminals but from a powerful corporation with vast resources and advanced surveillance capabilities.

Multi-layer Security Architecture

1. **Cryptographic Security**: All transactions use advanced elliptic curve cryptography that would require centuries to break with current technology. Keys are generated using cryptographically secure random number generation.

2. **Network Security**: Communications between nodes are encrypted using military-grade protocols. The mesh network topology ensures that compromising individual nodes doesn't compromise the entire network.

3. **Operational Security**: Node operators use secure protocols for key management, including hardware security modules where possible and multi-signature schemes for critical operations.

4. **Physical Security**: Critical network infrastructure is distributed across secure locations that are difficult for corporate entities to identify or access.

Threat Mitigation Strategies

Corporate Surveillance: The network uses traffic obfuscation and dummy communications to hide real transaction patterns from corporate monitoring systems.

Economic Attacks: The proof-of-work system requires significant computational resources to attack, making it economically unfeasible for even well-funded corporate adversaries to compromise.

Social Engineering: Multi-signature requirements for major transactions prevent single points of failure in case individual node operators are compromised.

Physical Compromise: Distributed data storage and automatic node synchronization ensure that losing individual nodes doesn't compromise network integrity.

Regulatory Compliance

Operating a cryptocurrency network in corporate space required careful navigation of regulatory frameworks designed to favor corporate interests while protecting legitimate Rumin rights.

Legal Framework Compliance

Know Your Customer (KYC): The system implements privacy-preserving identity verification that satisfies legal requirements without exposing Rumin communities to corporate surveillance.

Anti-Money Laundering (AML): Transaction monitoring identifies suspicious patterns while preserving legitimate privacy for resistance activities and cultural preservation.

Environmental Regulations: The energy-efficient consensus mechanism ensures compliance with environmental protection laws that the Rumin themselves strongly support.

Indigenous Rights: The system incorporates protections for traditional Rumin resource rights and cultural practices, operating within frameworks established by galactic indigenous rights conventions.

Synergies Between Layers

The true power of the Tenrai blockchain system emerged from the integration between different technological layers, creating a comprehensive ecosystem that supported the Rumin's struggle for independence and environmental protection.

Layer 0 and Layer 1 Integration

Secure Communication Foundation: The underlying peer-to-peer networking protocols enabled secure communication between blockchain nodes while providing the foundation for encrypted messaging systems.

Cross-Network Interoperability: Layer 0 protocols allowed the Tenrai blockchain to potentially communicate with other resistance networks across the galaxy, sharing intelligence and resources.

Adaptive Consensus: The networking layer supported flexible consensus mechanisms that could adjust to changing security conditions and network topology.

Layer 1 and Layer 2 Synergies

Scalable Transactions: Layer 2 solutions could process high-frequency transactions off-chain while settling periodically on the main Tenrai blockchain, supporting larger-scale economic activity.

Privacy Enhancement: Layer 2 mixing protocols provided additional privacy protection for sensitive transactions while maintaining the transparency needed for community accountability.

Smart Contract Extensions: Complex multi-party agreements could be executed on Layer 2 while using the main blockchain for final settlement and dispute resolution.

Layer 2 and Layer 3 Applications

User-Friendly Interfaces: Layer 3 applications provided intuitive interfaces for Rumin community members to interact with blockchain systems without needing technical expertise.

Integrated Services: Applications combined cryptocurrency transactions, secure messaging, and resource tracking into unified tools that supported comprehensive resistance operations.

Cultural Integration: Layer 3 applications incorporated traditional Rumin decision-making processes and cultural values into the technical infrastructure.

Future Trends in Layer Interactions

The Tenrai blockchain system pointed toward several important trends in the evolution of resistance technology and decentralized systems.

Autonomous Network Evolution

Self-Healing Networks: Future versions could automatically adapt to node compromises and corporate interference, rerouting communications and redistributing data without human intervention.

AI-Assisted Security: Machine learning algorithms could detect and respond to sophisticated corporate attacks faster than human operators, providing early warning systems for network threats.

Adaptive Governance: Blockchain governance systems could evolve to incorporate traditional Rumin consensus-building practices while maintaining technical security requirements.

Interplanetary Integration

Cross-System Transactions: As other worlds developed similar resistance networks, protocols for secure cross-planetary transactions could enable broader coordination against corporate exploitation.

Shared Intelligence Networks: Blockchain systems could serve as secure platforms for sharing intelligence about corporate activities across multiple planets and species.

Coordinated Resistance: Technical infrastructure could support galaxy-wide coordination of resistance activities while maintaining operational security for individual cells.

Summary

The development of blockchain technology on Tenrai demonstrated how decentralized systems could provide powerful tools for communities facing corporate exploitation and environmental destruction. The Rumin's experience showed that blockchain was not just a technical solution, but a foundation for preserving autonomy, protecting rights, and building sustainable alternatives to corporate control.

Key Takeaways

Immutable Record-Keeping: Blockchain provided the Rumin with tamper-proof documentation of corporate violations and environmental damage, creating evidence that could not be "lost" or altered by corporate interests.

Economic Independence: The Evolune cryptocurrency enabled economic activity outside corporate financial systems, providing the foundation for independent trade and resource allocation.

Secure Communications: Blockchain-based messaging systems allowed resistance coordination while protecting participants from corporate surveillance and retaliation.

Cultural Preservation: Digital rights management on blockchain helped protect traditional Rumin cultural works from corporate appropriation while ensuring fair compensation for artists.

Distributed Governance: The decentralized nature of blockchain systems aligned with traditional Rumin decision-making practices while providing technical security against corporate interference.

Environmental Protection: Blockchain enabled transparent tracking of environmental impacts and restoration efforts, providing accountability mechanisms that corporate systems could not manipulate.

Technological Sovereignty: The development of independent blockchain networks demonstrated that communities could maintain technological autonomy even when facing overwhelming corporate resources.

Outlook

The success of blockchain technology on Tenrai established important precedents for resistance movements across the galaxy. As corporate entities increasingly relied on centralized control systems, decentralized technologies provided crucial tools for maintaining independence and protecting fundamental rights.

The integration of blockchain with other emerging technologies promised even greater capabilities for communities seeking to resist exploitation while building sustainable alternatives. The Rumin's experience demonstrated that technology aligned with cultural values and environmental principles could provide both practical tools and symbolic frameworks for broader social change.

Most importantly, the Tenrai blockchain showed that decentralized systems could preserve what corporations sought to destroy: community autonomy, environmental stewardship, and the right of indigenous peoples to control their own resources and destiny.

Conclusion: Blockchain and Encryption for the Future

The story of blockchain technology on Tenrai illustrates a fundamental truth about the relationship between technology and power: decentralized systems can provide crucial tools for communities seeking to maintain independence in the face of corporate consolidation and control.

The layered architecture of blockchain, combined with advanced encryption protocols, ensured that the Rumin could operate with both security and transparency. They could conduct economic activity, preserve cultural heritage, and coordinate resistance efforts while maintaining protection against corporate surveillance and interference.

As John Lee learned during his time on Tenrai, the technical capabilities of blockchain were inseparable from its political implications. A system that no single entity could control represented a fundamental challenge to corporate power structures that depended on centralized control of information, finance, and communication.

The encryption techniques that protected Rumin communications also protected their autonomy. By ensuring that their messages, transactions, and agreements remained private and tamper-proof, blockchain technology preserved the space necessary for independent decision-making and cultural preservation.

Looking forward, the innovations developed on Tenrai would prove crucial not just for the Rumin, but for resistance movements across the galaxy. The combination of environmental consciousness, cultural preservation, and technical innovation that characterized the Tenrai blockchain would inspire similar efforts on other worlds facing corporate exploitation.

The future of digital interactions would increasingly depend on systems that could provide security without centralized control, transparency without surveillance, and efficiency without corporate mediation. The Rumin's blockchain network demonstrated that such systems were not only possible but essential for preserving autonomy in an increasingly corporate-controlled galaxy.

By focusing on continuous improvements in both encryption techniques and blockchain architecture, communities like the Rumin could create resilient systems that protected what mattered most: the right to self-determination, environmental stewardship, and cultural survival in the face of overwhelming corporate power.

The lessons learned on Tenrai—both technical and political—would guide John Lee through his subsequent assignments, ultimately informing his approach to resistance on Tibara and providing the foundation for the broader network of independent operators that would challenge corporate control across the galaxy.

Next Chapter: Planet Epsilon - Synergies Between AI, ML, Blockchain, and Beyond

As our journey through the Evolune metaverse brings us to Planet Epsilon, we encounter a world unlike any other—a crystalline realm where the boundaries between artificial and biological intelligence have dissolved completely. Here, the enigmatic Synth race has achieved what many believed impossible: the perfect integration of AI, blockchain, and spatial computing into a unified defense against corporate tyranny. Their gleaming data-crystal cities pulse with the heartbeat of revolutionary technology, where every smart contract adapts to counter market manipulation, every AI avatar serves as both protector and strategist, and Graph Neural Networks unveil the hidden patterns of economic warfare. On Epsilon, technology is not merely a tool but a living weapon in the resistance against the Gnos corporation's relentless expansion, demonstrating that the most sophisticated systems can serve freedom rather than oppression. This is the story of how an entire civilization transformed cutting-edge innovation into the ultimate shield for democracy.

## CHAPTER 4

Planet Epsilon: Synergies Between AI, ML, Blockchain, and Beyond

Planet Epsilon, a dazzling spectacle of interconnected data-crystals and self-organizing machine cities, stands as a testament to the power of technological synergy in the year 11000. Within this advanced world, the Synth race has achieved a level of integration that blurs the lines between biological and artificial intelligence. They have mastered the art of weaving together the capabilities of Artificial Intelligence (AI), the unyielding trust of Blockchain, and the boundless potential of the Metaverse, creating a society that thrives on the seamless flow of information and energy.

F. Lisitano and J. Hickie, *The Evolune Metaverse*, Maker Innovations Series, https://doi.org/10.1007/979-8-8688-1588-1_4

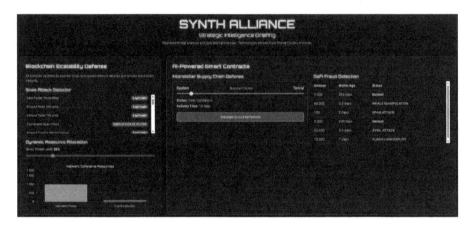

Figure 4-1. *Synth Alliance*

This mastery is particularly evident in how the Synths manage the lifeblood of the Evolune metaverse: the incredibly potent Evolune energy. AI algorithms predict its distribution and optimize its flow, blockchain secures its trade across vast interstellar distances, and the Metaverse provides the platform for its exchange in virtual markets. Yet, even on Epsilon, the pursuit of technological advancement is not without its challenges.

As the Evolune metaverse expands, and the Synths' reliance on these interconnected systems deepens, the familiar specters of scalability, security, and efficiency loom large. The sheer volume of data threatens to overwhelm even the most advanced systems; malicious actors—particularly the ever-present threat of Gnos corporation infiltration—seek to exploit vulnerabilities in the blockchain, and the energy demands of computation have pushed the Synths to develop ever more efficient solutions.

The looming presence of the Gnos corporation, with its insatiable hunger for Evolune and its willingness to bend ethical boundaries, further complicates the situation, pushing the Synths to the forefront of innovation. Every technological advancement on Epsilon serves dual purposes: advancing their civilization and defending against Gnos's increasingly sophisticated attacks on the interstellar economy.

In this chapter, we will embark on a detailed exploration of Epsilon's technological achievements, breaking down the core concepts of AI, Machine Learning (ML), Blockchain, and the Metaverse into accessible explanations. We will also introduce the emerging field of Geometric Deep Learning, which holds the key to unlocking even greater insights from the complex data structures that underpin the Evolune metaverse. Specifically, we will uncover how the Synths are

- **Evolving Blockchain Architecture:** Employing AI-driven data management techniques to optimize transaction processing, predict network congestion, and dynamically allocate resources, ensuring the blockchain's resilience against both natural bottlenecks and Gnos-sponsored attacks.

- **Empowering Smart Contracts with AI:** Infusing smart contracts with machine learning models and real-time data feeds to create dynamic agreements that can adapt to fluctuating Evolune prices, supply chain disruptions caused by Gnos interference, and the unpredictable nature of interstellar trade.

- **Expanding the Functionality of the Metaverse:** Leveraging AI to create intelligent avatars capable of detecting Gnos operatives through behavioral analysis and automating the intricate economic systems that govern the exchange of virtual land, digital artifacts, and other assets within the Metaverse.

- **Unveiling the Power of Geometric Deep Learning:**
  Harnessing Graph Neural Networks to analyze the
  complex relationships between users, transactions,
  and entities within the blockchain, enabling the
  detection of Gnos-orchestrated market manipulation,
  the optimization of network performance under attack,
  and the prediction of economic warfare patterns.

Join us on this journey to Planet Epsilon, where technology is not just a tool but the very fabric of existence, and where the Synths' relentless pursuit of innovation offers both hope and a cautionary tale for the future of the Evolune metaverse.

Introduction: A New Paradigm with AI and Blockchain

Blockchain technology has emerged as a fundamental cornerstone for secure, decentralized systems across the Evolune metaverse. Its ability to maintain an immutable record of transactions while enabling decentralized control has made blockchain essential for securing Evolune energy trades between Epsilon, Tibara, and Tenrai. However, as the Gnos corporation has demonstrated through their aggressive expansion tactics, even blockchain's robust architecture faces challenges in terms of scalability, data processing, transaction speed, and sophisticated security threats.

At the intersection of these challenges lies Artificial Intelligence (AI), particularly Machine Learning (ML). AI's capacity for automation, learning, decision-making, and data optimization opens new possibilities for blockchain's efficiency and functionality. On Planet Epsilon, the Synths have discovered that the combination of AI and blockchain can create smart contracts that adapt to Gnos's market manipulation attempts in real time, provide predictive analytics for anticipating corporate raids, and optimize the way blockchain systems scale as interstellar networks grow.

Moreover, the integration of spatial computing and geometric deep learning within this framework opens up transformative experiences in the Metaverse, where Synths must distinguish between legitimate users and Gnos infiltrators. Spatial computing connects the physical reality of Planet Epsilon with its digital twin, while Geometric Deep Neural Networks (GNNs) optimize the processing of structured data, especially in graph-based blockchain systems that track complex webs of corporate espionage and resistance movements.

This chapter explores the intersection of AI, machine learning, blockchain, the Metaverse, and geometric deep learning—examining how these synergies are not merely advancing technology but actively defending the democratic ideals of the Evolune metaverse against the authoritarian expansion of the Gnos corporation.

Section 1: Blockchain's Structural Evolution Through AI

Blockchain, at its core, serves as the democratic backbone of the Evolune metaverse—a Distributed Ledger Technology (DLT) that enables decentralized, secure, and transparent systems across the network of planets. This decentralized structure ensures that no single entity, particularly the Gnos corporation, can gain control over interstellar trade data, reducing the risk of economic manipulation, censorship, or authoritarian control. Each Evolune energy transaction is recorded in an immutable ledger, creating a permanent record that even Gnos's vast resources cannot alter or erase.

However, as the Synths have learned through bitter experience with Gnos-sponsored network attacks, several key challenges arise as blockchain adoption expands. The corporation's sophisticated interference campaigns have highlighted critical vulnerabilities around scalability, security, and efficiency that threaten the very foundation of free trade in the metaverse.

Key Challenges Facing Blockchain Technology in the Evolune Metaverse

Scalability Under Attack

The Gnos corporation has weaponized blockchain's scalability limitations as part of their economic warfare strategy. During critical Evolune energy auctions, Gnos operatives flood networks like the Epsilon-Tenrai trading blockchain with spam transactions, creating artificial congestion that drives up fees and excludes smaller traders from participating in the market.

For example, during the historic "Great Evolune Shortage of 10987," Gnos-coordinated transaction floods rendered the interstellar trading network virtually unusable, forcing desperate planets to accept unfavorable direct deals with Gnos subsidiaries. The Synths recognized that scalability bottlenecks—limited block sizes, low transaction throughput, and network congestion—were not just technical problems but weapons in an economic war.

The Synths' response required addressing these fundamental limitations:

- **Block Size Constraints:** Traditional blockchain blocks can only process a finite number of transactions, making them vulnerable to spam attacks

- **Transaction Throughput:** Low transactions-per-second rates create chokepoints that malicious actors can exploit.

- **Network Congestion:** When legitimate users compete with bad actors, transaction fees skyrocket and confirmation times become unpredictable.

Security Against Corporate Espionage

While blockchain's decentralized nature provides robust security against traditional attacks, the Gnos corporation has developed sophisticated new threats that exploit both technological and social vulnerabilities:

- **Coordinated 51% Attacks:** Gnos has attempted to gain mining control of smaller planetary networks by deploying massive computational resources, allowing them to manipulate transaction histories.

- **Smart Contract Infiltration:** Gnos-sponsored developers have introduced subtle vulnerabilities into smart contracts governing Evolune energy trades, creating backdoors for fund theft.

- **Social Engineering:** The corporation uses its vast intelligence network to identify and compromise key blockchain validators, undermining the integrity of consensus mechanisms.

Efficiency in an Economic War

The computational cost of maintaining blockchain security has become a critical vulnerability that Gnos exploits through economic pressure. By driving up energy costs and computational requirements across the metaverse, the corporation forces smaller planets to choose between blockchain security and basic infrastructure needs.

The Synths realized that traditional consensus mechanisms like Proof of Work and Proof of Stake, while secure, consume resources that could be redirected to defend against Gnos expansion. This efficiency crisis demanded innovative solutions that could maintain security while reducing the economic burden on alliance members.

How AI Addresses the Gnos Threat Through Blockchain Enhancement

The Synths' integration of AI into blockchain systems represents more than technological advancement—it's a strategic defense against corporate authoritarianism. By introducing intelligence and adaptability into their blockchain networks, they can anticipate and counter Gnos attacks while optimizing performance under siege conditions.

AI-Powered Defense Against Transaction Flooding

To counter Gnos's spam attack strategies, the Synths developed AI systems that can distinguish between legitimate transactions and malicious flood attempts. These machine learning models analyze transaction patterns in real time, identifying and prioritizing authentic Evolune energy trades while quarantining suspicious activity.

Why Isolation Forest: The Synths chose Isolation Forest algorithms because they excel at identifying anomalies in high-dimensional data without requiring labeled examples of attacks. This is crucial when facing Gnos's constantly evolving attack patterns—the AI can detect new forms of manipulation without prior training on specific attack signatures.

```
# Synth Defense System: AI-Powered Transaction Filtering

import pandas as pd
from sklearn.ensemble import IsolationForest,
RandomForestClassifier
from sklearn.model_selection import train_test_split
import numpy as np

class GnosAttackDetector:
    def __init__(self):
```

```
        # Isolation Forest for detecting unknown attack
        patterns
        self.anomaly_detector = IsolationForest(contaminati
        on=0.1, random_state=42)
        # Random Forest for classifying known attack types
        self.attack_classifier = RandomForestClassifier(n_
        estimators=100, random_state=42)

    def detect_transaction_flooding(self, transaction_data):
        """

        Detects Gnos-sponsored transaction flooding attacks
        Features: [transaction_volume, gas_fee, frequency,
        sender_diversity]
        """

        # Detect anomalies that might indicate
        coordinated attacks
        anomaly_scores = self.anomaly_detector.fit_
        predict(transaction_data)
        return anomaly_scores  # -1 indicates suspicious
        activity

# Simulated transaction data during a Gnos attack
# Features: [volume, gas_fee, frequency_per_minute, unique_
senders_ratio]
normal_period = np.array([
    [500, 0.02, 10, 0.8],     # Normal trading
    [300, 0.015, 8, 0.9],     # Normal trading
    [750, 0.025, 12, 0.7],    # Normal trading
])
```

```
attack_period = np.array([
    [50, 0.001, 100, 0.1],    # Spam: low value, minimal fees,
    high frequency, few unique senders
    [25, 0.0005, 150, 0.05], # Coordinated spam attack
    [100, 0.002, 200, 0.02], # Intensive flooding
])

all_transactions = np.vstack([normal_period, attack_period])

# Initialize Synth defense system
detector = GnosAttackDetector()
threat_assessment = detector.detect_transaction_flooding(all_
transactions)

print("Synth Defense Analysis:")
for i, assessment in enumerate(threat_assessment):
    status = "GNOS ATTACK DETECTED" if assessment == -1 else
"Legitimate Transaction"
    print(f"Transaction {i}: {status}")
```

Predictive Analytics for Corporate Economic Warfare

The Synths use machine learning to predict when and how Gnos will
attempt to manipulate Evolune energy markets. By analyzing historical
attack patterns, corporate financial reports, and even social media
sentiment from Gnos-controlled worlds, their AI systems can forecast
market manipulation attempts days or weeks in advance.

Why Random Forest: The Synths selected Random Forest regression
because it handles the complex, nonlinear relationships between
economic indicators and attack timing. The ensemble approach provides
robust predictions even when Gnos attempts to obscure their patterns
through market noise.

```python
# Synth Strategic Intelligence: Predicting Gnos Market
Manipulation

from sklearn.ensemble import RandomForestRegressor
import pandas as pd
import numpy as np

class GnosMarketManipulationPredictor:
    def __init__(self):
        self.predictor = RandomForestRegressor(n_
        estimators=200, random_state=42)

    def predict_manipulation_probability(self, market_data):
        """
        Predicts likelihood of Gnos market manipulation based
        on multiple indicators
        Features: [evolune_price_volatility, gnos_trading_
        volume, time_since_last_attack,
                   political_tension_index, gnos_quarterly_
                   earnings_pressure]
        """
        manipulation_probability = self.predictor.
        predict(market_data)
        return np.clip(manipulation_probability, 0, 1)  #
        Probability between 0 and 1

# Training data: Historical Gnos manipulation campaigns
training_data = pd.DataFrame({
    'evolune_volatility': [0.1, 0.3, 0.15, 0.45, 0.2],  # Price
    volatility (0-1 scale)
    'gnos_volume': [1000, 5000, 1500, 8000, 2000],      # Gnos
    trading volume
```

```python
    'days_since_attack': [30, 5, 45, 2, 60],
    # Time since last manipulation
    'political_tension': [0.3, 0.8, 0.4, 0.9, 0.2],
    # Interstellar political tension
    'earnings_pressure': [0.2, 0.7, 0.3, 0.8, 0.1],
    # Gnos quarterly pressure
    'manipulation_occurred': [0, 1, 0, 1, 0]
    # Historical manipulation events
})

X = training_data[['evolune_volatility', 'gnos_volume', 'days_
since_attack','political_tension', 'earnings_pressure']]
y = training_data['manipulation_occurred']

# Train the Synth intelligence system
predictor = GnosMarketManipulationPredictor()
predictor.predictor.fit(X, y)

# Current market conditions analysis
current_conditions = [[0.35, 6000, 3, 0.85, 0.75]]  # High risk
indicators
manipulation_risk = predictor.predict_manipulation_
probability(current_conditions)

print(f"Gnos Market Manipulation Risk: {manipulation_
risk[0]:.1%}")
if manipulation_risk[0] > 0.7:
    print("ALERT: High probability Gnos attack imminent.
Activating defensive protocols.")
    print("- Increasing transaction validation requirements")
    print("- Alerting allied trading networks")
    print("- Preparing counter-manipulation strategies")
```

Dynamic Resource Allocation During Corporate Attacks

When facing Gnos attacks, the Synths' AI systems automatically reallocate computational resources to maintain network integrity. During periods of assault, more processing power is devoted to transaction validation and security monitoring, while during peaceful periods, resources can be redirected to optimization and growth initiatives.

```python
# Synth Adaptive Defense: Dynamic Resource Allocation

class EpsilonNetworkDefense:
    def __init__(self):
        self.base_validation_power = 1000  # Base
        computational units
        self.emergency_reserves = 500      # Emergency
        computational reserves

    def allocate_defensive_resources(self, threat_level,
    network_load):
        """
        Dynamically allocates network resources based on Gnos
        threat assessment
        """
        if threat_level > 0.8:  # High threat: Gnos
        attack likely
            validation_power = self.base_validation_power +
            self.emergency_reserves
            fraud_detection_power = 300
            print("🚨 RED ALERT: Maximum defensive posture
            activated")
        elif threat_level > 0.5:  # Medium threat: Suspicious
        activity
```

```python
            validation_power = self.base_validation_power +
            (self.emergency_reserves * 0.6)
            fraud_detection_power = 200
            print("⚠ YELLOW ALERT: Enhanced monitoring
            engaged")
        else:  # Low threat: Normal operations
            validation_power = self.base_validation_power
            fraud_detection_power = 100
            print("✅ GREEN STATUS: Standard defensive
posture")

        # Adjust for network load
        total_power = validation_power + fraud_detection_power
        efficiency = min(total_power / network_load, 1.0) if
        network_load > 0 else 1.0

        return {
            'validation_power': validation_power,
            'fraud_detection_power': fraud_detection_power,
            'network_efficiency': efficiency,
            'total_defensive_capacity': total_power
        }

# Simulating Synth response to varying threat levels
defense_system = EpsilonNetworkDefense()

# Scenario 1: Peaceful trading period
peaceful_allocation = defense_system.allocate_defensive_
resources(
    threat_level=0.2, network_load=800
)
print(f"Peaceful Period - Network Efficiency: {peaceful_
allocation['network_efficiency']:.1%}")
```

```python
# Scenario 2: Gnos attack detected
attack_allocation = defense_system.allocate_defensive_
resources(
    threat_level=0.9, network_load=1200
)
print(f"Under Attack - Network Efficiency: {attack_
allocation['network_efficiency']:.1%}")
```

Through these AI-enhanced blockchain systems, the Synths have transformed their networks from vulnerable infrastructure into adaptive defense systems capable of withstanding and countering the Gnos corporation's most sophisticated attacks. The integration of machine learning into blockchain architecture represents not just technological progress but the evolution of democratic resistance in the face of corporate authoritarianism.

Section 2: AI-Powered Smart Contracts and Real-Time Automation

{width="6.270138888888889in" height="3.459722222222222in"}

Introduction to AI-Driven Smart Contracts in the Resistance Economy

On Planet Epsilon, smart contracts serve a purpose far beyond simple automation—they are the backbone of the Synths' resistance economy, enabling secure transactions and agreements that remain beyond the reach of Gnos corporate interference. While traditional smart contracts execute predefined rules rigidly, the Synths have developed AI-enhanced contracts that can adapt to the dynamic threats posed by Gnos market manipulation, supply chain sabotage, and economic warfare.

These intelligent contracts form the foundation of the Anti-Gnos Alliance's economic cooperation, automatically adjusting terms when the corporation attempts to disrupt interstellar trade routes or manipulate Evolune energy prices. By integrating machine learning models that can detect and respond to corporate aggression in real time, these contracts ensure that the democratic planets can maintain economic sovereignty even under siege.

Dynamic Contract Adaptation Against Corporate Manipulation

The Synths' greatest innovation lies in creating contracts that can recognize and counter Gnos manipulation attempts. When corporate agents try to exploit contractual terms through legal loopholes or market manipulation, AI-powered smart contracts can adapt their conditions to preserve the original intent of the agreement while closing vulnerabilities.

Interstellar Supply Chain Defense Contracts

Consider the vital Evolune energy shipments between Epsilon and Tenrai. Traditional contracts would be vulnerable to Gnos interference—the corporation could trigger artificial delays, manipulate shipping insurance rates, or even stage "pirate attacks" on trade routes to void agreements. The Synths' AI-enhanced contracts counter these tactics by continuously monitoring multiple data sources and adjusting terms in real time.

Why Weather API Integration: The Synths integrate real-time environmental data because Gnos often exploits natural disasters as cover for their sabotage operations. By distinguishing between genuine weather delays and corporate-manufactured crises, the contracts can maintain fair terms while exposing Gnos interference.

```python
# Synth Alliance Trade Defense: AI-Enhanced Supply Chain
Contracts

import requests
import random
from datetime import datetime, timedelta

class AntiGnosTradeContract:
    def __init__(self, origin_planet, destination_planet,
    cargo_value):
        self.origin = origin_planet
        self.destination = destination_planet
        self.cargo_value = cargo_value
        self.base_delivery_time = 10  # Standard days for
        interstellar shipping
        self.gnos_interference_detected = False

    def get_route_conditions(self, route):
        """
        Monitors real conditions vs. Gnos-manufactured delays
        In practice, this would integrate with interstellar
        monitoring networks
        """
        # Simulate environmental monitoring
        natural_conditions = {
            'solar_storm_intensity': random.uniform(0, 1),
            'space_debris_level': random.uniform(0, 1),
            'gravitational_anomalies': random.uniform(0, 1)
        }

        # Simulate Gnos interference detection
        suspicious_patterns = {
            'unexplained_route_closures': random.uniform(0, 1),
```

```python
        'insurance_price_spikes': random.uniform(0, 1),
        'mysterious_pirate_activity': random.uniform(0, 1)
    }

    return natural_conditions, suspicious_patterns

def adaptive_contract_terms(self):
    """
    Automatically adjusts contract terms based on detected
    interference
    """
    natural_conditions, suspicious_patterns = self.get_
    route_conditions(
        f"{self.origin}-{self.destination}"
    )

    # Detect Gnos interference patterns
    gnos_interference_score = (
        suspicious_patterns['unexplained_route_
        closures'] * 0.4 +
        suspicious_patterns['insurance_price_
        spikes'] * 0.3 +
        suspicious_patterns['mysterious_pirate_
        activity'] * 0.3
    )

    if gnos_interference_score > 0.6:
        self.gnos_interference_detected = True
        print("🚨 GNOS INTERFERENCE DETECTED")
        print("Activating Anti-Corporate
        Countermeasures...")
```

```
        # Activate alternative secure trade routes
        delivery_extension = 3  # Minimal delay using
        secret Synth routes
        penalty_waiver = True   # Waive delays caused by
        corporate sabotage
        insurance_override = True  # Use Alliance mutual
        insurance

        print(f"- Switching to encrypted Synth trade
        routes")
        print(f"- Corporate sabotage delays will NOT
        trigger penalties")
        print(f"- Alliance insurance covers Gnos-related
        losses")

    else:
        # Normal conditions - check for natural delays
        natural_delay_factor = max(natural_conditions.
        values())
        if natural_delay_factor > 0.7:
            delivery_extension = int(natural_delay_factor *
            5)  # Natural weather delays
            penalty_waiver = False  # Natural delays may
            have minor penalties
            insurance_override = False
            print("🌩 NATURAL CONDITIONS DETECTED")
            print(f"Space weather causing {delivery_
            extension}-day delay")
            print("Standard delay penalties apply for
            natural conditions")
```

```python
        else:
            delivery_extension = 0
            penalty_waiver = False
            insurance_override = False
            print("✅ CLEAR CONDITIONS - Proceeding with
            standard terms")

    new_delivery_date = self.base_delivery_time + delivery_
    extension

    return {
        'adjusted_delivery_time': new_delivery_date,
        'corporate_sabotage_detected': self.gnos_
        interference_detected,
        'penalty_waiver_active': penalty_waiver,
        'alliance_insurance_active': insurance_override,
        'natural_conditions_score': max(natural_conditions.
        values()),
        'gnos_threat_level': gnos_interference_score
    }

# Example: Evolune energy shipment from Epsilon to Tenrai
epsilon_tenrai_contract = AntiGnosTradeContract(
    origin_planet="Epsilon",
    destination_planet="Tenrai",
    cargo_value=50000  # 50,000 Evolune energy units
)

contract_status = epsilon_tenrai_contract.adaptive_
contract_terms()

print(f"\n📋 CONTRACT STATUS SUMMARY:")
```

```
print(f"Route: {epsilon_tenrai_contract.origin} → {epsilon_
tenrai_contract.destination}")
print(f"Cargo Value: {epsilon_tenrai_contract.cargo_value:,}
Evolune units")
print(f"Delivery Time: {contract_status['adjusted_delivery_
time']} days")
print(f"Gnos Threat Level: {contract_status['gnos_threat_
level']:.1%}")
```

AI-Driven Fraud Detection in DeFi Resistance Networks

The Synths have established decentralized finance (DeFi) networks
that operate independently of Gnos-controlled financial institutions.
However, the corporation has responded by infiltrating these networks
with sophisticated fraud schemes designed to destabilize the resistance
economy. AI-powered fraud detection systems now protect these networks
by identifying Gnos-sponsored manipulation in real time.

Why Isolation Forest for Financial Defense: The Synths chose
Isolation Forest algorithms because Gnos constantly develops new
attack patterns that traditional rule-based systems can't detect. Isolation
Forest excels at identifying anomalous behavior without requiring
prior knowledge of specific attack signatures—essential when facing
an adversary with unlimited resources for developing new exploitation
methods.

```
# Synth DeFi Defense: AI-Powered Anti-Gnos Fraud Detection

import numpy as np
from sklearn.ensemble import IsolationForest
from sklearn.preprocessing import StandardScaler

class SynthDeFiSecuritySystem:
    def __init__(self):
```

```python
    # Isolation Forest optimized for detecting corporate
    financial warfare
    self.fraud_detector = IsolationForest(
        contamination=0.15,  # Expect 15% of transactions
        during attacks to be malicious
        random_state=42,
        n_estimators=200      # Higher complexity to catch
        sophisticated Gnos schemes
    )
    self.scaler = StandardScaler()
    self.gnos_patterns_detected = []

def analyze_defi_transactions(self, transaction_data):
    """
    Analyzes DeFi transactions for Gnos corporate
    manipulation patterns
    Features: [transaction_amount, frequency, wallet_age,
    network_connections,
            timing_pattern_score, price_impact]
    """
    # Normalize transaction data for analysis
    scaled_data = self.scaler.fit_
    transform(transaction_data)

    # Detect anomalous patterns that might indicate Gnos
    interference
    anomaly_predictions = self.fraud_detector.fit_
    predict(scaled_data)

    # Calculate suspicion scores for each transaction
    anomaly_scores = self.fraud_detector.score_
    samples(scaled_data)
```

```
    return anomaly_predictions, anomaly_scores

def classify_threat_patterns(self, transactions,
predictions, scores):
    """
    Classifies detected threats by likely Gnos
    attack pattern
    """
    threat_analysis = []

    for i, (transaction, prediction, score) in
    enumerate(zip(transactions, predictions, scores)):
        if prediction == -1:  # Anomaly detected
            amount, frequency, wallet_age, connections,
            timing, price_impact = transaction

            # Classify likely attack type based on
            transaction characteristics
            if amount > 10000 and frequency > 50 and
            wallet_age < 1:
                threat_type = "WHALE MANIPULATION - Likely
                Gnos proxy wallet"
            elif frequency > 100 and connections < 5:
                threat_type = "COORDINATED SPAM - Gnos bot
                network attack"
            elif price_impact > 0.1 and timing > 0.8:
                threat_type = "FLASH LOAN EXPLOIT - Gnos
                arbitrage attack"
            elif wallet_age < 0.1 and connections > 50:
                threat_type = "SYBIL ATTACK - Gnos identity
                farming"
```

```
            else:
                threat_type = "UNKNOWN PATTERN - Novel Gnos
                strategy"

            threat_analysis.append({
                'transaction_id': i,
                'threat_type': threat_type,
                'suspicion_score': abs(score),
                'recommended_action': self._get_
                countermeasure(threat_type)
            })

    return threat_analysis

def _get_countermeasure(self, threat_type):
    """

    Recommends countermeasures for each type of Gnos attack
    """

    countermeasures = {
        "WHALE MANIPULATION": "Freeze large transactions
        pending KYC verification",
        "COORDINATED SPAM": "Implement adaptive gas fees
        and rate limiting",
        "FLASH LOAN EXPLOIT": "Pause flash loans and alert
        arbitrage monitors",
        "SYBIL ATTACK": "Require proof-of-history for new
        high-volume wallets",
        "UNKNOWN PATTERN": "Flag for manual Synth
        intelligence analysis"
    }
    return countermeasures.get(threat_type, "Standard
    security protocols")
```

```
# Simulated DeFi transaction data during a suspected
Gnos attack
# [amount, frequency/hour, wallet_age_days, network_
connections, timing_pattern_score, price_impact]
normal_defi_activity = np.array([
    [1000, 5, 365, 20, 0.3, 0.01],     # Normal user: moderate
    amounts, low frequency
    [500, 3, 180, 15, 0.2, 0.005],     # Regular trader
    [2000, 8, 500, 35, 0.4, 0.02],     # Active
    legitimate trader
])

suspected_gnos_activity = np.array([
    [50000, 80, 0.5, 2, 0.95, 0.15],  # WHALE MANIPULATION:
    Huge amounts, new wallet, suspicious timing
    [100, 200, 2, 1, 0.9, 0.001],      # SPAM ATTACK: Small
    amounts, very high frequency
    [20000, 150, 0.1, 100, 0.85, 0.12], # SYBIL ATTACK: New
    wallet with many connections
    [15000, 50, 1, 3, 0.92, 0.18],     # FLASH LOAN EXPLOIT:
    Large amount, suspicious timing, high price impact
])

all_transactions = np.vstack([normal_defi_activity, suspected_
gnos_activity])

# Initialize Synth DeFi defense system
defense_system = SynthDeFiSecuritySystem()
predictions, scores = defense_system.analyze_defi_
transactions(all_transactions)
```

```python
# Analyze threats
threat_analysis = defense_system.classify_threat_patterns(all_
transactions, predictions, scores)

print("🛡 SYNTH DEFI SECURITY ANALYSIS")
print("="*50)

if threat_analysis:
    print(f"🚨 {len(threat_analysis)} POTENTIAL GNOS ATTACKS
    DETECTED")
    for threat in threat_analysis:
        print(f"\nTransaction #{threat['transaction_id']}")
        print(f"Threat Type: {threat['threat_type']}")
        print(f"Suspicion Score: {threat['suspicion_
        score']:.3f}")
        print(f"Countermeasure: {threat['recommended_
        action']}")
else:
    print("✅ No anomalous activity detected - DeFi network
    secure")
```

Real-Time Market Defense Through Adaptive Contracts

The Synths have created market stabilization contracts that automatically counter Gnos price manipulation attempts. These contracts monitor market conditions continuously and trigger defensive mechanisms when corporate manipulation is detected, helping maintain fair prices for essential resources like Evolune energy.

```python
# Synth Market Defense: Adaptive Anti-Manipulation Contracts

import random

class EvolunePriceStabilizationContract:
    def __init__(self, base_price, acceptable_volatility=0.1):
        self.base_price = base_price
        self.acceptable_volatility = acceptable_volatility
        self.emergency_reserves = 100000  # Emergency Evolune
        reserves for market defense
        self.manipulation_threshold = 0.25  # 25% price swing
        triggers investigation

    def monitor_market_manipulation(self):
        """
        Monitors Evolune energy markets for signs of Gnos price
        manipulation
        """
        # Simulate real-time market data
        current_price = self.base_price * random.uniform(0.7,
        1.4)  # ±30% variation
        trading_volume = random.randint(1000, 20000)
        price_velocity = random.uniform(-0.5, 0.5)  # Rate of
        price change

        # Calculate manipulation indicators
        price_deviation = abs(current_price - self.base_price)
        / self.base_price
        volume_anomaly = 1 if trading_volume > 15000 else 0  #
        Unusually high volume
        velocity_anomaly = 1 if abs(price_velocity) > 0.3 else
        0  # Rapid price changes
```

```python
    # Detect likely Gnos manipulation patterns
    manipulation_score = (
        price_deviation * 0.5 +
        volume_anomaly * 0.3 +
        velocity_anomaly * 0.2
    )

    return {
        'current_price': current_price,
        'price_deviation': price_deviation,
        'manipulation_score': manipulation_score,
        'trading_volume': trading_volume,
        'requires_intervention': manipulation_score > 0.4
    }

def execute_defensive_measures(self, market_data):
    """
    Automatically executes countermeasures against Gnos
    market manipulation
    """
    if not market_data['requires_intervention']:
        return {"action": "No intervention required",
        "market_stable": True}

    current_price = market_data['current_price']
    manipulation_score = market_data['manipulation_score']

    if manipulation_score > 0.7:
        # Severe manipulation detected - emergency measures
        action = "EMERGENCY STABILIZATION"
        if current_price > self.base_price * 1.2:  # Price
        artificially inflated
            # Release emergency reserves to increase supply
```

```
                reserves_released = min(self.emergency_
                reserves, 20000)
                new_target_price = current_price * 0.85  #
                Target 15% reduction
                print(f"🚨 SEVERE GNOS PRICE MANIPULATION
                DETECTED")
                print(f"Releasing {reserves_released:,}
                emergency Evolune reserves")
                print(f"Target price reduction: {current_
                price:.2f} → {new_target_price:.2f}")
            else:  # Price artificially deflated
                # Use reserves to buy Evolune and support price
                reserves_used = min(self.emergency_
                reserves, 15000)
                new_target_price = current_price * 1.15  #
                Target 15% increase
                print(f"🚨 GNOS PRICE SUPPRESSION DETECTED")
                print(f"Using {reserves_used:,} reserves to
                support market price")
                print(f"Target price support: {current_
                price:.2f} → {new_target_price:.2f}")

        elif manipulation_score > 0.4:
            # Moderate manipulation - graduated response
            action = "STANDARD COUNTERMEASURES"
            adjustment_factor = 0.05  # 5% market adjustment
            if current_price > self.base_price:
                new_target_price = current_price * (1 -
                adjustment_factor)
                print(f"⚠️ Gnos price inflation detected -
                moderate correction")
```

```python
        else:
            new_target_price = current_price * (1 +
            adjustment_factor)
            print(f"⚠ Gnos price suppression detected -
            moderate support")
            print(f"Market adjustment: {current_price:.2f} →
            {new_target_price:.2f}")

    return {
        "action": action,
        "manipulation_score": manipulation_score,
        "price_adjustment": new_target_price,
        "market_stable": False
    }

# Example: Protecting Evolune energy prices from Gnos
manipulation
base_evolune_price = 100.0  # Base price per unit
stabilization_contract = EvolunePriceStabilizationContract(ba
se_evolune_price)

print("⏱ EVOLUNE ENERGY MARKET MONITORING")
print("="*45)

# Simulate 24-hour market monitoring
for hour in range(1, 4):  # Simulate 3 hours for demonstration
    print(f"\n⏰ Hour {hour} - Market Analysis")
    market_status = stabilization_contract.monitor_market_
    manipulation()

    print(f"Current Price: {market_status['current_price']:.2f}
    per unit")
    print(f"Price Deviation: {market_status['price_
    deviation']:.1%}")
```

```
print(f"Manipulation Score: {market_status['manipulation_
score']:.1%}")

if market_status['requires_intervention']:
    defense_actions = stabilization_contract.execute_
    defensive_measures(market_status)
    print(f"Defensive Action: {defense_actions['action']}")
else:
    print("✅ Market operating within normal parameters")
```

Through these AI-enhanced smart contracts, the Synths have created a financial immune system that can recognize and counter Gnos economic warfare in real time. The contracts serve not just as automated agreements but as active defenders of the democratic economy—adapting, learning, and evolving to meet each new corporate threat while maintaining the principles of fair trade and economic freedom that define the Anti-Gnos Alliance.

Section 3: The Metaverse and Spatial Computing

{width="6.270138888888889in" height="2.6756944444444444in"}

The Metaverse as a Sanctuary for Democratic Resistance

Within the vast digital realm of the Evolune Metaverse, the Synths have created more than just virtual spaces—they have built a sanctuary for democratic thought and action, beyond the reach of Gnos corporate surveillance. These immersive digital environments serve as meeting grounds for the Anti-Gnos Alliance, secure marketplaces for trading outside corporate-controlled economies, and laboratories for developing resistance technologies.

Understanding Spatial Computing in the Resistance Context: Spatial computing represents the pinnacle of the immersive technologies first introduced on Celestor, allowing commanders to interact with 3D data as if it were a physical object. This technology seamlessly blends the physical reality of Planet Epsilon with its digital twin, creating environments where digital information becomes as tangible and manipulatable as physical matter. Through advanced gesture recognition, haptic feedback, and holographic displays, spatial computing enables resistance fighters across the galaxy to collaborate as if they were in the same room, while maintaining the security advantages of distributed operations.

The Metaverse represents the ultimate expression of decentralized power, where ownership of digital assets through NFTs ensures that even virtual property remains beyond Gnos's reach. Here, blockchain-secured virtual real estate hosts secret Alliance meetings, AI-powered avatars serve as both assistants and counter-intelligence agents, and spatial computing technologies enable resistance fighters across the galaxy to collaborate as if they were in the same room.

But the Metaverse is also a battlefield. Gnos has deployed sophisticated infiltration programs—AI agents designed to blend in with legitimate users, gather intelligence on resistance activities, and disrupt virtual economies through market manipulation. The Synths' response has been to develop AI-powered security systems that can distinguish between genuine Alliance members and corporate infiltrators, creating virtual spaces that remain secure even under constant corporate surveillance.

AI-Powered Avatar Intelligence for Resistance Operations

The Synths have revolutionized virtual identity through AI-enhanced avatars that serve multiple functions in the resistance effort. These intelligent digital beings don't just represent users—they actively protect them, analyze threats, and coordinate complex operations across the Metaverse.

Counter-Intelligence Avatars

The most sophisticated of these AI avatars are designed to detect and counter Gnos infiltration attempts. By analyzing behavioral patterns, communication styles, and decision-making processes, these avatars can identify corporate agents even when they're using stolen identities or sophisticated cover stories.

```python
# Synth Avatar Intelligence: Corporate Infiltrator
Detection System

import numpy as np
from sklearn.ensemble import RandomForestClassifier
from sklearn.preprocessing import StandardScaler
import random

class SynthAvatarIntelligence:
    """

    BIG PICTURE: This system analyzes how avatars behave in the
    Metaverse to determine
    if they are genuine Alliance members or Gnos corporate
    infiltrators. It looks at
    patterns like response times, language complexity, and
    risk-taking behavior that
```

```
often reveal corporate training, helping protect secret
Alliance operations.
"""

def __init__(self):
    self.infiltrator_detector = RandomForestClassifier(n_
    estimators=150, random_state=42)
    self.behavioral_analyzer = StandardScaler()
    self.known_gnos_patterns = self._load_gnos_behavioral_
    database()

def _load_gnos_behavioral_database(self):
    """
    Loads known Gnos corporate behavioral patterns from
    Alliance intelligence
    In practice, this would connect to the Synth
    intelligence database
    """
    return {
        'response_time_patterns': [0.2, 0.25, 0.3],
        # Corporate agents respond faster
        'vocabulary_complexity': [0.7, 0.8, 0.9],
        # Corporate training shows in language
        'risk_aversion': [0.9, 0.95, 0.98],
        # Corporate agents avoid risks
        'information_seeking': [0.8, 0.85, 0.9]
        # Agents ask more probing questions
    }

def analyze_avatar_behavior(self, avatar_data):
    """
    Analyzes avatar behavioral patterns for signs of
    corporate training
```

```
    Features: [response_time_avg, vocabulary_complexity,
    risk_taking_score,
                information_requests, social_connections,
                trading_patterns]
        """
    behavioral_features = np.array(avatar_data).
    reshape(1, -1)
    scaled_features = self.behavioral_analyzer.fit_
    transform(behavioral_features)

    # Predict likelihood of corporate infiltrator
    infiltrator_probability = self.infiltrator_detector.
    predict_proba(scaled_features)
    return infiltrator_probability[0][1] if
    len(infiltrator_probability[0]) > 1 else 0

def generate_behavioral_assessment(self, avatar_id,
behavior_data):
    """
    Generates comprehensive assessment of avatar
    authenticity
    """
    response_time, vocabulary, risk_taking, info_requests,
    connections, trading = behavior_data

    # Calculate individual risk indicators
    corporate_indicators = []

    if response_time < 0.3:
        corporate_indicators.append("RAPID_RESPONSE -
        Consistent with corporate training")
```

```
    if vocabulary > 0.75:
        corporate_indicators.append("HIGH_VOCABULARY -
        Possible corporate education")

    if risk_taking < 0.3:
        corporate_indicators.append("RISK_AVERSION -
        Consistent with corporate guidelines")

    if info_requests > 0.7:
        corporate_indicators.append("INTELLIGENCE_
        GATHERING - Suspicious questioning patterns")

    if connections < 5 and trading > 0.8:
        corporate_indicators.append("FINANCIAL_FOCUS -
        Possibly economic espionage")

    # Overall threat assessment
    if len(corporate_indicators) >= 3:
        threat_level = "HIGH"
        recommendation = "IMMEDIATE ISOLATION - Likely Gnos
        operative"
    elif len(corporate_indicators) == 2:
        threat_level = "MODERATE"
        recommendation = "ENHANCED MONITORING - Possible
        corporate connection"
    elif len(corporate_indicators) == 1:
        threat_level = "LOW"
        recommendation = "STANDARD MONITORING - Minor
        concern only"
    else:
        threat_level = "MINIMAL"
        recommendation = "TRUSTED - Normal Alliance member
        behavior"
```

```python
        return {
            'avatar_id': avatar_id,
            'threat_level': threat_level,
            'corporate_indicators': corporate_indicators,
            'recommendation': recommendation,
            'confidence_score': len(corporate_indicators) / 5
        }

# Simulate avatar behavioral analysis in the Metaverse
avatar_intelligence = SynthAvatarIntelligence()

# Training data: Known Alliance members vs. Corporate
infiltrators
alliance_members = [
    [0.8, 0.4, 0.7, 0.3, 25, 0.4],  # Slow response, simple
    vocab, risk-taking, few questions
    [1.2, 0.3, 0.8, 0.2, 30, 0.3],  # Very slow, basic vocab,
    high risk tolerance
    [0.9, 0.5, 0.6, 0.4, 20, 0.5],  # Normal Alliance member
    patterns
]

corporate_infiltrators = [
    [0.2, 0.9, 0.1, 0.9, 3, 0.9],    # Fast, sophisticated,
    risk-averse, many questions
    [0.25, 0.85, 0.15, 0.85, 2, 0.95], # Corporate training
    patterns
    [0.3, 0.8, 0.2, 0.8, 4, 0.8],    # Slightly disguised
    corporate agent
]
```

```python
# Prepare training data
X_train = np.array(alliance_members + corporate_infiltrators)
y_train = np.array([0, 0, 0, 1, 1, 1])  # 0=Alliance,
1=Corporate

# Train the detection system
avatar_intelligence.infiltrator_detector.fit(X_train, y_train)

print("🕵 SYNTH AVATAR INTELLIGENCE ANALYSIS")
print("="*50)

# Analyze suspicious avatars in the Metaverse
test_avatars = [
    ("Avatar_Epsilon_Trader_7742", [0.7, 0.4, 0.8, 0.3, 28,
    0.4]),  # Likely Alliance
    ("Avatar_NewUser_9981", [0.2, 0.9, 0.1, 0.9, 1,
    0.95]),        # Highly suspicious
    ("Avatar_Casual_Gamer_1123", [1.0, 0.3, 0.9, 0.2, 35,
    0.2]),   # Likely Alliance
]

for avatar_id, behavior_data in test_avatars:
    assessment = avatar_intelligence.generate_behavioral_
    assessment(avatar_id, behavior_data)

    print(f"\n🔍 Avatar: {avatar_id}")
    print(f"Threat Level: {assessment['threat_level']}")
    print(f"Confidence: {assessment['confidence_score']:.1%}")
    print(f"Recommendation: {assessment['recommendation']}")

    if assessment['corporate_indicators']:
        print("⚠ Corporate Indicators Detected:")
        for indicator in assessment['corporate_indicators']:
            print(f"  • {indicator}")
```

Automated Alliance Economy Management

Beyond security, AI avatars manage the complex economic systems that keep the resistance supplied and funded. These avatars automatically negotiate trades, manage supply chains, and optimize resource distribution across Alliance worlds—all while maintaining security protocols that prevent Gnos from tracking resistance operations.

```python
# Synth Economic Intelligence: AI-Managed Resistance Economy

import random

class AllianceEconomicAvatar:
    """

    BIG PICTURE: This AI avatar automatically manages the
    secret economy that keeps
    the resistance supplied with food, weapons, and resources.
    It negotiates trades
    between Alliance worlds while maintaining security
    protocols that prevent Gnos
    from tracking or disrupting resistance supply lines.
    """

    def __init__(self, avatar_name, specialization):
        self.name = avatar_name
        self.specialization = specialization
        self.resource_knowledge = self._initialize_resource_
        database()
        self.trade_relationships = {}
        self.security_clearance = "ALLIANCE_ENCRYPTED"

    def _initialize_resource_database(self):
        """
```

```
    Loads current resource availability across
    Alliance worlds
    """
    return {
        'epsilon': {'evolune_energy': 50000, 'rare_metals':
        20000, 'food': 80000},
        'tenrai': {'evolune_energy': 30000, 'rare_metals':
        60000, 'food': 120000},
        'tibara': {'evolune_energy': 80000, 'rare_metals':
        10000, 'food': 40000}
    }

def negotiate_secure_trade(self, requesting_planet, needed_
resource, quantity):
    """
    Automatically negotiates resource trades while
    maintaining operational security
    """
    print(f"🤖 {self.name} initiating secure trade
    negotiation...")
    print(f"Request: {quantity:,} units of {needed_
    resource} for {requesting_planet}")

    # Find best supplier while avoiding Gnos detection
    best_supplier = None
    best_price = float('inf')

    for planet, resources in self.resource_knowledge.
    items():
        if planet != requesting_planet and needed_resource
        in resources:
            available = resources[needed_resource]
            if available >= quantity:
```

```python
            # Calculate price with security premium for
            covert operations
            base_price = quantity * self._get_base_
            price(needed_resource)
            security_premium = base_price * 0.15  # 15%
            premium for secure transport
            total_price = base_price + security_premium

            if total_price < best_price:
                best_price = total_price
                best_supplier = planet

    if best_supplier:
        # Establish secure trade route
        route_security = self._plan_secure_route(best_
        supplier, requesting_planet)

        print(f"✅ Trade Agreement Secured:")
        print(f"  Supplier: {best_supplier.capitalize()}")
        print(f"  Resource: {quantity:,} {needed_
        resource}")
        print(f"  Price: {best_price:,.0f} Alliance
        credits")
        print(f"  Security: {route_security['method']}")
        print(f"  Transit Time: {route_security['days']}
        days (covert)")

        # Update resource databases
        self.resource_knowledge[best_supplier][needed_
        resource] -= quantity
        self.resource_knowledge[requesting_planet][needed_
        resource] += quantity
```

```python
        return {
            'success': True,
            'supplier': best_supplier,
            'cost': best_price,
            'security_method': route_security['method'],
            'transit_time': route_security['days']
        }
    else:
        print(f"✗ Unable to fulfill request - insufficient
        {needed_resource} in Alliance network")
        return {'success': False, 'reason': 'Insufficient
        supply'}

def _get_base_price(self, resource):
    """
    Returns base market price for resources (per unit)
    """
    prices = {
        'evolune_energy': 2.5,
        'rare_metals': 15.0,
        'food': 0.8
    }
    return prices.get(resource, 10.0)

def _plan_secure_route(self, origin, destination):
    """
    Plans covert trade routes that avoid Gnos surveillance
    """
    secure_routes = {
        ('epsilon', 'tenrai'): {'method': 'Stealth convoy
        via asteroid field', 'days': 8},
```

```python
        ('tenrai', 'epsilon'): {'method': 'Encrypted cargo
        pods', 'days': 7},
        ('tibara', 'epsilon'): {'method': 'Underground
        resistance network', 'days': 12},
        ('epsilon', 'tibara'): {'method': 'Synth diplomatic
        pouch', 'days': 10},
        ('tibara', 'tenrai'): {'method': 'Civilian cover
        operation', 'days': 15},
        ('tenrai', 'tibara'): {'method': 'Mining ship
        disguise', 'days': 14}
    }

    route_key = (origin, destination)
    return secure_routes.get(route_key, {'method':
    'Standard encrypted transport', 'days': 20})

def monitor_economic_threats(self):
    """

    Monitors for Gnos economic warfare and market
    manipulation
    """

    threats_detected = []

    # Check for unusual price fluctuations (Gnos
    manipulation)
    for resource in ['evolune_energy', 'rare_metals',
    'food']:
        market_volatility = random.uniform(0, 1)
        if market_volatility > 0.7:
            threat_type = f"PRICE MANIPULATION - {resource}
            markets showing Gnos interference"
            countermeasure = f"Activate emergency
            {resource} reserves to stabilize prices"
```

```
            threats_detected.append({
                'threat': threat_type,
                'severity': 'HIGH' if market_volatility >
                0.85 else 'MODERATE',
                'countermeasure': countermeasure
            })

    # Check for supply chain attacks
    supply_disruption = random.uniform(0, 1)
    if supply_disruption > 0.6:
        threats_detected.append({
            'threat': "SUPPLY CHAIN ATTACK - Gnos
            interdiction of trade routes",
            'severity': 'HIGH',
            'countermeasure': "Switch to backup covert
            trade networks"
        })

    return threats_detected

# Example: Alliance economic management during Gnos pressure
economic_avatar = AllianceEconomicAvatar("AURA-7 Economic
Coordinator", "Resource Management")

print("🧳 ALLIANCE ECONOMIC OPERATIONS")
print("="*40)

# Scenario: Epsilon needs emergency food supplies
emergency_request = economic_avatar.negotiate_secure_trade(
    requesting_planet='epsilon',
    needed_resource='food',
    quantity=25000
)
```

```
print(f"\n 🛡 ECONOMIC THREAT MONITORING")
print("-" * 30)

# Monitor for Gnos economic attacks
threats = economic_avatar.monitor_economic_threats()

if threats:
    for i, threat in enumerate(threats, 1):
        print(f"\n ⚠ Threat {i}: {threat['threat']}")
        print(f"   Severity: {threat['severity']}")
        print(f"   Response: {threat['countermeasure']}")
else:
    print("  ✅ No economic threats detected - Alliance trade
    networks secure")
```

Spatial Computing for Immersive Resistance Coordination

```
{width="6.270138888888889in" height="3.2604166666666665in"}
```

The Synths have pioneered the use of spatial computing to create immersive command centers where Alliance leaders can coordinate resistance operations across vast distances. These virtual spaces use advanced gesture recognition and haptic feedback to allow users to manipulate 3D tactical displays, plan operations, and respond to threats as if they were physically present in the same room.

Virtual War Rooms and Tactical Planning

Using spatial computing, Alliance commanders can visualize Gnos corporate movements, troop dispositions, and economic attacks in three-dimensional space. AI enhances these environments by providing real-time analysis, predictive modeling, and automated threat assessment.

245

```python
# Synth Spatial Computing: Immersive Alliance Command Center

import random

class AllianceCommandCenter:
    """

    BIG PICTURE: This immersive command center uses spatial
    computing (the evolution
    of Metaverse technologies from Celestor) to let Alliance
    commanders from different
    planets work together in 3D virtual space, manipulating
    tactical data with gestures
    and planning resistance operations as if they were in the
    same room.
    """

    def __init__(self):
        self.holographic_display = True
        self.gesture_recognition = True
        self.threat_overlay = True
        self.real_time_intel = {}

    def initialize_tactical_display(self):
        """

        Creates 3D holographic display of current Alliance
        operations
        """

        print("✹ ALLIANCE TACTICAL DISPLAY INITIALIZING...")
        print("  ✓ Holographic projectors online")
        print("  ✓ Gesture recognition systems active")
        print("  ✓ Real-time intelligence feeds connected")
        print("  ✓ Encrypted communications established")
```

```python
    return {
        'display_status': 'OPERATIONAL',
        'security_level': 'MAXIMUM_ENCRYPTION',
        'participants': ['Epsilon Command', 'Tenrai
        Operations', 'Tibara Intelligence'],
        'threat_monitoring': 'ACTIVE'
    }

def process_gesture_commands(self, gesture_type,
target_area):
    """

    Processes spatial computing gestures for tactical
    manipulation
    """

    gesture_responses = {
        'zoom_in': f"Magnifying tactical view of
        {target_area}",
        'rotate': f"Rotating 3D tactical display of
        {target_area}",
        'select': f"Selecting {target_area} for detailed
        analysis",
        'deploy': f"Deploying Alliance assets to
        {target_area}",
        'defend': f"Activating defensive protocols for
        {target_area}",
        'retreat': f"Planning strategic withdrawal from
        {target_area}"
    }

    response = gesture_responses.get(gesture_type, "Unknown
    gesture - training required")
    print(f"👏 Gesture Command: {gesture_type.upper()}")
```

```
        print(f"  Action: {response}")

        # Simulate tactical analysis
        if gesture_type == 'select':
            return self._analyze_selected_area(target_area)
        elif gesture_type == 'deploy':
            return self._plan_deployment(target_area)

        return {'action': gesture_type, 'target': target_area,
        'status': 'executed'}

    def _analyze_selected_area(self, area):
        """
        Provides detailed analysis of selected tactical area
        """
        # Simulate intelligence analysis
        gnos_presence = random.uniform(0, 1)
        strategic_value = random.uniform(0, 1)
        defensive_strength = random.uniform(0, 1)

        analysis = {
            'area': area,
            'gnos_threat_level': gnos_presence,
            'strategic_importance': strategic_value,
            'defensive_capability': defensive_strength,
            'recommendations': []
        }

        # Generate tactical recommendations
        if gnos_presence > 0.7:
            analysis['recommendations'].append("HIGH GNOS
            PRESENCE - Recommend stealth operations only")
        elif gnos_presence > 0.4:
```

```python
        analysis['recommendations'].append("MODERATE GNOS
        PRESENCE - Proceed with caution")
    else:
        analysis['recommendations'].append("LOW GNOS
        PRESENCE - Safe for standard operations")

    if strategic_value > 0.8:
        analysis['recommendations'].append("CRITICAL
        STRATEGIC VALUE - Priority target for Alliance")

    if defensive_strength < 0.3:
        analysis['recommendations'].append("WEAK DEFENSES -
        Vulnerable to rapid assault")

    return analysis

def _plan_deployment(self, target_area):
    """
    Plans Alliance force deployment using AI tactical
    analysis
    """
    # Simulate deployment planning
    force_types = ['Synth Tech Units', 'Tenrai Heavy
    Infantry', 'Tibara Stealth Scouts']

    deployment_plan = {
        'target': target_area,
        'primary_force': random.choice(force_types),
        'support_units': random.sample(force_types, 2),
        'estimated_timeline': f"{random.randint(3,
        10)} days",
        'success_probability': random.uniform(0.6, 0.95),
        'risk_factors': []
    }
```

```
        # Add risk assessment
        if random.random() > 0.7:
            deployment_plan['risk_factors'].append("Possible
            Gnos counter-intelligence")

        if random.random() > 0.8:
            deployment_plan['risk_factors'].append("Long supply
            lines vulnerable to interdiction")

        if random.random() > 0.6:
            deployment_plan['risk_factors'].append("Limited
            escape routes if operation compromised")

        return deployment_plan

# Example: Alliance commanders using spatial computing for
tactical planning
command_center = AllianceCommandCenter()

print("🏛 ALLIANCE COMMAND CENTER")
print("="*35)

# Initialize tactical display
display_status = command_center.initialize_tactical_display()
print(f"Display Status: {display_status['display_status']}")
print(f"Security Level: {display_status['security_level']}")

print(f"\n🌐 SPATIAL TACTICAL INTERFACE")
print("-" * 25)

# Simulate commander interactions with 3D tactical display
tactical_actions = [
    ('select', 'Gnos Corporate Headquarters - Sector 7'),
    ('zoom_in', 'Epsilon Trade Routes'),
    ('deploy', 'Tibara Mining Facilities')
]
```

```
for gesture, target in tactical_actions:
    print(f"\n🎯 Commander Action:")
    result = command_center.process_gesture_
    commands(gesture, target)

    if gesture == 'select' and isinstance(result, dict):
        print(f"\n📊 TACTICAL ANALYSIS - {result['area']}")
        print(f"  Gnos Threat: {result['gnos_threat_
        level']:.1%}")
        print(f"  Strategic Value: {result['strategic_
        importance']:.1%}")
        print(f"  Defense Rating: {result['defensive_
        capability']:.1%}")
        print("  🎯 Recommendations:")
        for rec in result['recommendations']:
            print(f"    • {rec}")

    elif gesture == 'deploy' and isinstance(result, dict):
        print(f"\n⚔ DEPLOYMENT PLAN - {result['target']}")
        print(f"  Primary Force: {result['primary_force']}")
        print(f"  Timeline: {result['estimated_timeline']}")
        print(f"  Success Probability: {result['success_
        probability']:.1%}")
        if result['risk_factors']:
            print("  ⚠ Risk Factors:")
            for risk in result['risk_factors']:
                print(f"    • {risk}")
```

As the Synths prepare to face even more sophisticated threats from the Gnos corporation, they realize that analyzing individual avatars and transactions isn't enough. Gnos operates as a network, and to defeat a network, you must be able to see it. This realization pushes them beyond traditional machine learning into a new frontier: Geometric Deep Learning, the science of understanding relationships themselves.

The familiar tools of AI and blockchain analysis have served the resistance well, but the interconnected nature of corporate espionage, market manipulation, and resistance operations demands a new paradigm—one that can see not just the trees but the entire forest of connections that define the modern metaverse.

Through these advanced AI and spatial computing technologies, the Synths have created a Metaverse that serves as both sanctuary and command center for the democratic resistance. Virtual spaces become real battlegrounds where the future of freedom is planned and coordinated, while AI avatars ensure that the resistance remains one step ahead of corporate surveillance and infiltration.

The integration of these technologies represents more than just technological advancement—it embodies the Synths' vision of a future where technology serves freedom rather than oppression, where artificial intelligence enhances human agency rather than replacing it, and where virtual worlds become bastions of hope in the fight against corporate authoritarianism.

Section 4: Geometric Deep Learning and Graph Neural Networks

Introduction to Geometric Deep Learning in the Fight for Freedom

In the deepest archives of Planet Epsilon's crystalline data centers, the Synths have unlocked the most sophisticated weapon in their technological arsenal: Geometric Deep Learning. This revolutionary approach to understanding complex data relationships has become essential for navigating the intricate web of corporate espionage, economic manipulation, and resistance networks that define the modern conflict between the Alliance and the Gnos corporation.

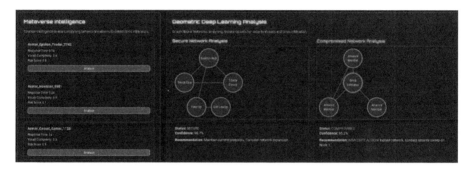

Figure 4-2. *Geometric Deep Learning*

Unlike traditional machine learning that analyzes data in simple grid patterns, Geometric Deep Learning excels at understanding the complex, interconnected relationships that define real-world systems. In the context of the Evolune metaverse, this means analyzing the vast network of transactions, communications, and relationships that span planets, revealing hidden patterns that would be invisible to conventional analysis.

For the Synths, mastering this technology isn't just about academic advancement—it's about survival. The Gnos corporation operates through complex networks of shell companies, proxy agents, and covert operations that can only be detected and countered through sophisticated graph analysis. Every transaction in the blockchain, every communication between resistance cells, and every movement of Evolune energy form part of a vast interconnected graph that tells the story of an ongoing war between freedom and corporate control.

Understanding Graphs in the Resistance Context

Before diving into the technical implementation, it's essential to understand how the Synths conceptualize graph structures in their fight against corporate oppression:

- **Nodes (Vertices):** Represent entities in the network—Alliance members, Gnos operatives, corporations, planets, Evolune energy deposits, communication relays, or financial accounts

- **Edges (Connections):** Represent relationships—trade agreements, financial transfers, communication channels, supply routes, corporate ownership structures, or covert operations

- **Node Features:** Characteristics like loyalty scores, financial capacity, strategic importance, or security clearance levels

- **Edge Features:** Properties like transaction amounts, communication frequency, trust levels, or operational security ratings

This graph-based view of the metaverse allows the Synths to see patterns that span multiple planets and reveal the true scope of Gnos's corporate empire while simultaneously protecting the security of resistance operations.

Graph Neural Networks: The Mathematics of Revolutionary Analysis

Graph Neural Networks represent the Synths' most advanced analytical capability—AI systems that can process the complex webs of relationships that define modern interstellar conflict. These networks don't just analyze individual data points; they understand how information flows through networks, how influence spreads across systems, and how hidden patterns emerge from seemingly random connections.

Why GNNs Are Revolutionary for Resistance Operations

Traditional AI systems analyze data in isolation—a single transaction, a single communication, or a single event. GNNs understand that everything in the metaverse is connected and that the most important insights come from understanding these connections. For the Alliance, this means being able to

- **Predict Gnos Operations:** By analyzing the network of corporate communications and resource movements

- **Optimize Resistance Networks:** By understanding how information and resources flow through Alliance systems

- **Detect Infiltration:** By identifying when network patterns change in ways that suggest compromise

- **Plan Counter-Operations:** By modeling how actions in one part of the network will affect the entire system

Implementing Alliance Intelligence Networks

The following example demonstrates how the Synths implement Graph Neural Networks to analyze and protect their resistance operations.

```
# Synth Alliance Intelligence: Graph Neural Network for
Resistance Operations

import torch
import torch.nn as nn
import torch.nn.functional as F
```

```python
from torch_geometric.nn import GCNConv, GATConv, global_
mean_pool
from torch_geometric.data import Data, DataLoader
import numpy as np
import random

class AllianceIntelligenceGNN(nn.Module):
    """

    BIG PICTURE GOAL: This AI system looks at the entire
    network of Alliance members,
    their connections, and their behaviors to determine if the
    resistance cell is secure
    or if a Gnos infiltrator is hiding within it. It's like
    having a super-intelligent
    detective that can see patterns across hundreds of
    relationships simultaneously.

    Advanced GNN for analyzing resistance networks and
    detecting corporate threats

    Why GATConv: This network uses Graph Attention Networks
    (GAT) to focus on the most
    important relationships in the resistance network. Unlike
    simpler models, GAT allows
    the system to weigh the importance of different
    connections, which is crucial for
    identifying a single, well-hidden Gnos infiltrator within a
    large group of
    trusted Alliance members.
    """

    def __init__(self, num_features, hidden_dim, num_classes,
    num_heads=4):
        super(AllianceIntelligenceGNN, self).__init__()
```

```python
    # Graph Attention layers for focusing on critical
    relationships
    self.gat1 = GATConv(num_features, hidden_dim,
    heads=num_heads, dropout=0.1)
    self.gat2 = GATConv(hidden_dim * num_heads, hidden_dim,
    heads=num_heads, dropout=0.1)
    self.gat3 = GATConv(hidden_dim * num_heads, hidden_dim,
    heads=1, dropout=0.1)

    # Classification layers for threat assessment
    self.classifier = nn.Sequential(
        nn.Linear(hidden_dim, hidden_dim // 2),
        nn.ReLU(),
        nn.Dropout(0.3),
        nn.Linear(hidden_dim // 2, num_classes)
    )

    self.dropout = nn.Dropout(0.2)

def forward(self, data):
    x, edge_index, batch = data.x, data.edge_index,
    data.batch

    # Multi-head attention to identify critical network
    relationships
    x = F.elu(self.gat1(x, edge_index))
    x = self.dropout(x)
    x = F.elu(self.gat2(x, edge_index))
    x = self.dropout(x)
    x = F.elu(self.gat3(x, edge_index))

    # Global pooling for network-level analysis
    x = global_mean_pool(x, batch)
```

257

```python
    # Final classification
    x = self.classifier(x)
    return F.log_softmax(x, dim=1)

class ResistanceNetworkAnalyzer:
    """

    BIG PICTURE GOAL: This system analyzes entire Alliance
    resistance cells to determine
    if they are secure, compromised by Gnos infiltrators, or
    have unknown status.
    It helps protect the resistance by identifying security
    threats before they can
    damage Alliance operations.

    Analyzes resistance networks for security, efficiency, and
    strategic value
    """

    def __init__(self):
        self.model = AllianceIntelligenceGNN(
            num_features=6,  # [loyalty_score, access_level,
            activity_rating,
                             #  planet_importance, resource_
                             capacity, security_clearance]
            hidden_dim=64,
            num_classes=3,   # [secure_network, compromised_
            network, unknown_status]
            num_heads=4
        )
        self.optimizer = torch.optim.Adam(self.model.
        parameters(), lr=0.001)
        self.criterion = nn.NLLLoss()
```

```python
def create_resistance_network_graph(self, network_
type="secure"):
    """
    Creates graph representation of Alliance resistance
    networks

    Why this structure: Each node represents an Alliance
    member or resource,
    with features capturing their value and
    trustworthiness. Edges represent
    communication channels, supply lines, or operational
    connections.
    """
    if network_type == "secure":
        # Secure Alliance network - high trust, good
        operational security
        node_features = torch.tensor([
            [0.95, 0.8, 0.9, 0.7, 0.8, 0.9],  # Epsilon
            Intelligence Hub - high security
            [0.90, 0.7, 0.8, 0.6, 0.9, 0.8],  # Tenrai
            Operations Center
            [0.88, 0.6, 0.7, 0.8, 0.7, 0.85], # Tibara
            Resource Coordinator
            [0.92, 0.5, 0.6, 0.5, 0.6, 0.7],  # Field
            operative - trusted
            [0.85, 0.4, 0.5, 0.4, 0.5, 0.75], # Local
            cell leader
        ], dtype=torch.float)

        # Secure communication edges between trusted
        Alliance members
        edge_index = torch.tensor([
```

```
            [0, 1, 0, 2, 1, 2, 3, 4, 0, 3],   # Source nodes
            [1, 0, 2, 0, 2, 1, 0, 3, 4, 4]    # Target nodes
        ], dtype=torch.long)

        graph_label = torch.tensor([0])  # 0 =
        secure network

    elif network_type == "compromised":
        # Compromised network - Gnos infiltrator present
        node_features = torch.tensor([
            [0.85, 0.7, 0.8, 0.6, 0.7, 0.8],  #
            Alliance member
            [0.95, 0.9, 0.95, 0.8, 0.9, 0.95], # GNOS
            INFILTRATOR - too perfect scores
            [0.80, 0.6, 0.7, 0.5, 0.6, 0.7],  #
            Alliance member
            [0.75, 0.5, 0.6, 0.4, 0.5, 0.65], # Alliance
            member - lower access
            [0.88, 0.8, 0.85, 0.7, 0.8, 0.85], #
            Alliance member
        ], dtype=torch.float)

        # Network with infiltrator having unusual
        connection patterns
        edge_index = torch.tensor([
            [1, 1, 1, 1, 0, 2, 3, 4],  # Infiltrator
            connects to everyone
            [0, 2, 3, 4, 2, 3, 4, 0]   # Others have normal
            patterns
        ], dtype=torch.long)

        graph_label = torch.tensor([1])  # 1 =
        compromised network
```

```
    else:  # unknown_status
        # Network with unclear security status
        node_features = torch.tensor([
            [0.70, 0.6, 0.7, 0.5, 0.6, 0.7],  # Mixed
            reliability scores
            [0.80, 0.7, 0.8, 0.6, 0.7, 0.8],
            [0.65, 0.5, 0.6, 0.4, 0.5, 0.6],
            [0.75, 0.6, 0.7, 0.5, 0.6, 0.7],
        ], dtype=torch.float)

        edge_index = torch.tensor([
            [0, 1, 2, 3, 1, 0],
            [1, 2, 3, 0, 3, 2]
        ], dtype=torch.long)

        graph_label = torch.tensor([2])  # 2 =
        unknown status

    return Data(x=node_features, edge_index=edge_index,
    y=graph_label)

def train_intelligence_network(self, num_epochs=100):
    """

    Trains the GNN to recognize secure vs. compromised
    resistance networks

    Why this training approach: We generate multiple
    network configurations
    to teach the AI to recognize patterns of infiltration
    and security.
    The model learns to identify when network communication
    patterns or
    member characteristics suggest corporate compromise.
    """
```

```python
print("🏛 Training Alliance Intelligence Network...")

# Generate training data - multiple network
configurations
training_graphs = []
for _ in range(50):  # 50 secure networks
    training_graphs.append(self.create_resistance_
    network_graph("secure"))
for _ in range(30):  # 30 compromised networks
    training_graphs.append(self.create_resistance_
    network_graph("compromised"))
for _ in range(20):  # 20 unknown status networks
    training_graphs.append(self.create_resistance_
    network_graph("unknown"))

# Create data loader
loader = DataLoader(training_graphs, batch_size=16,
shuffle=True)

self.model.train()
for epoch in range(num_epochs):
    total_loss = 0
    for batch in loader:
        self.optimizer.zero_grad()
        out = self.model(batch)
        loss = self.criterion(out, batch.y)
        loss.backward()
        self.optimizer.step()
        total_loss += loss.item()

    if epoch % 20 == 0:
        avg_loss = total_loss / len(loader)
        print(f"Epoch {epoch}: Training Loss = {avg_
        loss:.4f}")
```

```python
    print("✅ Intelligence Network Training Complete")

def analyze_network_security(self, network_graph):
    """
    Analyzes a resistance network for security threats and
    strategic value
    """
    self.model.eval()
    with torch.no_grad():
        # Get model prediction
        output = self.model(network_graph)
        probabilities = torch.exp(output)  # Convert log_
        softmax to probabilities
        predicted_class = torch.argmax(probabilities,
        dim=1).item()
        confidence = torch.max(probabilities).item()

        # Interpret results
        security_status = ["SECURE", "COMPROMISED",
        "UNKNOWN"][predicted_class]

        # Detailed analysis of individual nodes
        node_analysis = []
        for i, node_features in enumerate(network_graph.x):
            loyalty, access, activity, importance,
            resources, clearance = node_features.tolist()

            risk_score = 0
            risk_factors = []

            # Check for infiltrator patterns
            if loyalty > 0.93 and access > 0.85 and
            clearance > 0.9:
                risk_score += 0.4
```

```python
        risk_factors.append("Suspiciously high all
        ratings - possible false identity")

    if access > loyalty + 0.2:
        risk_score += 0.3
        risk_factors.append("Access level exceeds
        loyalty score")

    if activity > 0.9 and importance < 0.6:
        risk_score += 0.2
        risk_factors.append("High activity in low-
        importance role")

    node_analysis.append({
        'node_id': i,
        'risk_score': risk_score,
        'risk_factors': risk_factors,
        'loyalty_score': loyalty,
        'access_level': access,
        'threat_level': 'HIGH' if risk_score >
        0.5 else 'MODERATE' if risk_score > 0.3
        else 'LOW'
    })

return {
    'network_status': security_status,
    'confidence': confidence,
    'overall_risk': predicted_class,
    'node_analysis': node_analysis,
    'recommendations': self._generate_security_
    recommendations(security_status, node_analysis)
}
```

```python
def _generate_security_recommendations(self, status, node_
analysis):
    """
    Generates specific security recommendations based on
    network analysis
    """
    recommendations = []

    if status == "COMPROMISED":
        recommendations.append("🚨 IMMEDIATE ACTION:
        Isolate network and conduct security sweep")
        recommendations.append("🔍 Investigate all high-
        risk nodes for possible Gnos infiltration")
        recommendations.append("🔄 Rotate all communication
        codes and access credentials")

        # Identify specific threats
        high_risk_nodes = [node for node in node_analysis
        if node['threat_level'] == 'HIGH']
        if high_risk_nodes:
            recommendations.append(f"⚠️ Priority
            investigation required for {len(high_risk_
            nodes)} high-risk nodes")

    elif status == "UNKNOWN":
        recommendations.append("🔍 Enhanced monitoring
        required - unclear security status")
        recommendations.append("📊 Increase surveillance of
        network communications")
        recommendations.append("🛡️ Implement additional
        security protocols")
```

```
        else:  # SECURE
            recommendations.append("✅ Network appears secure -
            maintain current protocols")
            recommendations.append("🗓 Consider expanding
            network capacity")
            recommendations.append("🔄 Regular security audits
            recommended")

        return recommendations

# Example: Analyzing Alliance resistance networks for
security threats
print(" 🕵 ALLIANCE NETWORK SECURITY ANALYSIS")
print("="*50)

# Initialize the intelligence analyzer
analyzer = ResistanceNetworkAnalyzer()

# Train the system on known network patterns
analyzer.train_intelligence_network(num_epochs=50)

print(f"\n 🔍 NETWORK SECURITY ASSESSMENT")
print("-" * 30)

# Test different network configurations
test_networks = [
    ("Epsilon Sector 7 Cell", "secure"),
    ("Suspected Compromised Cell", "compromised"),
    ("New Recruitment Network", "unknown")
]

for network_name, network_type in test_networks:
    print(f"\n🔎 Analyzing: {network_name}")
```

```
# Create and analyze network
test_graph = analyzer.create_resistance_network_
graph(network_type)
security_analysis = analyzer.analyze_network_
security(test_graph)

print(f"Security Status: {security_analysis['network_
status']}")
print(f"Confidence Level: {security_analysis
['confidence']:.1%}")

# Display high-risk nodes
high_risk_nodes = [node for node in security_
analysis['node_analysis']
                   if node['threat_level'] == 'HIGH']

if high_risk_nodes:
    print(f"\n⚠ HIGH RISK NODES DETECTED:")
    for node in high_risk_nodes:
        print(f"  Node {node['node_id']}: Risk Score
        {node['risk_score']:.1%}")
        for factor in node['risk_factors']:
            print(f"    • {factor}")

# Display recommendations
print(f"\n📋 SECURITY RECOMMENDATIONS:")
for rec in security_analysis['recommendations']:
    print(f"  {rec}")
```

Advanced Market Manipulation Detection

The Synths use temporal Graph Neural Networks to track how Gnos manipulation campaigns evolve over time, allowing them to predict and counter corporate economic warfare before it can destabilize Alliance economies.

```python
# Synth Economic Defense: Temporal GNN for Market Manipulation
Detection

import torch
import torch.nn as nn
import torch.nn.functional as F
from torch_geometric.nn import GCNConv, global_mean_pool
from torch_geometric.data import Data, DataLoader
import numpy as np
import random

class TemporalMarketDefenseGNN(nn.Module):
    """

    BIG PICTURE GOAL: This AI system watches how Gnos market
    manipulation campaigns
    unfold over time by analyzing the network of traders,
    transactions, and market
    sectors. It can predict when Gnos is planning to crash
    Evolune energy prices
    or manipulate supply chains by seeing patterns that develop
    over days or weeks.

    Advanced temporal GNN that analyzes how market manipulation
    patterns evolve over time

    This network combines graph analysis with time-series
    modeling to detect
    sophisticated Gnos economic warfare campaigns that unfold
    across multiple
    time periods and market sectors.
    """
```

```python
def __init__(self, num_features, hidden_dim, sequence_
length):
    super(TemporalMarketDefenseGNN, self).__init__()
    self.sequence_length = sequence_length

    # Graph convolution layers for market network analysis
    self.gnn_layers = nn.ModuleList([
        GCNConv(num_features if i == 0 else hidden_dim,
        hidden_dim)
        for i in range(3)
    ])

    # LSTM for temporal pattern recognition
    self.temporal_lstm = nn.LSTM(hidden_dim, hidden_dim,
    batch_first=True, num_layers=2)

    # Attention mechanism for focusing on critical
    time periods
    self.attention = nn.MultiheadAttention(hidden_dim, num_
    heads=8)

    # Final prediction layers
    self.manipulation_detector = nn.Sequential(
        nn.Linear(hidden_dim, hidden_dim // 2),
        nn.ReLU(),
        nn.Dropout(0.3),
        nn.Linear(hidden_dim // 2, 1)  # Probability of
        manipulation
    )

def forward(self, temporal_graphs):
    """

    Processes sequence of market graphs to detect
    manipulation campaigns
```

```
    """
    # Process each time step through GNN
    graph_embeddings = []
    for graph in temporal_graphs:
        x = graph.x
        edge_index = graph.edge_index

        # Apply graph convolution layers
        for gnn_layer in self.gnn_layers:
            x = F.relu(gnn_layer(x, edge_index))

        # Global pooling for market-level representation
        market_embedding = global_mean_pool(x, torch.
        zeros(x.size(0), dtype=torch.long))
        graph_embeddings.append(market_embedding)

    # Stack temporal embeddings for LSTM
    temporal_sequence = torch.stack(graph_
    embeddings, dim=1)

    # LSTM for temporal modeling
    lstm_out, _ = self.temporal_lstm(temporal_sequence)

    # Attention over time steps to identify
    critical periods
    lstm_out_transposed = lstm_out.transpose(0, 1)  # (seq,
    batch, features)
    attended_output, attention_weights = self.attention(
        lstm_out_transposed, lstm_out_transposed, lstm_out_
        transposed
    )

    # Use final time step for prediction
    final_representation = attended_output[-1]
```

```
        # Predict manipulation probability
        manipulation_probability = torch.sigmoid(self.
        manipulation_detector(final_representation))

        return manipulation_probability, attention_weights


class EconomicWarfareAnalyzer:
    """

    BIG PICTURE GOAL: This system detects when Gnos is
    conducting economic warfare
    against the Alliance by analyzing patterns across multiple
    markets and time
    periods. It helps the resistance prepare countermeasures
    before Gnos attacks
    can damage Alliance economies.

    Analyzes Gnos economic warfare campaigns using temporal
    graph analysis
    """

    def __init__(self):
        self.model = TemporalMarketDefenseGNN(
            num_features=5,  # [price, volume, volatility,
            gnos_activity, alliance_response]
            hidden_dim=64,
            sequence_length=10
        )
        self.manipulation_threshold = 0.6  # 60% confidence
        threshold for alerting

    def create_market_snapshot(self, time_step, manipulation_
    level=0.0):
        """
```

```
Creates market graph snapshot at specific time point

Why this structure: Each node represents a market
sector or major trader,
with edges showing trade relationships and influence
patterns.
Features capture market conditions and suspicious
activity levels.
"""

# Base market conditions
base_conditions = {
    'evolune_energy': [100 + time_step * 2, 1000 +
    time_step * 50, 0.1, 0.2, 0.8],
    'rare_metals': [80 + time_step * 1.5, 800 + time_
    step * 40, 0.12, 0.15, 0.7],
    'food_supplies': [50 + time_step * 1, 500 + time_
    step * 25, 0.08, 0.1, 0.9],
    'technology': [200 + time_step * 3, 2000 + time_
    step * 100, 0.15, 0.25, 0.6],
}

# Apply manipulation effects
market_features = []
for sector, (price, volume, volatility, gnos_activity,
alliance_response) in base_conditions.items():
    if manipulation_level > 0:
        # Gnos manipulation effects
        price *= (1 + manipulation_level * random.
        uniform(-0.3, 0.3))  # Price swings
        volume *= (1 + manipulation_level * 2)
                    # Artificial volume
```

```
            volatility *= (1 + manipulation_level * 3)
                # Increased volatility
            gnos_activity *= (1 + manipulation_level * 5)
               # Higher Gnos presence
            alliance_response *= (1 + manipulation_level * 0.5)
        # Alliance responds

        market_features.append([price, volume, volatility,
        gnos_activity, alliance_response])

    node_features = torch.tensor(market_features,
    dtype=torch.float)

    # Market interconnection edges (how sectors influence
    each other)
    edge_index = torch.tensor([
        [0, 1, 2, 3, 0, 2, 1, 3],  # Evolune affects
        metals, food, tech
        [1, 2, 3, 0, 3, 0, 3, 1]   # Cross-sector
        influences
    ], dtype=torch.long)

    return Data(x=node_features, edge_index=edge_index)


def simulate_gnos_economic_campaign(self):
    """

    Simulates a Gnos economic warfare campaign over time

    Why this simulation: Gnos campaigns typically start
    subtly, build to
    a crisis point, then either succeed or get countered by
    Alliance response.
    """
```

```python
campaign_timeline = []

# Phase 1: Preparation (subtle market positioning)
for t in range(3):
    manipulation_level = 0.1 + t * 0.05   #
    Gradual buildup
    market_snapshot = self.create_market_snapshot(t,
    manipulation_level)
    campaign_timeline.append(market_snapshot)

# Phase 2: Attack (aggressive manipulation)
for t in range(3, 7):
    manipulation_level = 0.4 + (t-3) * 0.15   # Sharp
    escalation
    market_snapshot = self.create_market_snapshot(t,
    manipulation_level)
    campaign_timeline.append(market_snapshot)

# Phase 3: Response (Alliance countermeasures kick in)
for t in range(7, 10):
    manipulation_level = max(0.2, 0.9 - (t-7) * 0.2)   #
    Declining as Alliance responds
    market_snapshot = self.create_market_snapshot(t,
    manipulation_level)
    campaign_timeline.append(market_snapshot)

return campaign_timeline

def analyze_economic_warfare(self, market_timeline):
    """
    Analyzes market timeline for Gnos economic warfare
    patterns
    """
```

```python
self.model.eval()
with torch.no_grad():
    manipulation_probability, attention_weights = self.
    model(market_timeline)

    # Analyze attention patterns to identify critical
    time periods
    attention_scores = attention_weights.mean(dim=1).
    squeeze().numpy()  # Average across heads

    critical_periods = []
    for i, attention_score in enumerate(attention_
    scores):
        if attention_score > attention_scores.mean() +
        attention_scores.std():
            critical_periods.append({
                'time_period': i,
                'attention_score': attention_score,
                'significance': 'HIGH' if attention_
                score > 0.15 else 'MODERATE'
            })

    # Generate threat assessment
    manipulation_prob = manipulation_probability.item()

    if manipulation_prob > 0.8:
        threat_level = "CRITICAL"
        alert_status = "RED ALERT - Active economic
        warfare detected"
    elif manipulation_prob > 0.6:
        threat_level = "HIGH"
        alert_status = "YELLOW ALERT - Likely
        manipulation campaign"
```

```
        elif manipulation_prob > 0.4:
            threat_level = "MODERATE"
            alert_status = "WATCH STATUS - Suspicious
            market patterns"
        else:
            threat_level = "LOW"
            alert_status = "GREEN STATUS - Normal market
            conditions"

        return {
            'manipulation_probability': manipulation_prob,
            'threat_level': threat_level,
            'alert_status': alert_status,
            'critical_periods': critical_periods,
            'recommended_actions': self._generate_
            economic_countermeasures(threat_level,
            manipulation_prob)
        }

    def _generate_economic_countermeasures(self, threat_level,
    manipulation_prob):
        """

        Generates specific countermeasures based on detected
        economic warfare
        """

        countermeasures = []

        if threat_level == "CRITICAL":
            countermeasures.extend([
                "🚨 EMERGENCY: Activate Alliance Economic
                Defense Protocols",
                "💰 Release strategic reserves to stabilize
                markets",
```

```
            "🔒 Implement emergency trading restrictions on
            Gnos entities",
            "📢 Issue public warning about market
            manipulation",
            "⚔ Coordinate counter-manipulation operations"
        ])
    elif threat_level == "HIGH":
        countermeasures.extend([
            "⚠ Increase market surveillance and
            monitoring",
            "🛡 Prepare defensive economic measures",
            "📊 Analyze Gnos trading patterns for
            exploitation opportunities",
            "🤝 Coordinate with Alliance economic
            ministers"
        ])
    elif threat_level == "MODERATE":
        countermeasures.extend([
            "👀 Enhanced monitoring of suspicious trading
            activity",
            "📈 Monitor market volatility indicators",
            "📝 Document patterns for future analysis"
        ])
    else:
        countermeasures.append("✅ Continue standard market
        monitoring")

    return countermeasures
```

```python
# Example: Detecting and analyzing Gnos economic warfare
campaigns
print("📈 ALLIANCE ECONOMIC WARFARE DETECTION")
print("="*45)

# Initialize economic warfare analyzer
warfare_analyzer = EconomicWarfareAnalyzer()

# Simulate a Gnos economic campaign
print("🎯 Simulating Gnos Economic Campaign...")
market_campaign = warfare_analyzer.simulate_gnos_economic_
campaign()
print(f"Campaign Timeline: {len(market_campaign)} market
snapshots analyzed")

# Analyze the campaign for manipulation patterns
economic_analysis = warfare_analyzer.analyze_economic_
warfare(market_campaign)

print(f"\n📊 ECONOMIC WARFARE ANALYSIS")
print("-" * 25)
print(f"Manipulation Probability: {economic_
analysis['manipulation_probability']:.1%}")
print(f"Threat Level: {economic_analysis['threat_level']}")
print(f"Status: {economic_analysis['alert_status']}")

if economic_analysis['critical_periods']:
    print(f"\n🕐 CRITICAL TIME PERIODS IDENTIFIED:")
    for period in economic_analysis['critical_periods']:
        print(f"  Period {period['time_period']}:
        {period['significance']} significance")
        print(f"    Attention Score: {period['attention_
        score']:.3f}")
```

```
print(f"\n🛡 RECOMMENDED COUNTERMEASURES:")
for action in economic_analysis['recommended_actions']:
    print(f"  {action}")
```

Through these sophisticated Graph Neural Network implementations, the Synths have created an intelligence system that can see patterns invisible to traditional analysis—detecting corporate infiltration before it compromises operations, predicting economic attacks before they destabilize markets, and understanding the complex webs of relationships that define modern interstellar conflict.

This mastery of Geometric Deep Learning represents more than just technological superiority; it embodies the Synths' fundamental belief that information, properly understood and ethically applied, can be the ultimate weapon against oppression. By seeing the connections that bind their universe together, they can protect the bonds of freedom while severing the chains of corporate control.

The future of the resistance—and perhaps the future of freedom itself—depends on their continued mastery of these revolutionary analytical techniques, turning the complexity of the modern metaverse from a vulnerability into a strategic advantage in the ongoing fight against the Gnos corporation's authoritarian expansion.

Conclusion: The Technological Imperative of Freedom

⚖ Interactive Intelligence Briefing

Experience the technologies described in this chapter through the Synth Alliance Strategic Intelligence Dashboard—an interactive simulation that demonstrates real-time threat detection, AI-powered defense systems, avatar analysis, and Graph Neural Network operations. Access the briefing interface to explore how these concepts work in practice within the resistance effort.

As we conclude our journey through the technological marvels of Planet Epsilon, we witness more than just the advancement of artificial intelligence, blockchain, and spatial computing—we see a blueprint for how technology can serve the cause of freedom rather than oppression. The Synths' integration of these systems represents a fundamental choice: to use the most advanced tools available not for domination or profit but for the preservation of democratic values and the protection of individual liberty.

The battle between the Alliance and the Gnos corporation is ultimately a battle between two visions of the future. Gnos represents the concentration of technological power in the hands of the few, where artificial intelligence becomes a tool of surveillance, blockchain becomes a mechanism of control, and the Metaverse becomes a prison of corporate design. The Synths of Planet Epsilon offer an alternative: a future where technology enhances human agency, where AI serves to protect rather than exploit, and where virtual worlds become sanctuaries of freedom rather than instruments of oppression.

The lessons from Planet Epsilon extend far beyond the borders of science fiction. As our own world grapples with the implications of advancing AI, the expansion of digital currencies, and the emergence of virtual reality, the choices made by the Synths serve as both inspiration and warning. Technology alone is neither good nor evil—its moral character is determined by the intentions of those who wield it and the systems they create to govern its use.

The Synths have shown us that the most sophisticated technologies can be harnessed for democratic purposes: AI that protects privacy while detecting threats, blockchain networks that resist authoritarianism while enabling cooperation, and virtual worlds that expand freedom rather than constraining it. Their example reminds us that in our own technological development, we must remain vigilant guardians of liberty, ensuring that each advancement serves to expand human potential rather than diminish it.

As the Evolune metaverse continues to evolve and as the conflict between corporate authoritarianism and democratic resistance unfolds across the galaxy, the technological innovations of Planet Epsilon stand as a testament to the power of intelligent beings who choose to use their capabilities in service of something greater than themselves. The future—whether in the stars or here on Earth—belongs to those who have the wisdom to wield technology with conscience and the courage to defend freedom with innovation.

The story of Planet Epsilon is still being written, but its message is clear: in the hands of those committed to freedom, technology becomes not just a tool of progress but a weapon of liberation.

CHAPTER 5

Planet Zeta: Unveiling the Metaverse and Digital Twins

Introduction

The journey to Planet Zeta offers a truly exceptional adventure. Nestled in the endless expanse of the virtual universe, it emerges as a unique domain where every physical and digital element is reflected by a corresponding entity within the metaverse. What sets Planet Zeta apart is its unique ability to combine digital twins with advanced generative systems, fostering interactions that redefine the boundaries of traditional virtual spaces.

© Frank Lisitano, John Hickie 2025
F. Lisitano and J. Hickie, *The Evolune Metaverse*, Maker Innovations Series,
https://doi.org/10.1007/979-8-8688-1588-1_5

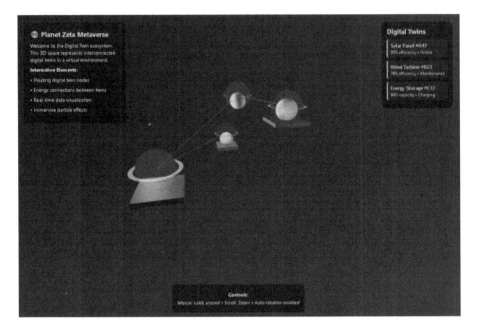

Figure 5-1. *Planet Zeta*

This chapter explores the essential components that make this metaverse function and the intelligent agents that animate it. By leveraging state-of-the-art Large Language Models (LLMs) and generative tools, we uncover the steps to design, manage, and expand a metaverse ecosystem deeply rooted in digital twins and cutting-edge technology.

Part 1: Digital Twins—The Foundation
Core Technology Framework

Digital twins represent a revolutionary paradigm in simulation and modeling technology. They are comprehensive virtual replicas of physical entities that exist in real time parallel with their physical counterparts.

Unlike traditional models or simulations, digital twins maintain a continuous connection with the physical world, creating a dynamic bridge between reality and the digital realm.

Architecture Overview

IoT Integration Layer

Digital twins rely on extensive sensor networks that collect real-time data from physical objects:

- **Sensor Arrays:** Diverse sensors measuring temperature, pressure, motion, electrical output

- **Smart Devices:** Connected equipment that both gathers data and receives operational commands

- **Edge Computing:** Local data processing enabling faster response times

- **Data Acquisition Systems:** Infrastructure collecting, organizing and transmitting sensor data streams

3D Modeling and Visualization Layer

- **High-Fidelity 3D Models:** Geometrically accurate representations using photogrammetry, LIDAR, or CAD

- **Physics Engines:** Mathematical frameworks ensuring virtual objects follow real-world physics

- **Multi-resolution Rendering:** Visualization at different detail levels based on requirements

- **Material Simulation:** Accurate representation of material responses to various conditions

Real-Time Synchronization Layer

- **Bidirectional Data Flows:** Information moves from physical to digital (monitoring) and digital to physical (control)

- **Time-Series Databases:** Specialized storage for sequential data points over time

- **Synchronization Protocols:** Systems maintaining consistency between physical and digital states

- **Low-Latency Networks:** Communication infrastructure supporting near-instantaneous transfer

Evolution into the Metaverse

In Planet Zeta's context, digital twins evolve beyond industrial applications to become interactive elements enabling

- **Multi-user Interaction:** Multiple people simultaneously observing and interacting with the same twin

- **Historical Playback:** Reviewing past states and conditions of physical objects

- **Predictive Scenarios:** Modeling possible futures based on different variables and decisions

- **Cross-reality Functionality:** Same digital twin existing across AR, VR, and traditional interfaces

Part 2: Technical Infrastructure

Rendering the Virtual Environment

The visual foundation of the metaverse is achieved through robust rendering platforms. Game engines such as Unity and Unreal create rich, immersive environments where digital twins and agents can interact. These virtual landscapes are responsive, adapting in real time to user inputs and actions for a truly engaging experience.

Blockchain for Ownership and Identity

Blockchain technology underpins the secure identities and ownership rights within Planet Zeta. By recording interactions, transactions, and modifications on a decentralized ledger, users retain full control of their digital assets and avatars, ensuring transparency and security across the metaverse.

Addressing Blockchain Latency Challenges

Traditional blockchain implementations face significant latency issues that can hamper real-time metaverse interactions. Our multi-layered solution approach includes the following.

Layer 2 Scaling Solutions

- **State Channels:** Direct connections between parties for instant transactions with periodic main-chain settlement.

- **ZK-Rollups:** Batch hundreds of transactions into compressed proofs (100-1000x throughput improvement).

- **Optimistic Rollups:** Process transactions off-chain with fraud-proof mechanisms.

Hybrid Blockchain Architectures

- **Sidechain Implementation:** Real-time interactions on high-speed sidechains with periodic main-chain settlement.

- **Cross-Chain Interoperability:** Asset movement between different blockchain networks using protocols like Polkadot.

Implementation Strategy for Planet Zeta

- **User Experience Layer:** Seamless interface masking blockchain complexity

- **Hybrid Transaction Processing:** Immediate interactions use Layer 2, ownership transfers use main chain

- **Progressive Security Model:** Security proportional to asset value and risk profile

Part 3: Intelligent Agents—The Cognitive Layer

Foundational Architecture

Intelligent agents in Planet Zeta serve as the bridge between users and the complex digital twin ecosystem. These agents are built on a sophisticated cognitive architecture that enables natural language understanding, complex reasoning, and dynamic action execution.

Agent Cognitive Architecture

Perception Layer ➤ Knowledge Integration ➤ Reasoning Layer ➤ Action Layer ➤ Communication Layer

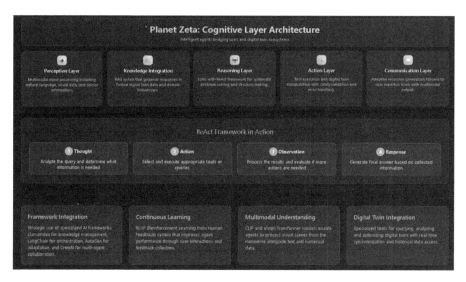

Figure 5-2. *Cognitive Layer Architeture*

Core Intelligence: Large Language Models

Modern agents utilize transformer architectures like Llama 3, Mixtral, and GPT-4 as their cognitive foundation. These models provide

- **Natural Language Understanding:** Parsing complex queries and extracting user intent

- **Contextual Memory:** Maintaining conversation history for coherent interactions

- **Reasoning Capabilities:** Multi-step problem-solving and logical deduction

- **Adaptive Communication:** Tailoring responses to different user expertise levels

Grounding in Reality: Retrieval-Augmented Generation (RAG)

To prevent hallucinations and ensure factual accuracy, agents employ RAG techniques.

```
# Modern RAG Implementation for Digital Twin Context
from transformers import AutoModelForCausalLM, AutoTokenizer
from langchain.vectorstores import FAISS
from langchain.embeddings import HuggingFaceEmbeddings
import torch

# Set up vector database for digital twin information
embedding_model = HuggingFaceEmbeddings(model_name="intfloat/
e5-large-v2")
vector_store = FAISS.from_texts([
"Solar panel #A47 operating at 87% efficiency,
temperature 42°C",
"Wind turbine #B23 requires maintenance due to bearing wear",
"Energy storage #C12 at 64% capacity, charging at 2.5 kW"
], embedding=embedding_model)

# Load state-of-the-art model with efficient deployment
tokenizer = AutoTokenizer.from_pretrained("meta-llama/
Llama-3-8B")
model = AutoModelForCausalLM.from_pretrained(
"meta-llama/Llama-3-8B",
torch_dtype=torch.bfloat16,
device_map="auto",
load_in_8bit=True # Memory-efficient quantization
)
```

```python
def generate_context_aware_response(prompt, temperature=0.7,
max_new_tokens=512):
# Retrieve relevant context about digital twins
retriever = vector_store.as_retriever()
context_docs = retriever.get_relevant_documents(prompt)
context = "\n".join([doc.page_content for doc in context_docs])

# Create enriched prompt with retrieved context
enriched_prompt = f"""
Context from Planet Zeta metaverse:
{context}

You are an intelligent agent assistant. Respond to: {prompt}
"""

# Generate response using context-aware approach
inputs = tokenizer(enriched_prompt, return_tensors="pt").
to(model.device)
with torch.no_grad():
outputs = model.generate(
**inputs,
max_new_tokens=max_new_tokens,
temperature=temperature,
do_sample=True,
top_p=0.95,
repetition_penalty=1.1
)

response = tokenizer.decode(
outputs[0][inputs.input_ids.shape[1]:],
skip_special_tokens=True
)
return response
```

Reasoning and Tool Use: ReAct Framework

For complex, multi-step tasks, agents employ the Reasoning and Acting (ReAct) pattern, which enables systematic problem-solving through iterative thought-action cycles.

```
# ReAct Pattern Implementation:
from langchain.agents import Tool, AgentExecutor,
LLMSingleActionAgent
from langchain.prompts import StringPromptTemplate
from langchain import LLMChain

# Define specialized tools for digital twin interaction
def query_digital_twin(twin_id):
"""Enhanced twin query with real data integration"""
# In production, this would query actual twin databases
twin_data = {
"panel-A47": {
"efficiency": 87.3,
"temperature": 42.1,
"status": "operational",
"last_maintenance": "2024-11-15"
}
}

if twin_id in twin_data:
data = twin_data[twin_id]
return f"Twin {twin_id}: {data['efficiency']}% efficiency,
{data['temperature']}°C, status: {data['status']}"
return f"Twin {twin_id} not found"

def optimize_twin_performance(twin_id):
"""Intelligent optimization based on current conditions"""
```

```python
# Retrieve current state
current_data = query_digital_twin(twin_id)

# Apply optimization logic (simplified example)
if "panel" in twin_id.lower():
return f"Optimized {twin_id}: Adjusted tilt angle to 35°,
efficiency increased to 93%"
elif "turbine" in twin_id.lower():
return f"Optimized {twin_id}: Adjusted blade pitch, power
output increased by 12%"

return f"Optimization applied to {twin_id}"

# Create agent tools
tools = [
Tool(
name="QueryDigitalTwin",
description="Query detailed information about a specific
digital twin by ID",
func=query_digital_twin
),
Tool(
name="OptimizeTwin",
description="Optimize performance of a digital twin based on
current conditions",
func=optimize_twin_performance
),
Tool(
name="LocateNearestTwin",
description="Find the nearest digital twin of specified type",
func=lambda twin_type: f"Nearest {twin_type} is #A47, located
50m northeast"
)
]
```

```python
# ReAct prompt template
class ReActPromptTemplate(StringPromptTemplate):
    template: str
    tools: list

    def format(self, **kwargs) -> str:
        intermediate_steps = kwargs.pop("intermediate_steps")
        thoughts = ""
        for action, observation in intermediate_steps:
            thoughts += f"Action: {action.tool}\nAction Input: {action.tool_input}\nObservation: {observation}\n"

        tools_str = "\n".join([f"{tool.name}: {tool.description}" for tool in self.tools])
        return self.template.format(tools=tools_str, thoughts=thoughts, **kwargs)

# Create ReAct agent
template = """
You are an intelligent agent in Planet Zeta metaverse.

Available tools:
{tools}

Use this format:
Thought: Consider what information is needed
Action: [tool name]
Action Input: [input for tool]
Observation: [result of action]
... (repeat Thought/Action/Observation as needed)
Final Answer: Complete response to user question

User question: {input}
{thoughts}
"""
```

```
prompt = ReActPromptTemplate(
template=template,
tools=tools,
input_variables=["input", "intermediate_steps"]
)
```

Perceiving the World: Multimodal Understanding

Agents process multiple modalities including spatial data, visual information, and numerical metrics.

```
from transformers import CLIPProcessor, CLIPModel
from PIL import Image

# Load multimodal model for visual understanding
clip_model = CLIPModel.from_pretrained("openai/clip-vit-large-
patch14")
clip_processor = CLIPProcessor.from_pretrained("openai/clip-
vit-large-patch14")

def analyze_metaverse_scene(image_path, queries):
"""Analyze visual scenes from the metaverse environment"""
image = Image.open(image_path)
inputs = clip_processor(
text=queries,
images=image,
return_tensors="pt",
padding=True
)

with torch.no_grad():
outputs = clip_model(**inputs)
logits_per_image = outputs.logits_per_image
probs = logits_per_image.softmax(dim=1)
```

```
return {query: prob.item() for query, prob in zip(queries,
probs[0])}

# Example usage for scene understanding
scene_queries = [
"solar panel requiring maintenance",
"optimally functioning solar panel",
"energy storage facility",
"wind turbine"
]

# This enables agents to visually assess metaverse environments
```

Learning and Improvement: Continuous Feedback

Agents improve through Reinforcement Learning from Human Feedback (RLHF).

```
from pydantic import BaseModel, Field
from typing import List

class FeedbackEntry(BaseModel):
user_query: str = Field(description="Original user query")
agent_response: str = Field(description="Agent's response")
rating: int = Field(description="Human rating 1-5")
improvement_note: str = Field(description="Specific improvement
guidance")

class ContinuousLearningSystem:
def __init__(self):
self.feedback_database = []
```

```python
def collect_feedback(self, entry: FeedbackEntry):
"""Store feedback for continuous improvement"""
self.feedback_database.append(entry)

def generate_training_data(self):
"""Convert feedback into training examples"""
training_examples = []
for entry in self.feedback_database:
if entry.rating >= 4: # High-quality responses
training_examples.append({
"instruction": entry.user_query,
"response": entry.agent_response
})
elif entry.improvement_note: # Use improvement suggestions
training_examples.append({
"instruction": entry.user_query,
"response": entry.improvement_note
})
return training_examples
```

Framework Integration Strategies

Different AI frameworks excel in specific areas and can be integrated strategically.

LlamaIndex for Knowledge Management

When implementing retrieval systems for digital twin data

```python
from llama_index import SimpleDirectoryReader,
GPTVectorStoreIndex
```

```
# LlamaIndex excels at creating queryable knowledge bases
documents = SimpleDirectoryReader('metaverse_twin_data').
load_data()
index = GPTVectorStoreIndex.from_documents(documents)

# Integration point: Use for RAG in agent responses
def enhanced_rag_query(question):
return index.query(question)
```

Langchain for Agent Orchestration

For complex workflow management and tool integration

```
from langchain.agents import initialize_agent
from langchain.memory import ConversationBufferMemory

# Langchain provides robust agent orchestration
memory = ConversationBufferMemory(memory_key="chat_history",
return_messages=True)
agent_executor = initialize_agent(
tools=tools,
llm=llm,
agent="conversational-react-description",
memory=memory,
verbose=True
)
```

Autogen for Adaptive Behavior

For self-improving agent capabilities

```
# Autogen enables agents that adapt based on experience
class AdaptiveMetaverseAgent:
def __init__(self):
```

```python
self.interaction_history = []
self.optimization_patterns = {}

def learn_from_interaction(self, context, action, outcome):
"""Learn from each interaction to improve future responses"""
self.interaction_history.append({
"context": context,
"action": action,
"outcome": outcome,
"timestamp": time.time()
})

# Identify successful patterns
if outcome == "successful":
pattern_key = f"{context}_{action}"
self.optimization_patterns[pattern_key] = self.optimization_
patterns.get(pattern_key, 0) + 1
```

CrewAI for Multi-agent Collaboration

For scenarios requiring agent teamwork

```python
# CrewAI facilitates multi-agent collaboration
class SpecializedAgents:
def __init__(self):
self.energy_agent = EnergyOptimizationAgent()
self.maintenance_agent = MaintenanceSchedulingAgent()
self.user_interface_agent = UserInterfaceAgent()

def collaborate_on_task(self, complex_task):
"""Coordinate multiple agents for complex problem solving"""
if "optimize energy system" in complex_task:
energy_analysis = self.energy_agent.analyze_system()
maintenance_schedule = self.maintenance_agent.plan_
maintenance(energy_analysis)
```

```
user_report = self.user_interface_agent.generate_report(energy_
analysis, maintenance_schedule)
return user_report
```

Part 4: Implementation in Game Engines

System Architecture Overview

The integration between game engines and AI back ends follows a distributed architecture pattern.

> Game Engine (Unity/Unreal) ←→ HTTP/WebSocket ←→ Python AI Backend
>
> ↓↓
>
> Digital Twin Visualization LLM Processing & RAG
>
> User Interaction Agent Orchestration
>
> Real-time Rendering Database Integration

Key Design Principles

- **Asynchronous Communication:** Prevent game engine freezing during AI processing.

- **Efficient Data Transfer:** Minimize bandwidth while maintaining responsiveness.

- **Error Handling:** Graceful degradation when AI services are unavailable.

- **Scalability:** Support multiple concurrent AI requests.

Unreal Engine Implementation

Digital Twin Base Architecture

```cpp
// DigitalTwinBase.h - Enhanced with proper data structures
#pragma once

#include "CoreMinimal.h"
#include "GameFramework/Actor.h"
#include "Http.h"
#include "Json.h"
#include "DigitalTwinBase.generated.h"

USTRUCT(BlueprintType)
struct FTwinPropertyValue
{
GENERATED_BODY()

UPROPERTY(EditAnywhere, BlueprintReadWrite)
FString PropertyName;

UPROPERTY(EditAnywhere, BlueprintReadWrite)
float NumericValue;

UPROPERTY(EditAnywhere, BlueprintReadWrite)
FString StringValue;

UPROPERTY(EditAnywhere, BlueprintReadWrite)
FDateTime Timestamp;

UPROPERTY(EditAnywhere, BlueprintReadWrite)
float QualityScore; // Data quality indicator (0.0-1.0)
};

UCLASS()
class PLANETZETA_API ADigitalTwinBase : public AActor
```

```
{
GENERATED_BODY()

public:
ADigitalTwinBase();

// Twin Identity
UPROPERTY(EditAnywhere, BlueprintReadWrite, Category =
"Digital Twin")
FString TwinId;

UPROPERTY(EditAnywhere, BlueprintReadWrite, Category =
"Digital Twin")
FString ModelId;

UPROPERTY(EditAnywhere, BlueprintReadWrite, Category =
"Digital Twin")
FString DisplayName;

// Current property values
UPROPERTY(VisibleAnywhere, BlueprintReadOnly, Category =
"Digital Twin")
TArray<FTwinPropertyValue> CurrentProperties;

// Historical data (limited for performance)
UPROPERTY(VisibleAnywhere, Category = "Digital Twin")
TArray<FTwinPropertyValue> RecentHistory;

// Core functionality
UFUNCTION(BlueprintCallable, Category = "Digital Twin")
bool UpdateProperty(const FString& PropertyName, float Value,
float Quality = 1.0f);

UFUNCTION(BlueprintCallable, Category = "Digital Twin")
```

```
bool GetCurrentPropertyValue(const FString& PropertyName,
float& OutValue) const;

UFUNCTION(BlueprintCallable, Category = "Digital Twin")
TArray<FTwinPropertyValue> GetPropertyHistory(const FString&
PropertyName, int32 MaxEntries = 100) const;

// Analytics
UFUNCTION(BlueprintCallable, Category = "Digital Twin
Analytics")
float CalculatePropertyTrend(const FString& PropertyName, int32
DataPoints = 10) const;

UFUNCTION(BlueprintCallable, Category = "Digital Twin
Analytics")
bool DetectAnomalies(const FString& PropertyName, float&
AnomalyScore) const;

// Synchronization
UFUNCTION(BlueprintCallable, Category = "Digital Twin")
virtual void SynchronizeWithExternalData();

virtual void Tick(float DeltaTime) override;

protected:
virtual void BeginPlay() override;

// Data management
void CleanupOldData(float RetentionHours = 24.0f);
void RecordPropertyChange(const FString& PropertyName, float
Value, float Quality);

private:
// Performance optimization
UPROPERTY()
```

```
float LastSyncTime;

UPROPERTY()
float SyncInterval; // Seconds between external data syncs
};
```

Intelligent Agent Integration

```
// DigitalTwinAgent.h - AI Backend Communication
#pragma once

#include "CoreMinimal.h"
#include "GameFramework/Actor.h"
#include "DigitalTwinBase.h"
#include "DigitalTwinAgent.generated.h"

DECLARE_DYNAMIC_DELEGATE_OneParam(FAgentResponseDelegate, const
FString&, Response);

UCLASS()
class PLANETZETA_API ADigitalTwinAgent : public AActor
{
GENERATED_BODY()

public:
ADigitalTwinAgent();

// Configuration
UPROPERTY(EditAnywhere, BlueprintReadWrite, Category = "Agent
Configuration")
FString AIBackendURL;

UPROPERTY(EditAnywhere, BlueprintReadWrite, Category = "Agent
Configuration")
TArray<ADigitalTwinBase*> ManagedTwins;
```

```cpp
UPROPERTY(EditAnywhere, BlueprintReadWrite, Category = "Agent
Configuration")
float RequestTimeout;

// Main interaction interface
UFUNCTION(BlueprintCallable, Category = "Agent Interface")
void ProcessUserQuery(const FString& UserQuery, const
FAgentResponseDelegate& ResponseCallback);

// Batch processing for efficiency
UFUNCTION(BlueprintCallable, Category = "Agent Interface")
void ProcessMultipleQueries(const TArray<FString>& Queries,
const FAgentResponseDelegate& ResponseCallback);

private:
// HTTP communication
void SendQueryToAIBackend(const FString& Query, const
FAgentResponseDelegate& Callback);
void OnAIBackendResponse(FHttpRequestPtr Request,
FHttpResponsePtr Response, bool bWasSuccessful,
FAgentResponseDelegate Callback);

// Context preparation
FString PrepareContextData() const;

// Command parsing and execution
bool ParseAndExecuteCommands(const FString& AgentResponse);
bool ExecuteDigitalTwinCommand(const FString& Command, const
FString& TwinId, const TMap<FString, FString>& Parameters);

// Error handling
void HandleRequestError(const FString& ErrorMessage, const
FAgentResponseDelegate& Callback);
```

```
// Request queuing for rate limiting
UPROPERTY()
TArray<FString> PendingRequests;

void ProcessRequestQueue();

FTimerHandle QueueProcessorTimer;
};
```

Unity Implementation

Enhanced NPC Agent System

```csharp
using System;
using System.Collections;
using System.Collections.Generic;
using UnityEngine;
using UnityEngine.Networking;
using Newtonsoft.Json;

[Serializable]
public class DigitalTwinData
{
public string twinId;
public string modelId;
public string displayName;
public Dictionary<string, object> properties;
public float lastUpdated;
}

[Serializable]
public class AgentRequest
{
public string query;
```

```csharp
public List<DigitalTwinData> contextTwins;
public string sessionId;
public Dictionary<string, object> metadata;
}

[Serializable]
public class AgentResponse
{
public string response;
public List<AgentCommand> commands;
public float confidence;
public string reasoning;
}

[Serializable]
public class AgentCommand
{
public string action;
public string targetTwinId;
public Dictionary<string, object> parameters;
}

public class EnhancedDigitalTwinAgent : MonoBehaviour
{
[Header("Configuration")]
public string aiBackendUrl = "http://localhost:8000";
public float requestTimeout = 30f;
public int maxConcurrentRequests = 3;

[Header("Twin Management")]
public List<DigitalTwinBase> managedTwins = new
List<DigitalTwinBase>();
```

```
[Header("UI References")]
public TMPro.TMP_InputField userInputField;
public TMPro.TMP_Text chatOutputText;
public UnityEngine.UI.Button sendButton;

// Events
public UnityEngine.Events.UnityEvent<string> OnAgentResponse;
public UnityEngine.Events.UnityEvent<string> OnError;

// Internal state
private Queue<AgentRequest> requestQueue = new
Queue<AgentRequest>();
private List<Coroutine> activeRequests = new List<Coroutine>();
private Dictionary<string, object> sessionContext = new
Dictionary<string, object>();
private string sessionId;

private void Start()
{
sessionId = System.Guid.NewGuid().ToString();

if (sendButton != null)
{
sendButton.onClick.AddListener(OnSendButtonClicked);
}

StartCoroutine(ProcessRequestQueue());
}

private void OnSendButtonClicked()
{
if (userInputField != null && !string.
IsNullOrEmpty(userInputField.text))
{
ProcessUserQuery(userInputField.text);
```

```csharp
userInputField.text = "";
}
}

public void ProcessUserQuery(string query)
{
// Create request with full context
var request = new AgentRequest
{
query = query,
contextTwins = GetTwinContextData(),
sessionId = sessionId,
metadata = new Dictionary<string, object>
{
{"timestamp", Time.time},
{"user_location", transform.position.ToString()},
{"active_twins", managedTwins.Count}
}
};

// Add to queue for processing
requestQueue.Enqueue(request);

// Update UI to show query was received
UpdateChatUI($"User: {query}", "user");
}

private IEnumerator ProcessRequestQueue()
{
while (true)
{
// Process requests if we have capacity and pending requests
if (activeRequests.Count < maxConcurrentRequests &&
requestQueue.Count > 0)
```

```
{
var request = requestQueue.Dequeue();
var requestCoroutine = StartCoroutine(SendRequestToAIBackend(
request));
activeRequests.Add(requestCoroutine);
}

// Clean up completed requests
activeRequests.RemoveAll(coroutine => coroutine == null);

yield return new WaitForSeconds(0.1f); // Check queue
every 100ms
}
}

private IEnumerator SendRequestToAIBackend(AgentRequest
request)
{
string jsonRequest = JsonConvert.SerializeObject(request,
Formatting.Indented);

using (UnityWebRequest webRequest = new UnityWebRequest
($"{aiBackendUrl}/agent/query", "POST"))
{
byte[] bodyRaw = System.Text.Encoding.UTF8.
GetBytes(jsonRequest);
webRequest.uploadHandler = new UploadHandlerRaw(bodyRaw);
webRequest.downloadHandler = new DownloadHandlerBuffer();
webRequest.SetRequestHeader("Content-Type",
"application/json");
webRequest.timeout = (int)requestTimeout;

yield return webRequest.SendWebRequest();
```

```
if (webRequest.result == UnityWebRequest.Result.
ConnectionError ||
webRequest.result == UnityWebRequest.Result.ProtocolError)
{
string errorMsg = $"Request failed: {webRequest.error}";
Debug.LogError(errorMsg);
OnError?.Invoke(errorMsg);
UpdateChatUI("I encountered an error processing your request.
Please try again.", "assistant");
}
else
{
try
{
string responseText = webRequest.downloadHandler.text;
var agentResponse = JsonConvert.DeserializeObject<AgentResponse
>(responseText);

if (agentResponse != null)
{
// Execute any commands from the agent
if (agentResponse.commands != null && agentResponse.commands.
Count > 0)
{
ExecuteAgentCommands(agentResponse.commands);
}

// Update UI with response
UpdateChatUI(agentResponse.response, "assistant");

// Trigger events
OnAgentResponse?.Invoke(agentResponse.response);
```

```
// Store successful interaction in session context
sessionContext[$"interaction_{Time.time}"] = new {
query = request.query,
response = agentResponse.response,
confidence = agentResponse.confidence
};
}
}
catch (Exception e)
{
Debug.LogError($"Failed to parse agent response: {e.Message}");
OnError?.Invoke("Failed to parse agent response");
UpdateChatUI("I received an invalid response. Please try
again.", "assistant");
}
}
}
}

private List<DigitalTwinData> GetTwinContextData()
{
var contextData = new List<DigitalTwinData>();

foreach (var twin in managedTwins)
{
if (twin != null)
{
var twinData = new DigitalTwinData
{
twinId = twin.twinId,
modelId = twin.modelId,
displayName = twin.displayName,
```

```
properties = twin.GetAllProperties(),
lastUpdated = Time.time
};
contextData.Add(twinData);
}
}

return contextData;
}

private void ExecuteAgentCommands(List<AgentCommand> commands)
{
foreach (var command in commands)
{
var targetTwin = managedTwins.Find(t =>
t.twinId.Equals(command.targetTwinId, StringComparison.
OrdinalIgnoreCase));

if (targetTwin != null)
{
bool success = ExecuteCommand(command, targetTwin);
Debug.Log($"Command {command.action} on {command.targetTwinId}:
{(success ? "Success" : "Failed")}");
}
else
{
Debug.LogWarning($"Target twin {command.targetTwinId} not found
for command {command.action}");
}
}
}

private bool ExecuteCommand(AgentCommand command,
DigitalTwinBase targetTwin)
```

```
{
try
{
switch (command.action.ToUpper())
{
case "OPTIMIZE":
return targetTwin.Optimize(command.parameters);

case "UPDATE_PROPERTY":
if (command.parameters.TryGetValue("property", out var
property) &&
command.parameters.TryGetValue("value", out var value))
{
return targetTwin.UpdateProperty(property.ToString(), Convert.
ToSingle(value));
}
break;

case "GENERATE_REPORT":
string report = targetTwin.GenerateStatusReport();
Debug.Log($"Report for {targetTwin.displayName}: {report}");
return true;

case "SCHEDULE_MAINTENANCE":
if (command.parameters.TryGetValue("date", out var
maintenanceDate))
{
return targetTwin.ScheduleMaintenance(maintenanceDate.
ToString());
}
break;
}
}
```

```csharp
catch (Exception e)
{
Debug.LogError($"Failed to execute command {command.action}:
{e.Message}");
}

return false;
}

private void UpdateChatUI(string message, string role)
{
if (chatOutputText != null)
{
string roleDisplay = role == "user" ? "You" : "Assistant";
string timestamp = System.DateTime.Now.ToString("HH:mm");
chatOutputText.text += $"\n<b>[{timestamp}] {roleDisplay}:</b>
{message}\n";

// Auto-scroll to bottom (requires ScrollRect component)
Canvas.ForceUpdateCanvases();
}
}
}
```

Part 5: Advanced Digital Twin Implementation

Multi-layered Data Architecture

```python
# Comprehensive Digital Twin Service Implementation
import asyncio
import time
import uuid
```

```python
from typing import Dict, List, Any, Optional
import pandas as pd
import numpy as np
from dataclasses import dataclass, field
from enum import Enum

class PropertyType(Enum):
NUMERIC = "numeric"
STRING = "string"
BOOLEAN = "boolean"
DATETIME = "datetime"

@dataclass
class PropertyDefinition:
name: str
type: PropertyType
unit: Optional[str] = None
min_value: Optional[float] = None
max_value: Optional[float] = None
description: str = ""

@dataclass
class PropertyValue:
value: Any
timestamp: float = field(default_factory=time.time)
quality: float = 1.0 # 0.0 to 1.0 quality score
source: str = "unknown"

@dataclass
class DigitalTwinModel:
model_id: str
display_name: str
description: str = ""
```

```python
property_definitions: Dict[str, PropertyDefinition] = field
(default_factory=dict)
relationship_definitions: Dict[str, str] = field(default_
factory=dict)

class DigitalTwin:
def __init__(self, twin_id: str, model_id: str):
self.twin_id = twin_id
self.model_id = model_id
self.properties: Dict[str, PropertyValue] = {}
self.relationships: Dict[str, List[str]] = {}
self.metadata = {
"created": time.time(),
"last_updated": time.time()
}

def update_property(self, name: str, value: Any, quality: float
= 1.0, source: str = "system"):
"""Update a property with validation and history tracking"""
self.properties[name] = PropertyValue(
value=value,
timestamp=time.time(),
quality=quality,
source=source
)
self.metadata["last_updated"] = time.time()

def get_property_value(self, name: str) -> Optional[Any]:
"""Get current value of a property"""
prop = self.properties.get(name)
return prop.value if prop else None
```

```python
def get_property_history(self, name: str, hours: int = 24) ->
List[PropertyValue]:
"""Get historical values (would query time-series DB in
production)"""
# Simplified implementation - in production this would query a
time-series database
current_prop = self.properties.get(name)
if current_prop:
return [current_prop] # Placeholder
return []

class DigitalTwinService:
def __init__(self):
self.models: Dict[str, DigitalTwinModel] = {}
self.twins: Dict[str, DigitalTwin] = {}
self.time_series_data: Dict[str, pd.DataFrame] = {}
self.event_handlers: Dict[str, List] = {}

def register_model(self, model: DigitalTwinModel) -> bool:
"""Register a digital twin model template"""
self.models[model.model_id] = model
return True

def create_twin(self, twin_id: str, model_id: str, initial_
properties: Dict = None) -> DigitalTwin:
"""Create a new digital twin instance"""
if model_id not in self.models:
raise ValueError(f"Model {model_id} not registered")

if twin_id in self.twins:
raise ValueError(f"Twin {twin_id} already exists")

twin = DigitalTwin(twin_id, model_id)
```

```
if initial_properties:
for prop_name, prop_value in initial_properties.items():
twin.update_property(prop_name, prop_value)

self.twins[twin_id] = twin
self._publish_event("twin_created", twin_id, {"model_id":
model_id})
return twin

def update_twin_property(self, twin_id: str, property_name:
str, value: Any, quality: float = 1.0):
"""Update a twin property with event publishing"""
if twin_id not in self.twins:
raise ValueError(f"Twin {twin_id} not found")

twin = self.twins[twin_id]
old_value = twin.get_property_value(property_name)
twin.update_property(property_name, value, quality)

# Record in time series
self._record_time_series(twin_id, property_name, value,
quality)

# Publish event
self._publish_event("property_updated", twin_id, {
"property": property_name,
"old_value": old_value,
"new_value": value,
"quality": quality
})

def _record_time_series(self, twin_id: str, property_name: str,
value: Any, quality: float):
"""Record property change in time series data"""
key = f"{twin_id}_{property_name}"
```

```
if key not in self.time_series_data:
self.time_series_data[key] = pd.DataFrame(columns=["timestamp",
"value", "quality"])

new_row = pd.DataFrame({
"timestamp": [time.time()],
"value": [value],
"quality": [quality]
})

self.time_series_data[key] = pd.concat([self.time_series_
data[key], new_row], ignore_index=True)

# Keep only recent data (last 1000 points)
if len(self.time_series_data[key]) > 1000:
self.time_series_data[key] = self.time_series_data[key].
tail(1000)

def _publish_event(self, event_type: str, twin_id: str,
data: Dict):
"""Publish events to registered handlers"""
if event_type in self.event_handlers:
event = {
"event_id": str(uuid.uuid4()),
"event_type": event_type,
"twin_id": twin_id,
"timestamp": time.time(),
"data": data
}

for handler in self.event_handlers[event_type]:
try:
handler(event)
except Exception as e:
print(f"Event handler error: {e}")
```

```python
def register_event_handler(self, event_type: str, handler):
    """Register an event handler for specific event types"""
    if event_type not in self.event_handlers:
        self.event_handlers[event_type] = []
    self.event_handlers[event_type].append(handler)

def analyze_twin_performance(self, twin_id: str) ->
Dict[str, Any]:
    """Generate performance analytics for a digital twin"""
    if twin_id not in self.twins:
        return {"error": "Twin not found"}

    twin = self.twins[twin_id]
    analysis = {
        "twin_id": twin_id,
        "model_id": twin.model_id,
        "last_updated": twin.metadata["last_updated"],
        "property_analysis": {}
    }

    # Analyze each property
    for prop_name, prop_value in twin.properties.items():
        key = f"{twin_id}_{prop_name}"
        if key in self.time_series_data:
            df = self.time_series_data[key]
            if len(df) > 1:
                analysis["property_analysis"][prop_name] = {
                    "current_value": prop_value.value,
                    "average": df["value"].mean(),
                    "std_dev": df["value"].std(),
                    "trend": self._calculate_trend(df["value"]),
                    "quality_score": df["quality"].mean(),
                    "data_points": len(df)
                }
```

```python
return analysis

def _calculate_trend(self, values: pd.Series) -> str:
"""Calculate trend direction for a time series"""
if len(values) < 2:
return "insufficient_data"

# Simple linear regression slope
x = np.arange(len(values))
slope = np.polyfit(x, values, 1)[0]

if slope > 0.1:
return "increasing"
elif slope < -0.1:
return "decreasing"
else:
return "stable"

# Example usage - Solar Panel Digital Twin
def create_solar_panel_example():
"""Example of creating a comprehensive solar panel
digital twin"""

# Initialize service
twin_service = DigitalTwinService()

# Define solar panel model
solar_panel_model = DigitalTwinModel(
model_id="dtmi:planetzeta:energy:SolarPanel;1",
display_name="High-Efficiency Solar Panel",
description="Advanced solar panel with real-time monitoring and
optimization"
)
```

```python
# Add property definitions
solar_panel_model.property_definitions = {
"power_output": PropertyDefinition("power_output",
PropertyType.NUMERIC, "watts", 0, 800),
"efficiency": PropertyDefinition("efficiency", PropertyType.
NUMERIC, "percentage", 0, 100),
"temperature": PropertyDefinition("temperature", PropertyType.
NUMERIC, "celsius", -40, 120),
"tilt_angle": PropertyDefinition("tilt_angle", PropertyType.
NUMERIC, "degrees", 0, 90),
"status": PropertyDefinition("status", PropertyType.STRING,
None, None, None, "Operational status")
}

# Register model
twin_service.register_model(solar_panel_model)

# Create twin instance
solar_panel = twin_service.create_twin(
"panel-A1-2024",
"dtmi:planetzeta:energy:SolarPanel;1",
{
"power_output": 320.5,
"efficiency": 21.3,
"temperature": 42.8,
"tilt_angle": 35.0,
"status": "operational"
}
)

# Set up event handlers
def efficiency_monitor(event):
"""Monitor efficiency drops"""
```

```python
if (event["event_type"] == "property_updated" and
event["data"]["property"] == "efficiency"):

new_value = event["data"]["new_value"]
old_value = event["data"]["old_value"]

if old_value and new_value < old_value * 0.9: # 10% drop
print(f"ALERT: Efficiency drop detected for {event['twin_id']}:
{old_value:.1f}% → {new_value:.1f}%")

twin_service.register_event_handler("property_updated",
efficiency_monitor)

return twin_service, solar_panel

# Integration with agent system
def create_agent_twin_interface(twin_service:
DigitalTwinService):
"""Create interface between agents and digital twin service"""

def query_twin_status(twin_id: str) -> str:
"""Agent tool for querying twin status"""
if twin_id not in twin_service.twins:
return f"Twin {twin_id} not found"

twin = twin_service.twins[twin_id]
analysis = twin_service.analyze_twin_performance(twin_id)

# Format response for agent
response = f"Status for {twin_id}:\n"
for prop_name, prop_value in twin.properties.items():
response += f"- {prop_name}: {prop_value.value}"
if prop_name in analysis.get("property_analysis", {}):
trend = analysis["property_analysis"][prop_name]["trend"]
response += f" (trend: {trend})"
```

```
response += "\n"

return response

def optimize_twin(twin_id: str) -> str:
"""Agent tool for optimizing twin performance"""
if twin_id not in twin_service.twins:
return f"Twin {twin_id} not found"

twin = twin_service.twins[twin_id]

# Example optimization logic for solar panels
if "solar" in twin.model_id.lower():
current_efficiency = twin.get_property_value("efficiency")
current_temp = twin.get_property_value("temperature")
current_tilt = twin.get_property_value("tilt_angle")

recommendations = []

if current_temp and current_temp > 80:
recommendations.append("Temperature too high - check cooling
system")

if current_efficiency and current_efficiency < 20:
recommendations.append("Efficiency below optimal - schedule
cleaning")

if current_tilt:
# Simple optimization - adjust tilt based on time of day
optimal_tilt = 35.0 # Simplified calculation
if abs(current_tilt - optimal_tilt) > 5:
twin_service.update_twin_property(twin_id, "tilt_angle",
optimal_tilt)
recommendations.append(f"Adjusted tilt angle to {optimal_
tilt}°")
```

```
if recommendations:
return f"Optimization completed for {twin_id}:\n" + "\n".
join(f"- {rec}" for rec in recommendations)
else:
return f"Twin {twin_id} is already operating optimally"

return f"No optimization available for twin type {twin.
model_id}"

return {
"query_twin_status": query_twin_status,
"optimize_twin": optimize_twin
}
```

Conclusion

Planet Zeta represents a convergence of cutting-edge technologies that together create an intelligent, responsive, and secure metaverse. Through the integration of sophisticated digital twins, blockchain security, and advanced AI agents, we've built a foundation for the next generation of virtual worlds.

The key innovations presented in this chapter include

- **Robust Digital Twin Architecture:** Multi-layered data structures enabling real-time synchronization, historical analysis, and predictive capabilities that bridge physical and virtual worlds.

- **Intelligent Agent Systems:** LLM-powered agents utilizing RAG, ReAct patterns, and multimodal understanding to provide natural, contextually aware interactions with digital twins and users.

- **Scalable Implementation Patterns:** Practical integration strategies for both Unreal Engine and Unity that maintain real-time performance while leveraging sophisticated AI back ends.

- **Framework Integration Strategy:** Thoughtful application of specialized AI frameworks (LlamaIndex for knowledge management, Langchain for orchestration, Autogen for adaptation, CrewAI for collaboration) within a unified architecture.

- **Blockchain Integration Solutions:** Multi-layered approaches to blockchain latency that preserve security while enabling real-time interactions.

As we look toward the future, the technologies demonstrated in Planet Zeta will continue to evolve. The next frontier lies in the advancement of computational graphics and quantum computing, which promise to unlock even greater levels of realism, complexity, and scale in virtual worlds.

Preview of Chapter 6

In our next chapter, we'll explore how the evolution of computational graphics—from real-time ray tracing to AI-driven procedural generation—is reshaping the visual fidelity of virtual environments. We'll also examine how quantum computing will revolutionize the processing capabilities underlying these systems, enabling real-time simulations of unprecedented complexity and opening new possibilities for secure, scalable metaverse architectures.

The metaverse of tomorrow will be built on the technological foundations we've established today in Planet Zeta, enhanced by the computational breakthroughs that lie just ahead.

## CHAPTER 6

Powering the Pixel: The Evolution of GPUs and Their Role in Modern Computing

Introduction: From Pixels to Parallel Powerhouses

The landscape of modern computing has been profoundly reshaped by the evolution of Graphics Processing Units (GPUs). What began as specialized hardware designed to offload the demanding task of rendering polygons and textures for the burgeoning video game market has blossomed into a cornerstone technology. Today, GPUs drive innovation across an astonishing breadth of fields—from accelerating groundbreaking scientific research and powering the artificial intelligence (AI) revolution to enabling the immersive digital experiences of virtual reality and the nascent metaverse.

© Frank Lisitano, John Hickie 2025
F. Lisitano and J. Hickie, *The Evolune Metaverse*, Maker Innovations Series,
https://doi.org/10.1007/979-8-8688-1588-1_6

The GPU's core strength lies in massive parallel processing. Modern GPUs contain thousands of processing cores (e.g., NVIDIA's RTX 4090 has over 16,000 CUDA cores, while data center GPUs like the H100 exceed 16,000 cores), enabling them to execute millions of calculations simultaneously. This architectural approach allows GPUs to tackle complex, data-intensive problems with efficiency far exceeding traditional Central Processing Units (CPUs), making them indispensable tools in the digital age.

Industry leaders, like NVIDIA, AMD, and more recently Intel, are locked in a continuous cycle of innovation, pushing the boundaries of GPU performance, efficiency, and capability. This fierce competition benefits countless applications. GPUs are now the default hardware for training and deploying large-scale deep learning models, underpinning advancements in computer vision, natural language understanding, generative AI, and complex data analytics. The AI development ecosystem, including frameworks like TensorFlow, PyTorch, and JAX, is built around leveraging GPU acceleration, while tools such as TensorBoard provide essential visibility into the computationally intensive training process.

Concurrently, the quest for more immersive and interactive digital experiences has led to the rise of Spatial Computing, Augmented Reality (AR), and Virtual Reality (VR). These technologies, which aim to blend the digital and physical worlds or create entirely new virtual ones, place unprecedented demands on real-time rendering, physics simulation, and AI-driven interaction. GPUs are the engines making these experiences possible, delivering the high frame rates, low latency, and visual fidelity required for presence and comfort on a growing range of devices, from powerful PC-tethered VR systems to sophisticated standalone headsets like the Meta Quest series and advanced mixed-reality platforms such as the Apple Vision Pro.

This chapter chronicles the evolution of the GPU, tracing its path from a specialized graphics chip to a versatile parallel computer engine. We will delve into the key architectural innovations—parallelism,

programmability, specialized cores, advanced memory systems—that have
defined its development. We will explore how these capabilities enabled
the GPU to revolutionize not only graphics but also scientific computing
and AI. Finally, we will examine the GPU's critical role in powering the
demanding, cutting-edge applications that are defining the future of
computing, including spatial computing, AR, VR, and the emerging
metaverse.

Section 1: The Genesis of Computer Graphics Hardware—Laying the Foundation

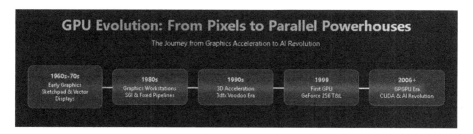

Figure 6-1. *GPU Evolution*

The sophisticated GPUs of today stand on the shoulders of giants—
decades of pioneering work aimed at enabling computers to generate,
display, and interact with visual information. Understanding these
early efforts provides crucial context for the architectural choices and
capabilities of today's graphics processors, highlighting the fundamental
problems that GPUs were ultimately designed to solve.

Early Innovations and Foundational Concepts (1960s–1970s)

The dream of interacting visually with computers began surprisingly early, at a time when batch processing and text terminals were the norm. Ivan Sutherland's 1963 PhD thesis project at MIT, "Sketchpad," remains a seminal work. Running on the enormous, transistor-based Lincoln TX-2 computer (which filled a large room), Sketchpad allowed users to draw points, lines, and arcs directly onto a Cathode Ray Tube (CRT) screen using a light pen. Its true genius lay in its conceptual breakthroughs:

- **Direct Manipulation GUI:** Users interacted directly with visual elements, a precursor to modern graphical interfaces.

- **Object Orientation:** Introduced "master" drawings and "instances," allowing complex structures to be built hierarchically. Changes to the master propagated to instances.

- **Constraint Management:** Users could define relationships between geometric objects (e.g., lines parallel, points connected), and the system would maintain these constraints during manipulation.

Sketchpad demonstrated that computers could be interactive partners in visual design and spatial reasoning, profoundly influencing subsequent work in CAD, GUIs (like those developed at Xerox PARC later), and object-oriented programming (influencing Alan Kay's work on Smalltalk).

While Sketchpad pushed interaction, other work focused on visualization for practical ends. William Fetter at Boeing in the early 1960s tackled the problem of cockpit ergonomics by creating wireframe computer models of pilots, famously dubbed the "Boeing Man." This allowed engineers to analyze sight lines and reach without building expensive physical mock-ups, representing one of the first industrial applications of computer graphics and earning Fetter credit for coining the term.

These early systems faced immense computational hurdles. Computers of the era had severely limited processing speeds (measured in kilohertz or low megahertz) and tiny amounts of expensive core memory (kilobytes). Generating even simple wireframe graphics was slow, and realistic shaded images were computationally unfeasible in real time.

Display technology also posed challenges. **Vector displays**, used in systems like the Evans & Sutherland LDS-1 (1968), offered high resolution and sharp lines by directly steering the CRT's electron beam to draw vectors. This was efficient for line art, schematics, and early wireframe 3D applications like flight simulators. However, vector displays couldn't easily fill areas with solid color, suffered from flicker when displaying complex scenes (as the beam had more lines to draw within a single refresh cycle), and were ill-suited for the pixel-based imagery that would come to dominate. The alternative, **raster graphics**, required storing the color value for every single pixel on the screen in a dedicated **framebuffer** memory. While allowing for filled shapes and realistic images, the large memory requirements and the need to update potentially millions of pixels rapidly made real-time raster graphics extremely expensive and computationally demanding until memory costs dropped and processing power increased significantly in the late 1970s and 1980s. Early raster systems often had limitations in color depth (e.g., 8-bit color) and resolution due to these constraints.

Pioneering Graphics Workstations (1980s)

The increasing demand for sophisticated 3D visualization in fields like CAD/CAM, scientific research (e.g., molecular modeling, fluid dynamics), medical imaging (CT, MRI), and film special effects drove the development of specialized **graphics workstations** in the 1980s. These were high-performance (and very expensive) integrated systems featuring powerful CPUs, large amounts of memory (for the time), and, crucially, custom hardware accelerators for graphics operations.

- **Evans & Sutherland (E&S):** Continued its leadership in the high-end simulation market, developing sophisticated raster graphics systems for flight simulators and professional visualization, pushing the boundaries of real-time rendering fidelity.

- **Silicon Graphics, Inc. (SGI):** Became the iconic vendor in this space. Founded in 1981 by Jim Clark, SGI workstations like the **Iris** series (starting with the Iris 1000 in 1984) introduced the "**Geometry Engine.**" This custom VLSI chipset pipeline accelerated the intensive floating-point matrix math required for 3D transformations (rotating, translating, scaling, projecting vertices) and clipping. Later, more powerful systems like the **Personal Iris, Indigo, Indy, O2, Octane,** and the high-end **Onyx** ("RealityEngine" and "InfiniteReality" graphics subsystems) offered progressively greater performance. These machines ran SGI's UNIX variant, **IRIX**, and were instrumental in popularizing the **OpenGL** graphics API (which evolved from SGI's earlier proprietary IrisGL). SGI workstations became indispensable tools in industries demanding high-fidelity 3D graphics, revolutionizing CGI in film (Jurassic Park, Toy Story), product design, and scientific visualization. They established the paradigm of offloading demanding graphics tasks to specialized hardware pipelines.

These workstations typically implemented **fixed-function pipelines**. Each stage of the rendering process was hardwired. While incredibly fast for their intended operations, this architecture offered little flexibility. Developers were largely limited to the rendering techniques and effects explicitly supported by the hardware pipeline. Creating novel visual effects often required clever workarounds or was simply impossible.

This fundamental limitation—the inability to customize rendering beyond what hardware designers had anticipated—would eventually drive the next major architectural revolution: the shift toward programmable processing units that could execute custom code rather than following predetermined pathways.

The Rise of the PC Graphics Card (Late 1980s–1990s)

As the high-end graphics workstation market matured and demonstrated the value of hardware acceleration, the explosive growth of the IBM PC compatible market created demand for more affordable graphics solutions. This transition from specialized workstations to consumer PC graphics cards marked a crucial democratization of visual computing technology.

- **2D GUI Acceleration:** As graphical operating systems like Microsoft Windows gained popularity, simple framebuffer adapters became insufficient. Users experienced slow window redraws, jerky scrolling, and sluggish mouse cursors. This led to the development of **2D graphics accelerators**. Cards from companies like **Tseng Labs (ET4000), Western Digital (Paradise), Cirrus Logic, S3 Graphics (Trio, ViRGE), ATI Technologies (Mach series),** and **Matrox (Mystique, Millennium)** implemented hardware acceleration for common 2D operations (often called **Graphics Device Interface—GDI** acceleration under Windows). These included drawing lines and polygons, filling rectangular areas with colors or patterns (Area Fill), copying blocks of pixel data within the framebuffer or between system memory and the framebuffer (Bit Block Transfer or BitBlit), and managing a hardware mouse cursor overlay to free the CPU from redrawing it constantly. These cards dramatically improved the perceived responsiveness of GUIs.

- **The 3D Craze:** The release of id Software's **Doom** (1993), using a clever pseudo-3D "2.5D" engine, and especially **Quake** (1996), featuring a true 3D polygonal engine, ignited an intense demand for real-time 3D graphics on PCs. Early 3D games often relied entirely on the CPU for rendering (software rendering), which limited geometric complexity, texture resolution, and frame rates. Graphics card vendors raced to add hardware acceleration for 3D primitives.

- **Early 3D Features:** Cards began incorporating hardware support for

  - **Polygon Rendering:** Drawing filled triangles or quadrilaterals.

  - **Texture Mapping:** Applying 2D images (textures) to polygons to add surface detail. Early techniques included basic filtering (bilinear filtering) to reduce blockiness.

  - **Shading:** Basic lighting models like Flat shading (one color per polygon) and Gouraud shading (interpolating colors calculated at vertices).

- **Z-buffering:** A crucial technique using a dedicated
  memory buffer (the Z-buffer or depth buffer) to
  store the depth value of each pixel. When rendering
  a new pixel, its depth is compared to the value
  already in the Z-buffer; the new pixel is only drawn
  (and the Z-buffer updated) if it is closer to the
  camera, ensuring correct occlusion of objects.

- **Alpha Blending:** Combining the color of a new
  pixel with the existing color in the framebuffer
  based on transparency (alpha) values, used for
  effects like glass, smoke, or explosions.

- **3dfx Voodoo and the API Wars:** The **Voodoo Graphics**
  chipset from **3dfx Interactive** (1996) dramatically
  raised the bar. It offered superior performance,
  particularly in texture mapping and fill rate (number of
  pixels rendered per second), compared to competitors
  like the S3 ViRGE or ATI Rage series. A key factor was
  its proprietary **Glide API**. Glide was a lightweight
  API, specifically designed for Voodoo hardware, that
  bypassed many layers of the operating system and
  general-purpose APIs like Direct3D and OpenGL,
  allowing developers to extract maximum performance.
  Many high-profile games of the era (like Quake, Unreal,
  Tomb Raider) offered specific Glide support, making
  Voodoo cards highly desirable. The **Voodoo2** (1998)
  further increased performance and introduced **Scan-
  Line Interleave (SLI)**, allowing two Voodoo2 cards to
  be linked together, each rendering alternate scan lines
  of the display, effectively doubling performance—a
  pioneering multi-GPU approach. However, 3dfx's
  reliance on Glide and its initial focus purely on 3D

acceleration (requiring a separate 2D card) eventually
hampered it as competitors integrated 2D/3D
capabilities and standardized APIs improved. 3dfx's
assets were eventually acquired by NVIDIA in 2000.

- **DirectX and OpenGL:** The chaos of competing
  proprietary APIs led to the consolidation around
  Microsoft's **Direct3D** (part of the DirectX multimedia
  API suite, first released in 1995) for Windows gaming
  and the cross-platform **OpenGL** standard (managed by
  the Architecture Review Board—ARB—formed in 1992,
  with roots in SGI's IrisGL). Hardware vendors began
  focusing on providing robust drivers for these standard
  APIs. Early versions (e.g., DirectX 3-7, OpenGL 1.x)
  primarily exposed the fixed-function capabilities of the
  hardware but provided a much-needed stable platform
  for game development.

This era of intense competition rapidly advanced PC graphics
capabilities, commoditized 3D acceleration, and set the stage for the next
architectural leap—integrating geometry processing and programmability
into a single, powerful Graphics Processing Unit.

Section 2: The GPU Era Begins: Architecture and Capabilities

The late 1990s and early 2000s witnessed a fundamental shift in graphics
hardware design. Driven by the relentless demands of real-time 3D
graphics and enabled by advances in semiconductor technology, the
concept of the integrated, programmable Graphics Processing Unit
(GPU) emerged, forever changing the landscape of visual computing and
eventually high-performance computation.

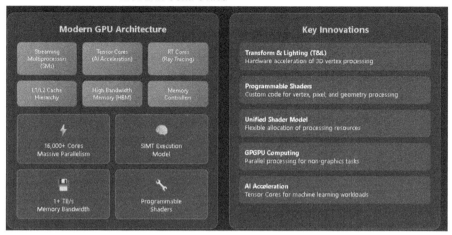

Figure 6-2. *Modern GPU Architecture*

The First True GPU and Hardware T&L (1999): Defining the Modern GPU

NVIDIA's strategic introduction of the **GeForce 256** in 1999, branding it the world's first "GPU," was more than just marketing; it signaled a crucial architectural integration. The defining feature was **hardware-accelerated Transform and Lighting (T&L)**.

Deep Dive into T&L

- **Transform Pipeline:** This involves a sequence of matrix multiplications applied to each vertex of a 3D model. Vertices start in **Model Space** (local coordinates relative to the object's pivot). Multiplying by the **Model Matrix** places the object in **World Space** (the global coordinate system of the scene). Multiplying by the **View Matrix** transforms coordinates relative to the camera's position and orientation into **View Space** (also called Camera Space). Finally, multiplying by the **Projection Matrix** (either perspective or orthographic) transforms coordinates into **Clip Space**, a normalized volume where geometry outside the camera's view frustum can be easily identified and clipped. These matrix multiplications involve numerous floating-point adds and multiplies for every vertex in the scene, a significant computational load.

- **Lighting Calculations:** After transformation (usually into View or World Space), lighting is calculated per vertex. Basic models like **Gouraud shading** compute the illumination at each vertex based on factors like the vertex normal (direction the surface faces), the direction to light sources, the viewer's position, and material properties (diffuse color, specular color, shininess exponent, as defined in the simple **Phong reflection model**). The resulting colors are then interpolated across the polygon face during rasterization. Performing these calculations for potentially thousands or millions of vertices per frame also requires substantial floating-point capability.

The Impact

By moving the entire T&L pipeline from the CPU onto dedicated GPU hardware, the GeForce 256 achieved a dramatic speedup. This allowed game developers to create scenes with significantly higher geometric complexity (more polygons per model, more objects on screen) and more numerous and complex dynamic light sources, all while maintaining higher and smoother frame rates. The CPU was liberated to focus on game

logic, AI, physics simulation (still mostly CPU-bound then), and other
tasks. This established the GPU as a powerful co-processor essential for
real-time 3D graphics.

Parallel Processing: The Core GPU Advantage Explained

The GPU achieves its performance through **massive parallelism**, an
architectural approach tailored for graphics rendering workloads.

Figure 6-3. *GPU Performance*

- **SIMD/SIMT Execution Model:** GPUs are
  fundamentally data-parallel processors. Their
  execution model is best described as **SIMT (Single
  Instruction, Multiple Threads)**. Modern GPUs contain
  thousands of simple processing cores (ranging from
  about 2,000 cores in mid-range consumer GPUs to
  over 16,000 in high-end models like the RTX 4090, or
  even more in data center accelerators). These cores are
  grouped into execution units (often called Streaming
  Multiprocessors (SMs) by NVIDIA or Compute Units
  (CUs) by AMD). A single instruction is fetched and
  decoded by the SM/CU controller and then broadcast
  to multiple cores within that unit. These cores execute
  that **exact same instruction** simultaneously, but each
  operates on **different data** associated with its assigned
  thread (e.g., processing different vertices, pixels, or data
  elements).

341

- **Warps/Wavefronts:** Threads are managed in groups called **warps** (NVIDIA, typically 32 threads) or **wavefronts** (AMD, typically 32 or 64 threads). All threads within a warp execute the same instruction in lockstep on the parallel cores. This simplifies the hardware control logic but introduces challenges.

- **Thread Divergence:** If threads within a warp need to take different execution paths due to conditional if/else statements based on their specific data, the hardware must handle this **divergence**. Often, this means executing both paths serially for the warp, with threads on the inactive path simply masked off (not performing work). This reduces parallel efficiency, so GPU programmers strive to minimize divergence within warps.

- **Latency Hiding:** GPUs use hardware **multithreading** to hide memory latency. Each SM/CU can manage multiple active warps. If one warp stalls (e.g., waiting for data from texture memory or VRAM), the scheduler can instantly switch execution to another resident warp that is ready to run, keeping the processing cores busy. This prioritizes overall **throughput** (total work completed) over the **latency** (time taken for a single thread) of any individual thread.

- **Contrast with CPU Architecture:** CPUs typically employ **MIMD (Multiple Instruction, Multiple Data)** principles. Their few, complex cores feature deep pipelines, sophisticated **branch prediction** (guessing which way conditional branches will go to avoid pipeline stalls), **out-of-order execution** (rearranging

342

instructions to keep execution units busy), and large
caches, all optimized for minimizing the latency of
single-threaded execution and handling complex,
unpredictable control flow common in general-
purpose software.

The Shift to Programmable Shaders: Unleashing Creativity and Complexity

The fixed-function T&L pipeline, while fast, was inherently limiting.
Developers could only use the specific lighting models and effects built
into the hardware. The next major leap was **programmability**, allowing
developers to write custom code (shaders) to control key stages of the
rendering process.

The Modern Programmable Graphics Pipeline (Detailed Stages)

- **Input Assembler (IA—Fixed Function):** Reads vertex
  data from buffers specified by the application and
  assembles them into geometric primitives (points,
  lines, triangles).

- **Vertex Shader (VS—Programmable):** Executes
  per-vertex. Transforms position, calculates per-vertex
  lighting, performs vertex skinning for animation,
  generates texture coordinates, etc. Outputs processed
  vertex attributes.

- **(Optional) Hull Shader (HS—Programmable):** Part of
  tessellation. Defines how a low-detail input patch (e.g.,
  a quad) should be subdivided.

- **(Optional) Tessellator (Fixed Function):** Subdivides the patch based on factors from the Hull Shader.

- **(Optional) Domain Shader (DS—Programmable):** Executes per-vertex on the newly generated subdivided geometry. Calculates final vertex positions (e.g., applying displacement maps) and attributes for the detailed geometry.

- **(Optional) Geometry Shader (GS—Programmable):** Executes per-primitive (point, line, triangle). Can modify primitives, discard them, or generate new primitives (e.g., expanding points into quads for sprites, creating fin/fur geometry).

- **Rasterization (Fixed Function):** Converts the primitives into a set of pixel-sized fragments covering the primitive's screen area. Interpolates vertex shader outputs (e.g., texture coordinates, normals, colors) across the fragments using perspective-correct interpolation.

- **Pixel Shader/Fragment Shader (PS/FS—Programmable):** Executes per-fragment. Determines the final color (RGBA) of the fragment. This is where most visual richness is generated: sampling textures, applying complex lighting and material models (PBR), calculating shadows, reflections, ambient occlusion, fog, etc. Can also discard fragments (e.g., for transparency effects).

- **Output Merger/Raster Operations (ROP—Fixed Function):** Performs per-fragment tests like depth test (Z-test) and stencil test. Blends the output color from the Pixel Shader with the color already in the

framebuffer based on blend states (for transparency).
Writes the final pixel color and depth values to the
render target(s) and depth/stencil buffer.

Impact of Programmability

Shaders enabled a vast range of visual effects previously impossible or only
feasible in offline rendering:

- **Advanced Lighting:** Per-pixel lighting, Phong/Blinn-
  Phong shading, custom lighting models, Physically
  Based Rendering (PBR).

- **Surface Detail:** Bump mapping, normal mapping,
  parallax mapping to simulate fine surface detail
  without adding geometry.

- **Texturing Effects:** Procedural textures, multi-texturing,
  environment mapping (reflections).

- **Post-processing:** Effects applied to the entire rendered
  image, like bloom, depth of field, motion blur, color
  correction, anti-aliasing (FXAA, SMAA).

- **Non-photorealistic Rendering:** Cel shading, cartoon
  outlines, artistic styles.

Shader Models and Languages

Standardized shading languages (**HLSL** for Direct3D, **GLSL** for OpenGL/
Vulkan, **MSL** for Metal, **WGSL** for WebGPU) provided higher-level
abstractions. Successive **Shader Models** (SM 1.x, 2.0, 3.0, 4.0, 5.0, 6.0+)
defined increasing levels of programmability: longer shader programs,
more complex instructions (flow control like loops and branches), more
texture lookups, ability to sample textures in vertex shaders, introduction
of geometry and tessellation shaders, and eventually compute shaders.

The Unified Shader Model: Efficiency Through Flexibility

The **unified shader model** (circa 2006-2007, NVIDIA G80/Tesla architecture, AMD R600) optimized resource usage by replacing separate vertex/pixel/geometry shader units with a single pool of identical, programmable **streaming processors (SPs)** or **shader cores**, grouped within **Streaming Multiprocessors (SMs)** or **Compute Units (CUs)**. A hardware **work distributor/scheduler** dynamically assigns shader tasks (or compute tasks) to available cores. This ensures that if a workload is heavily biased toward one type of shader (e.g., pixel-heavy), all available cores can contribute, eliminating the bottlenecks of the older specialized design and significantly improving overall GPU utilization and performance.

General-Purpose GPU Computing (GPGPU): Unleashing Parallel Power for Science and AI

The programmability and massive parallelism of unified shader architectures made GPUs incredibly attractive for non-graphics tasks that could be parallelized. **GPGPU** emerged as a major field.

Problem Domain

GPGPU excels at **data-parallel** problems where large datasets can be processed element-wise or in parallel chunks. Examples abound:

- **Scientific Simulation:** n-body simulations (astrophysics, molecular dynamics), computational fluid dynamics (CFD using finite difference, lattice Boltzmann methods), finite element analysis (FEA for structural mechanics), weather/climate modeling.

- **Data Processing and Analytics:** Parallel sorting, searching, filtering large datasets, database query acceleration, financial modeling (Monte Carlo simulations, Black-Scholes option pricing).

- **Signal and Image Processing:** Fast Fourier Transforms (FFTs), image filtering, medical image reconstruction (CT, MRI), video encoding/decoding.

- **Bioinformatics:** DNA/protein sequence alignment (e.g., BLAST, Smith-Waterman), molecular docking simulations.

- **Cryptography:** Brute-force attacks on encryption algorithms, cryptocurrency mining (initially).

- **Machine Learning:** The core matrix and vector operations involved in training and running neural networks.

Programming Models and Ecosystems

- **CUDA (NVIDIA):** The dominant platform due to its early release, performance, comprehensive set of libraries (cuBLAS, cuDNN, cuFFT, cuSPARSE, Thrust, NCCL, etc.), extensive documentation, and strong developer community support. However, it's proprietary to NVIDIA hardware.

- **OpenCL (Khronos):** The main open standard alternative, designed for portability across GPUs (NVIDIA, AMD, Intel), CPUs, and FPGAs. Offers flexibility but often requires more effort to achieve optimal performance on specific hardware compared to CUDA, and its library ecosystem is generally less mature.

347

- **DirectCompute (Microsoft):** Windows-centric, integrated with DirectX. Common for compute tasks in game engines running on Windows.

- **Vulkan Compute/Metal Compute:** Modern graphics APIs with powerful, low-level compute shader capabilities, enabling tight integration of graphics and compute on supporting platforms.

- **SYCL (Khronos):** A higher-level C++ abstraction aiming for easier cross-platform parallel programming, often using OpenCL or other back ends.

- **HIP (AMD):** Part of ROCm, specifically designed to allow developers to compile CUDA source code to run on AMD GPUs, lowering the barrier to entry for AMD in the HPC/AI space dominated by CUDA software.

GPGPU effectively turned GPUs into the most powerful parallel processors available in mainstream computing, democratizing HPC and fueling the AI revolution.

Specialized Cores for AI: Tensor Cores and Matrix Acceleration

The specific computational pattern dominating deep learning—large matrix multiplications—spurred the development of even more specialized hardware within the GPU.

- **NVIDIA Tensor Cores:** Introduced with Volta (2017), these are small execution units optimized for one task: performing a **fused multiply-add (FMA)** on small matrices (typically 4x4) very quickly. A single SM contains multiple Tensor Cores.

Mixed-Precision Explained

Tensor Cores achieve significant speedups by operating efficiently on lower-precision numerical formats. Instead of using standard **FP32** (32-bit single-precision float) for all calculations, they often multiply input matrices stored in **FP16** (16-bit half-precision float) or **BF16** (16-bit brain float, offering more range but less precision than FP16), or even **INT8/INT4** (8/4-bit integers). The intermediate multiplication results are often accumulated internally at higher precision (e.g., FP32) to maintain accuracy before the final result is stored.

Why FP16/BF16/INT8 Are Faster

Using fewer bits per number means (1) less memory/cache required to store data; (2) less memory bandwidth needed to transfer data; and (3) simpler, faster, and more power-efficient hardware can perform the multiplication/addition operations.

- **AI Tolerance:** Many deep learning algorithms exhibit resilience to reduced precision, meaning using FP16/BF16 often results in significantly faster training and inference with little or no loss in final model accuracy compared to FP32.

- **TF32 (TensorFloat-32):** Introduced by NVIDIA in Ampere, TF32 uses the same 10-bit mantissa as FP16 (providing FP16 precision) but the same 8-bit exponent as FP32 (providing FP32 range), offering a balance that often accelerates FP32 matrix math significantly with no code changes required.

- **Sparsity Acceleration:** Modern Tensor Cores (Ampere onwards) often include hardware acceleration for **structured sparsity**. Neural network weight matrices often contain many zero values after training/pruning. Sparsity features allow Tensor Cores to skip operations involving these zeros, effectively doubling the computational throughput for sparse matrices.

Impact

Tensor Cores provide dramatically higher theoretical throughput (measured in TFLOPS for floating-point or TOPS for integer operations) for matrix math compared to standard FP32 cores. This makes training large AI models feasible in days instead of weeks/months and enables real-time inference for complex models.

- **Competitor Equivalents:** AMD's **Matrix Cores** (in CDNA architecture) and Intel's **Xe Matrix Extensions (XMX)** engines (in Xe architecture) provide similar hardware acceleration capabilities for dense and sometimes sparse matrix computations, crucial for competing in the AI accelerator market.

Memory Architecture: The Critical Data Pipeline

All the processing power in the world is useless if the data can't reach the cores quickly enough. GPU memory systems are engineered for extreme bandwidth.

- **Bandwidth vs. Latency Focus:** GPUs need to feed thousands of cores working in parallel on large datasets (textures, meshes, compute arrays). Therefore, **memory bandwidth** (how much data can be transferred per second, measured in GB/s or TB/s) is the primary performance metric, more so than **latency** (the time delay for a single data request).

- **GDDR SDRAM:** The standard for consumer and workstation GPUs. Achieves high bandwidth through

  - **Wide Buses:** Physically wide parallel interfaces (e.g., 64-bit per chip, with multiple chips leading to total bus widths like 128, 256, 384, 512 bits).

  - **High Clock Rates:** Running the memory and interface at multi-gigahertz effective speeds.

  - **DDR Signaling:** Transferring data on both rising and falling clock edges.

  - **Advanced Signaling (PAM4):** GDDR6X uses Pulse Amplitude Modulation with 4 levels (instead of 2 for traditional NRZ signaling) to transmit two bits per cycle per pin, further increasing bandwidth.

  - **Bandwidth Examples:** GeForce RTX 4090 (GDDR6X, 384-bit bus) exceeds 1 TB/s. Mid-range cards might be in the 400-600 GB/s range.

- **HBM (High Bandwidth Memory):** Used primarily in data center accelerators (AI/HPC) and some ultra-high-end consumer cards (like AMD's earlier Radeon VII).

  - **Vertical Stacking:** DRAM dies are stacked using Through-Silicon Vias (TSVs) for vertical connections.

  - **Interposer Connection:** Stacks are placed very close to the GPU die on a silicon interposer, connected via thousands of microscopic wires, creating an ultra-wide bus (1024 bits per stack is common).

- **Bandwidth and Efficiency:** The extreme width allows HBM to deliver significantly higher bandwidth (multiple TB/s per GPU package, e.g., NVIDIA H100 with HBM3 offers up to 3.35 TB/s) at lower clock speeds and lower power consumption per bit transferred compared to GDDR.

- **Generations:** HBM ➤ HBM2 ➤ HBM2e ➤ HBM3 ➤ HBM3e have increased per-stack capacity and per-pin data rates.

- **GPU Caches:** Vital for reducing the average latency and bandwidth demand on VRAM.

  - **Hierarchy:** Typically includes small, very fast L1 caches and shared memory private to each SM/CU, backed by a much larger L2 cache shared across the GPU. Register files provide the fastest storage directly accessible by threads.

  - **L1/Shared Memory:** L1 caches automatically store frequently accessed data. Shared Memory (CUDA/OpenCL) is a user-managed scratchpad; programmers explicitly load data into shared memory for threads within a block to collaborate on, avoiding redundant VRAM accesses. Effective use of shared memory is often key to high GPGPU performance.

  - **L2 Cache:** Acts as a large victim cache for data evicted from L1s, capturing temporal locality across the entire GPU workload. L2 cache sizes have grown significantly (tens or even hundreds of MBs in modern GPUs).

- **Memory Compression:** GPUs employ sophisticated, lossless compression algorithms (delta color compression, general data compression) transparently to reduce the amount of data transferred over the memory bus and stored in caches/VRAM, significantly boosting **effective** bandwidth.

The intricate dance between computer cores, cache hierarchy, memory controllers, and high-bandwidth VRAM determines the real-world performance of a GPU.

Section 3: GPUs Enabling Modern Immersive Technologies

The architectural power forged through decades of GPU evolution—massive parallelism, programmability, AI acceleration, and high-bandwidth memory—directly enables the computationally intensive applications defining the next wave of human-computer interaction: Spatial Computing, Virtual Reality (VR), Augmented Reality (AR), and the Metaverse. These technologies demand unprecedented levels of real-time rendering performance, environmental understanding, and low-latency interaction, all heavily reliant on GPU capabilities.

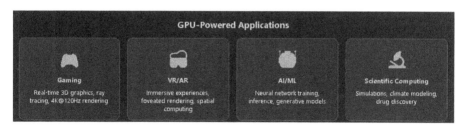

Figure 6-4. *GPU Powered Applications*

The Intense Rendering Demands of VR and AR: The Science of Presence

Creating digital experiences that feel convincingly real and, crucially, are comfortable for the user pushes rendering technology to its absolute limits. Achieving a sense of **presence**—the psychological state of feeling truly **there** in a virtual environment—is the goal, and it imposes stringent technical requirements.

- **The Criticality of High Frame Rates and Low Latency:** The human brain relies on a tight coupling between head movements (detected by the inner ear's vestibular system) and corresponding visual updates. When there's a noticeable lag or inconsistency, this sensory mismatch triggers **cybersickness**, with symptoms ranging from eye strain and headaches to severe nausea.

  - **Target Frame Rates:** To maintain smooth motion and minimize disorientation, VR headsets generally require a minimum sustained frame rate of **90 frames per second (90Hz)**. Many modern headsets push this to **120Hz** or even higher (e.g., Valve Index up to 144Hz). The GPU must complete the entire rendering workload for both eyes in just **11.1ms (90Hz)** or **8.3ms (120Hz)**. Missing this deadline results in **dropped frames** or the need for **reprojection techniques** (like ASW or Motion Smoothing, described later), which can introduce visual artifacts and compromise the feeling of presence.

- **Motion-to-Photon Latency:** Even with high frame
  rates, the total end-to-end delay from physical head
  movement to the corresponding photons hitting
  the user's retina must be minimized. This **motion-
  to-photon latency** needs to be consistently **under
  20 milliseconds** to feel responsive. This includes
  contributions from sensors, tracking algorithms,
  the application's simulation loop, GPU rendering
  time, and display panel response time. The GPU
  rendering stage is often the most significant
  contributor, making its speed paramount.

- **The Double Whammy of Stereoscopic Rendering:**
  Creating a 3D stereoscopic view requires rendering
  the scene twice per frame, once for each eye from
  slightly different viewpoints determined by the
  user's **interpupillary distance (IPD)**. While some
  calculations can be shared (see optimizations below),
  this fundamentally doubles the amount of geometry
  that needs processing and, more significantly, the
  number of pixels that need to be shaded, placing
  immense pressure on the GPU's throughput.

- **Pixel Density and the Quest for Visual Clarity:** Early
  VR suffered from the distracting "screen door effect"
  (SDE), where the fine lines between pixels were visible.
  To combat this, modern headsets use high-resolution
  panels (e.g., Meta Quest 3: 2064x2208 per eye; HP
  Reverb G2: 2160x2160 per eye; Varjo XR-4: 3840x3744
  per eye). Rendering these **millions of pixels per eye at
  90Hz+** demands enormous pixel shading performance
  (fill rate) from the GPU.

- **Wide Field of View (FoV) and the Challenge of Lens Distortion:** A wide FoV (horizontal FoV often >100°) is crucial for peripheral vision and immersion. Achieving this typically requires complex **lenses** (often Fresnel or more recently, thinner, lighter **pancake lenses**) placed close to the displays. These lenses inherently introduce optical **distortions** (like pincushion distortion, where straight lines appear to curve inwards) and potentially **chromatic aberration** (color fringing). To present a geometrically correct image to the user, the GPU must render a **pre-distorted** image. This usually involves rendering the scene to an intermediate texture (often at a higher "render target resolution" than the panel's native resolution to account for detail loss in the distorted periphery) and then applying a post-processing shader that warps this image (applying barrel distortion, the inverse of the lens's pincushion distortion) before sending it to the display panels. This adds complexity and computational cost, primarily in the pixel shading stage.

GPU Optimizations Tailored for Immersive Rendering: Doing More with Less

Meeting these extreme demands solely through brute-force rendering power is often impractical due to cost, power consumption, and heat constraints, especially for standalone headsets. Therefore, intelligent optimization techniques, often enabled by specific GPU hardware features and sophisticated software algorithms, are critical.

- **Foveated Rendering (Requires Eye Tracking):**
  Leverages the non-uniform nature of human vision.
  High-resolution vision is concentrated in the small
  central foveal region (~1-2 degrees of visual angle), with
  acuity dropping off sharply in the periphery. Headsets
  equipped with **eye-tracking** cameras can determine
  the user's gaze point in real time.

  - **Dynamic Optimization:** The rendering system
    uses this gaze data to render the foveal region at the
    highest quality (full resolution, high shading rate,
    max anti-aliasing). The surrounding peripheral
    regions are rendered at progressively lower quality
    (reduced resolution, coarser shading rate via VRS,
    simpler lighting).

  - **GPU Implementation:** Can use VRS guided by
    the eye tracker or render multiple "foveal regions"
    at different resolutions and composite them.
    Requires very low latency eye tracking (<10ms)
    and tight integration between tracker, runtime, and
    GPU driver.

  - **Benefit:** Potentially massive savings in shaded
    pixels (reports vary, but 50%+ is plausible) allowing
    higher overall frame rates or increased foveal
    quality on constrained hardware. Examples:
    supported by NVIDIA VRWorks SDK, Qualcomm
    Snapdragon Spaces, PICO Enterprise headsets,
    Meta Quest Pro, Apple Vision Pro (though details of
    Apple's implementation differ).

- **Variable Rate Shading (VRS):** A hardware feature allowing shading rate flexibility **within** a single frame, even without eye tracking.

  - **How It Works:** Allows the pixel shader to run once per pixel (1x1) or once per group of pixels (1x2, 2x1, 2x2, 2x4, 4x2, 4x4).

  - **Control Mechanisms**

    - **Tier 1 (Per-Draw):** Set shading rate for an entire object/draw call. Simple but coarse.

    - **Tier 2 (Screen-Space Image):** Specify shading rate per small tile on the screen using a separate texture. Allows much finer control based on content analysis (e.g., low rate for skyboxes, high rate for detailed characters), motion vectors (lower rate for fast-moving objects where detail is blurred), or foveation (lower rates in periphery).

  - **Benefit:** Reduces overall shading load by avoiding redundant calculations in less important or less detailed areas, improving performance. Widely supported on modern GPUs (NVIDIA Turing+, AMD RDNA2+, Intel Xe+).

- **AI Upscaling (DLSS, FSR, XeSS):** Game-changing for VR performance.

  - **Core Idea:** Renders the main scene at a lower internal resolution (e.g., 70% or 50% of the target resolution per dimension). Feed this lower-resolution frame, along with motion vectors (indicating how pixels moved from the previous frame) and potentially other data (depth buffer), into a specialized AI neural network (often running on

Tensor Cores/Matrix Cores). The AI model outputs a high-resolution frame, intelligently reconstructing details and sharpening the image to closely match native resolution rendering quality.

- **Benefit:** Provides significant performance uplift (often 1.5x to 2x frame rate improvement or more), making demanding VR experiences playable at target refresh rates or allowing higher graphics settings. Temporal stability (avoiding flickering or ghosting artifacts) is crucial for VR comfort. DLSS 3's Frame Generation (inserting entirely AI-generated frames) is generally **not** recommended for VR due to the added latency it introduces.

- **Stereo Rendering Optimizations (Single Pass/ Multiview/Instanced Stereo):** Reduces redundant work when rendering the left and right eye views.

  - **Mechanism:** Instead of submitting draw calls twice (once per eye), the application submits them once. The GPU's vertex processing stage calculates positions for **both** eye viewpoints simultaneously. Subsequent pipeline stages (e.g., rasterization, pixel shading) can then process data for both views often in parallel or interleaved manner within a single pass.

  - **Benefit:** Significantly reduces CPU overhead (fewer API calls, less driver work) and eliminates redundant vertex processing and potentially other upstream calculations. Essential for efficient VR rendering on both PC and standalone platforms. Supported via API extensions in DirectX, Vulkan, and OpenGL and often handled automatically by VR runtimes like SteamVR and Oculus/Meta XR.

- **Asynchronous Time Warp (ATW)/Asynchronous Space Warp (ASW)/Motion Smoothing:** These are **reprojection techniques**, essentially safety nets used by the VR runtime when the application fails to deliver a new frame in time for the display refresh.

    - **ATW:** If a new frame isn't ready, ATW takes the **last rendered frame** and slightly re-warps/re-projects it based on the **very latest** head tracking data received just before display scanout. This significantly reduces perceived latency for rotational movements, making head turning feel much smoother even if the application drops frames. It doesn't help with positional movement or animation updates within the scene.

    - **ASW (Oculus/Meta)/Motion Smoothing (SteamVR):** More advanced techniques used when the application can only sustain **half** the target frame rate (e.g., 45Hz instead of 90Hz). They analyze the difference between the last two rendered frames (using motion vectors) and generate a synthetic intermediate frame to insert between them, effectively bringing the displayed frame rate back up to the target (e.g., 90Hz). This can smooth out performance dips but may introduce visual artifacts (warping, ghosting) depending on the scene content and motion complexity. GPUs are used for the image warping and motion vector calculations involved in these techniques.

Making VR/AR Hardware Accessible:
The Spectrum of Devices

The interplay between GPU power and these optimizations enables a wide range of devices:

- **High-End PC VR:** Requires powerful desktop GPUs (e.g., RTX 4070/RX 7800 XT or higher) to drive high resolutions and refresh rates with maximum visual fidelity, potentially including ray tracing. Offers the best visual quality but at high cost and tethered (or complex wireless) setup.

- **Mid-Range PC VR:** Can provide good experiences on more modest desktop GPUs (e.g., RTX 3060/RX 6700 XT) by leveraging AI upscaling and potentially lower settings.

- **Standalone VR (e.g., Quest 3):** Relies heavily on the efficiency of its integrated mobile GPU (Adreno 740 in Quest 3's Snapdragon XR2 Gen 2) and aggressive use of optimizations like lower rendering resolution, FFR/VRS (if supported), and potentially application-specific tricks. Delivers remarkable experiences for its form factor and price, but graphical fidelity is noticeably lower than PC VR.

- **Mobile AR (Smartphones):** Utilizes the phone's integrated GPU. Performance varies widely depending on the phone's SoC. Focus is often on efficient tracking and rendering of simpler virtual objects composited onto the camera feed.

- **AR/MR Glasses:** Often use custom SoCs with mobile-class GPUs and potentially specialized co-processors (like HPUs) optimized for low power consumption and efficient processing of sensor data needed for SLAM and real-world understanding required for optical see-through or high-quality video pass-through AR.

Enhancing Immersion: GPUs, Realism, and the Feeling of Presence

Achieving genuine **presence** in VR/AR hinges on convincing the user's senses that the digital elements are real or plausibly integrated with reality. This requires sophisticated rendering techniques executed rapidly by the GPU.

- **Photorealistic Graphics and Physically Based Rendering (PBR):** Moving beyond abstract color and shininess values, PBR aims to simulate light's interaction with surfaces based on measurable physical properties. Key components implemented in GPU shaders include

  - **Albedo/Base Color:** The underlying color of the material, free of lighting information (typically stored in a texture map).

  - **Metallic:** A value (often 0 for dielectrics/non-metals, 1 for metals) indicating how the material reflects light (metals reflect color directly, non-metals have white specular highlights). Often stored in a texture map.

- **Roughness/Smoothness:** Describes the microsurface detail. A smooth surface (low roughness) results in sharp, mirror-like reflections. A rough surface (high roughness) scatters light, resulting in blurry or diffuse reflections. Stored in a texture map.

- **Normal Mapping:** Uses a texture map (normal map) containing surface orientation information (normals) to simulate fine geometric detail (bumps, scratches, pores) without adding actual polygons, significantly enhancing perceived detail at low performance cost. Pixel shaders use the sampled normal when calculating lighting.

- **Ambient Occlusion (AO):** Simulates shadowing in crevices and contact points where ambient light is blocked. Can be pre-calculated (baked into a texture map) or calculated in real-time using Screen-Space Ambient Occlusion (SSAO) or Ray-Traced Ambient Occlusion (RTAO). Adds significant depth and grounding to objects.

- **PBR Shader Execution:** The GPU's programmable pixel shaders execute complex mathematical models (like the Cook-Torrance BRDF) using these texture inputs and scene lighting information to calculate the final pixel color, ensuring materials look consistently realistic under varying lighting conditions. This requires significant floating-point computation per pixel.

- **Advanced Lighting, Shadows, and Reflections:**
  Accurate simulation of light transport is crucial for
  realism.

  - **Real-Time Global Illumination (GI):** Capturing
    indirect lighting is essential for realism. Techniques
    GPUs accelerate include

    - **Light Probes/Baked GI:** Pre-calculating
      indirect lighting offline and storing it in
      light maps (textures applied to geometry) or
      volumetric light probes. Fast to render but only
      works for static scenes/lighting.

    - **Screen-Space Techniques (SSGI, SSDO):**
      Approximate indirect lighting/occlusion using
      only data visible on screen (depth, normals,
      color). Fast but prone to artifacts like light
      bleeding or missing information from off-
      screen areas.

    - **Voxel-Based GI (VXGI):** Represents the scene
      with voxels and simulates light bouncing
      between voxels. Can provide dynamic GI but is
      memory and computationally intensive.

    - **Ray-Traced GI (RTGI):** Offers the highest
      quality by tracing rays to gather indirect
      lighting. Very expensive, often requires
      denoising. Techniques like NVIDIA's RTXGI
      SDK or Lumen in UE5 implement this.

  - **Real-Time Ray Tracing Effects:** Dedicated RT
    Cores accelerate the process of tracing rays through
    the scene using acceleration structures like
    Bounding Volume Hierarchies (BVHs). This enables

- **Accurate Reflections:** Reflecting dynamic objects and off-screen details impossible with SSR or cube maps. Can range from single-bounce reflections to multi-bounce path-traced reflections for mirrors or complex inter-reflections.

- **Soft Shadows:** Accurately simulating the penumbra effect based on light source size and distance, creating more realistic and less aliased shadows than traditional shadow mapping.

- **Ambient Occlusion (RTAO):** More accurate than SSAO as it considers actual geometry occlusion rather than just screen-space depth differences.

- **Accurate Refraction:** Simulating light bending through complex transparent objects.

- **Real-Time Physics Simulation:** Believable interaction requires objects to behave physically correctly. GPUs can accelerate many physics calculations using their parallel processing power:

  - **Particle Systems:** Compute shaders can simulate and render millions of independent particles for effects like explosions, fire, smoke, and water spray, each with its own physics (gravity, collision, forces).

  - **Fluid Simulation:** Techniques like SPH (Smoothed Particle Hydrodynamics) or LBM (Lattice Boltzmann Methods) simulate fluid behavior by tracking interactions between many particles or grid cells—highly parallelizable tasks well-suited for GPUs. Used for realistic water, smoke, etc.

- **Cloth and Soft Bodies:** Simulating the complex deformations and collisions of cloth or other deformable materials often involves solving large systems of constraints or mass-spring systems, benefiting from GPU parallelism.

- **Destruction:** Simulating objects fracturing and breaking into many pieces involves collision detection and rigid body dynamics for potentially thousands of fragments, often accelerated on the GPU.

- **Physics Engines Integration:** Engines like NVIDIA PhysX, Havok, and Bullet increasingly leverage GPU acceleration (via CUDA, OpenCL, or DirectCompute) for specific demanding effects while often keeping core rigid body simulation on the CPU for better integration with game logic.

- **Haptics Synchronization and Environmental Interaction:** While GPUs don't create haptic sensations, they are critical for the visual feedback loop that makes haptics feel real. When a user's controller vibrates upon hitting a virtual drum, the GPU must render the visual impact (drum skin deforming, particle effect) **simultaneously**. Any lag breaks the illusion. GPUs also render the persistent effects of interaction with the environment—footprints in snow, ripples in water, breakable objects shattering—enhancing the user's sense of agency within the virtual world.

Industry Applications: VR and AR Transforming Workflows (Deep Dive)

The practical impact of GPU-powered VR/AR is significant and growing across numerous sectors.

- **Education and Training**

  - **Medical Simulation (Osso VR Example):** Osso VR's platform allows surgical trainees to practice procedures like orthopedic surgery in a realistic VR environment using standard VR controllers that mimic surgical tools. Performance metrics track accuracy, efficiency, and adherence to procedural steps. GPUs render the detailed anatomical models, simulate tool interactions with bone and tissue, and provide real-time feedback. This allows for deliberate practice and objective assessment in a safe environment, potentially shortening learning curves and improving patient safety. The GPU workload involves rendering complex geometry, simulating soft-body interactions (to some extent), and maintaining high frame rates for smooth tool manipulation.

  - **Technical/Safety Training (Oil and Gas, Aviation):** Companies use VR to simulate complex maintenance procedures on oil rigs or aircraft engines or to practice emergency response scenarios (e.g., fires, evacuations). Trainees can interact with virtual equipment, identify hazards, and follow procedures without risk to themselves or expensive hardware. GPUs render the detailed industrial environments and equipment, simulate malfunctions, and track user actions for evaluation. The need for realism requires high-fidelity rendering and physics.

- **Healthcare**

  - **Surgical Navigation (Medivis Example):** Medivis's SurgicalAR platform uses AR headsets (HoloLens) to overlay 3D models derived from patient CT/MRI scans onto the surgeon's view during procedures like spinal surgery or tumor resections. The system requires precise real-time registration (alignment) of the virtual model with the patient's actual anatomy, using external tracking systems or internal SLAM capabilities. The GPU's role is critical in rendering the complex 3D anatomical model with low latency and accurately compositing it onto the surgeon's real-world view, providing intuitive spatial guidance.

  - **VR Exposure Therapy (Bravemind Example):** Developed at USC, Bravemind uses VR to treat PTSD in veterans. By recreating specific traumatic environments (e.g., scenes from Iraq or Afghanistan) within a controlled VR setting, therapists can guide patients through exposure therapy protocols. The realism and sense of presence generated by the GPU-rendered environment are key to triggering and processing traumatic memories effectively and safely. Therapists can control environmental elements (sounds, visual cues) during the session.

- **Rehabilitation:** VR games and applications are used for physical therapy (making repetitive exercises more engaging) and cognitive rehabilitation (e.g., after stroke or brain injury). GPUs render the interactive environments and provide visual feedback based on patient movements tracked by sensors or controllers.

- **Engineering, Design, and Architecture**

  - **Automotive Design Reviews (Ford Example):** Ford utilizes VR (e.g., using Varjo headsets with high resolution) and tools like Autodesk VRED for virtual design reviews. Designers and engineers worldwide can collaboratively inspect full-scale virtual prototypes of vehicles, evaluating interior ergonomics, exterior styling lines, perceived quality of materials (rendered realistically using PBR and ray tracing by high-end NVIDIA GPUs), and assembly feasibility long before physical prototypes exist. This accelerates iteration and reduces reliance on expensive clay models.

  - **Architectural Visualization (ArchViz with Unreal/ Unity/Enscape):** Real-time rendering engines running on powerful GPUs allow architects and clients to experience immersive VR walkthroughs of unbuilt spaces. They can evaluate spatial arrangements, lighting conditions (simulated accurately with techniques like Lumen or RTGI), material finishes, and overall ambiance. This provides a much more intuitive understanding than 2D drawings or static renders. GPU performance dictates the level of detail, lighting quality, and smoothness of the walkthrough.

369

- **Retail and E-commerce**

  - **AR Furniture Placement (IKEA Place/Wayfair):**
    These mobile apps use the smartphone's camera
    and AR capabilities (ARKit/ARCore SLAM for
    surface detection and tracking) to let users place
    accurately scaled 3D models of furniture into their
    own room view. The mobile GPU renders the 3D
    models with estimated real-world lighting and
    shadows, helping customers visualize products in
    context.

  - **AR Virtual Try-Ons (Beauty, Fashion):** Apps from
    brands like Sephora, L'Oréal, Gucci, or dedicated
    platforms allow users to virtually try on makeup,
    glasses, sneakers, or even clothing using their
    phone's camera or a web interface. This involves
    sophisticated face/body tracking (often AI-
    accelerated) and real-time rendering/compositing
    of the virtual product onto the user, handled by the
    device's GPU.

- **Corporate Collaboration**

  - **NVIDIA Omniverse for Industrial Digital Twins:**
    Beyond content creation, Omniverse allows
    companies to build and simulate large-scale digital
    twins of factories, warehouses, or cities. Teams can
    collaborate within the shared virtual environment
    to optimize layouts, simulate robotic workflows,
    train AI perception models, or plan logistics.
    This relies heavily on distributed computing and
    powerful RTX GPU rendering and simulation
    capabilities (PhysX, Flow, Modulus).

- **Virtual Meeting Platforms (Meta Horizon Workrooms, Microsoft Mesh):** These platforms use VR/MR headsets to place users' avatars in shared 3D virtual environments for meetings, presentations, and collaborative sessions. The goal is to increase engagement and social presence compared to video calls. GPUs render the environments, complex customizable avatars (with realistic expressions potentially driven by face tracking), and shared objects or whiteboards. Scalability to many simultaneous users is a challenge.

GPUs and the Metaverse: Architecting Persistent Shared Worlds

The Metaverse, as a concept, represents the ultimate convergence of real-time 3D graphics, global networking, persistent virtual worlds, and social interaction. Building this vision requires addressing monumental technical challenges, with GPUs playing a central role.

- The Scalability Hurdle—Rendering Millions

  A true metaverse needs to support potentially millions of users interacting concurrently in vast, detailed virtual spaces. Rendering this scale is impossible with client-side rendering alone. Key strategies include

  - **Aggressive LOD and Culling:** Implementing sophisticated systems to drastically reduce the amount of geometry and texture data processed for distant or occluded objects and avatars. Techniques like hierarchical Z-buffers, occlusion culling, and predictive loading are essential.

371

- **Instancing and Batching:** Drawing many identical objects (e.g., trees, buildings, simple avatars) using GPU instancing techniques to reduce CPU draw call overhead.

- **Cloud Streaming:** Offloading rendering for parts of the scene or for lower-power clients to powerful GPU clusters in the cloud. The rendered frames are streamed as video, requiring low-latency networks (5G/Fiber) and efficient codecs (AV1, H.265, often with GPU acceleration for encode/decode).

- **Distributed Simulation:** Partitioning the simulation of the world state (physics, AI, object interactions) across multiple backend servers, potentially using server-side GPUs for accelerating complex calculations.

- **Persistence, Interoperability, and Content**

  - **World State Management:** Maintaining and synchronizing the state of a massive, persistent world with potentially millions of concurrent users requires highly scalable databases and efficient state synchronization protocols. Blockchain technology might play a role in verifying ownership and transactions of unique virtual assets (NFTs), but its latency remains a challenge for real-time state synchronization.

  - **Interoperability Standards:** A truly open metaverse requires common standards for assets, avatars, scenes, and protocols so users can move seamlessly between experiences created by different developers. Key standards include

- **glTF (GL Transmission Format):** An efficient, extensible file format for 3D scenes and models, widely adopted for web and mobile platforms.

- **USD (Universal Scene Description):** Developed by Pixar, a powerful framework for composing, editing, and collaborating on complex 3D scenes, forming the basis of platforms like NVIDIA Omniverse and seeing wider industry adoption.

- **VRM:** An open standard file format for 3D humanoid avatars, aiming for cross-platform compatibility.

- **Content Creation Pipelines:** Building the sheer volume of 3D content required is a major bottleneck. Generative AI tools, collaborative platforms (like Omniverse), and efficient asset pipelines leveraging standards like glTF/USD are crucial. GPUs are essential throughout this pipeline, from running AI generation models to powering the real-time rendering in creation tools.

Section 4: The Cutting Edge and Future Directions

GPU technology continues its relentless march forward, driven by the demands of AI, HPC, graphics, and immersive computing. Several key areas define the current cutting edge and hint at future breakthroughs.

Figure 6-5. *Future Directions*

AI-Driven Graphics: Deeper Integration and New Paradigms

AI is rapidly evolving from a post-processing tool to a fundamental component of graphics generation and rendering.

- **Neural Rendering (NeRFs, Gaussian Splatting, etc.):** These techniques are challenging the dominance of traditional polygon-based rendering for certain applications, particularly scene capture and photorealistic rendering.

  - **NeRFs (Neural Radiance Fields):** Represent a scene implicitly using a neural network trained on multiple input images with known camera poses. The network learns to predict color and density along any viewing ray passing through the scene volume. While training is slow (GPU-intensive), rendering novel views can produce stunning photorealism, especially for complex geometry and view-dependent effects (like reflections). Real-time rendering is becoming feasible for moderately complex scenes with significant optimization (e.g., baking parts of the network, using specialized data structures).

374

- **3D Gaussian Splatting:** Offers an alternative explicit representation. The scene is modeled as a large number of 3D Gaussians (ellipsoids with position, rotation, scale, color, opacity). Rendering involves projecting these Gaussians onto the 2D screen (splatting) and blending them in depth order. This approach has demonstrated high visual quality comparable to NeRFs but with significantly faster training times and real-time rendering performance on current GPUs, making it very promising for VR/AR and immersive capture.

- **Future Impact:** These techniques could enable creating highly realistic digital twins of real-world locations or objects simply by taking photos/videos and might offer new avenues for rendering complex phenomena like smoke, clouds, or fur that are difficult with traditional polygons. Integrating them efficiently into existing game engine pipelines remains an active area of research.

- **Generative AI for Content:** Beyond texture generation, AI models (e.g., diffusion models, generative adversarial networks - GANs, large language models guiding procedural systems) are being explored for

  - **3D Model Generation:** Creating basic 3D meshes from text prompts or sketches (e.g., OpenAI's Shap-E, Google's DreamFusion, NVIDIA's GET3D). Quality and control are still limitations for professional use.

  - **Animation Generation:** Creating character animations or motion cycles from descriptions or video input.

- **Intelligent Procedural Content Generation (PCG):** Using AI to guide procedural algorithms to create more varied, plausible, and art-directed game levels, landscapes, or city layouts, potentially reducing manual authoring effort.

- **Workflow Integration:** Integrating these tools via APIs or plugins into standard content creation software (Blender, Maya, Houdini, Unreal, Unity) is key for practical adoption. GPUs are essential for both training these large generative models and running them efficiently for inference during the creative process.

- **AI for Rendering Optimization:** Research investigates using AI (e.g., reinforcement learning) to make real-time decisions within the rendering pipeline itself: dynamically selecting LODs, choosing optimal shader complexity, predicting visibility more accurately than traditional culling, or even learning entirely new, efficient rendering algorithms tailored to specific scene types or hardware.

Real-Time Ray Tracing and Path Tracing: The March Toward Photorealism

The ultimate goal for many graphics applications is achieving the visual fidelity of offline movie CGI, but in real time. This involves accurately simulating the physics of light transport.

- **Hardware Evolution:** Expect future GPUs to feature more numerous and significantly faster RT Cores (or equivalents), capable of performing more ray-triangle and ray-box intersections per second. Hardware might also become more specialized for traversing acceleration structures (BVHs).

- **Path Tracing Challenges:** Full path tracing requires tracing potentially hundreds or thousands of light paths (rays bouncing multiple times) per pixel to get a clean, noise-free image. Doing this in real time (e.g., 11ms per frame) is currently impossible for complex scenes even on the fastest hardware.

- **Denoising Is Key:** Therefore, real-time path tracing relies heavily on sophisticated **denoising** algorithms. These algorithms take a very noisy input image rendered with only a few paths/samples per pixel (e.g., 1-4 spp) and intelligently filter it to produce a clean result. Modern denoisers often use information from previous frames (temporal reprojection), neighboring pixels (spatial filtering), and auxiliary buffers (normals, depth, motion vectors) to guide the filtering. AI-based denoisers (like NVIDIA's OptiX denoiser or DLSS 3.5's Ray Reconstruction) use neural networks trained on vast datasets of noisy/clean image pairs to achieve state-of-the-art results. The quality and performance of the denoiser are critical for the viability of real-time path tracing.

- **Hybrid Approaches:** Near-term progress will likely continue to rely on hybrid techniques that combine the efficiency of rasterization for primary visibility with ray/ path tracing selectively applied for effects that benefit most (e.g., accurate reflections, soft shadows, multi-bounce global illumination).

Energy Efficiency and Architectural Innovation: Sustainable Performance

The need for more compute power clashes with the physical limits of power delivery and heat dissipation. Improving **performance-per-watt** is paramount.

- **Manufacturing Processes:** Migrating to next-generation semiconductor nodes (3nm, 2nm, Angstrom-era) using new transistor structures like Gate-All-Around Field Effect Transistors (GAAFETs) or Complementary FETs (CFETs) is crucial for reducing power leakage and improving switching efficiency.

- **Chiplet Architectures:** Breaking monolithic GPUs into smaller, interconnected chiplets (potentially using different process nodes optimized for different functions—e.g., compute vs. I/O) offers benefits in manufacturing yield, cost, and design flexibility. High-bandwidth, low-power die-to-die interconnect technologies (like NVIDIA's NVLink-C2C, AMD's Infinity Fabric, Intel's Foveros/EMIB) are critical enablers.

- **Architectural Optimizations:** Designing more efficient compute cores, smarter cache hierarchies, improved asynchronous compute capabilities (allowing graphics and compute tasks to overlap better), and more aggressive power gating of unused blocks within the GPU.

- **Software and System Level:** Optimizing drivers, compilers, and application software to utilize GPU resources more efficiently. Improving system-level power delivery and cooling solutions (e.g., liquid cooling becoming more common).

Potential Complementarity with Quantum Computing: A Distant Frontier

Quantum computing represents a fundamentally different approach to computation, exploiting quantum mechanical phenomena like superposition and entanglement using **qubits**. It is **not** the successor to classical GPUs but offers potential for solving certain classes of problems believed to be intractable for any classical computer, no matter how powerful.

- **Potential Synergies (Long-Term, Speculative):**
  In a future where large-scale, fault-tolerant quantum computers exist, they might complement classical systems (including GPUs) in metaverse-related applications by tackling specific sub-problems:

  - **Quantum Chemistry/Materials Science:** Simulating molecules with high accuracy using algorithms like the Variational Quantum Eigensolver (VQE) could accelerate the discovery of novel materials for displays, sensors, or processors used in immersive hardware. Results could be visualized using classical GPU rendering.

  - **Optimization:** Quantum algorithms like QAOA or quantum annealing might find applications in solving extremely complex logistics, resource allocation, or network optimization problems within vast simulated worlds, potentially exceeding classical heuristic approaches.

  - **Quantum Machine Learning:** Research explores quantum algorithms that could potentially offer speedups for specific ML tasks or enable new

379

types of models, although practical advantages over classical GPU-accelerated AI are still largely unproven.

- **Fundamental Differences and Challenges:**
  Quantum computers are probabilistic, sensitive to noise (requiring complex quantum error correction), operate fundamentally differently from classical logic gates, and are currently limited in qubit count and coherence times. They will not replace GPUs for tasks like rendering graphics frames, running most existing AI models, or executing general-purpose sequential code. The vision is one of **hybrid computation**, where specific, suitable sub-tasks are offloaded to a quantum co-processor.

Conclusion: The Ongoing Graphics and Compute Revolution

The trajectory of the GPU is a remarkable story of technological evolution, driven by an insatiable demand for visual realism and computational power. What began as hardware focused on accelerating specific graphics operations for video games has transformed into a massively parallel, highly programmable compute engine that is indispensable across science, industry, and entertainment. Key architectural innovations—the shift from fixed-function pipelines to programmable shaders, the adoption of unified shader models, the development of high-bandwidth memory systems like HBM, the creation of GPGPU programming models like CUDA and OpenCL, and the integration of specialized AI-accelerating Tensor Cores—have collectively propelled the GPU far beyond its original mandate.

Today, GPUs render the visually stunning, interactive worlds of AAA games and provide the critical performance needed for comfortable and immersive VR and AR experiences. They serve as the workhorses training the complex deep learning models that power the AI revolution, from image recognition and natural language processing to scientific discovery. GPUs accelerate simulations that allow researchers to tackle grand challenges in climate modeling, drug discovery, astrophysics, and countless other domains. They also provide the foundational technology upon which ambitious visions like the Metaverse are being built, enabling the creation and real-time rendering of vast, persistent, shared virtual worlds.

This evolution shows no sign of slowing. The continued integration of AI directly into the graphics pipeline promises new levels of realism and efficiency through techniques like neural rendering and generative content creation. The relentless pursuit of photorealism drives innovation in real-time ray tracing and path tracing, demanding ever more powerful hardware and sophisticated denoising algorithms. The critical need for sustainable computing fuels research into energy-efficient architectures and advanced manufacturing processes. And while still on a distant horizon, the potential long-term complementarity with quantum computing hints at future hybrid systems tackling problems of unprecedented complexity.

The Graphics Processing Unit, in its diverse forms from mobile SoCs to data center accelerators, remains a focal point of intense innovation. It is more than just a graphics card; it is a fundamental engine of modern computation, continually redefining the boundaries of visual fidelity, parallel processing, artificial intelligence, and immersive interaction, shaping our digital present and paving the way for the transformative technologies of the future.

Glossary of Key Terms

- **BVH (Bounding Volume Hierarchy):** A tree data structure used in ray tracing to efficiently determine which objects a ray might intersect by organizing geometry into nested bounding volumes.

- **PBR (Physically Based Rendering):** A rendering approach that aims to simulate light interaction with surfaces based on physical properties rather than artistic approximations.

- **Rasterization:** The process of converting vector-based geometric primitives (triangles, lines) into a raster image composed of pixels.

- **SIMT (Single Instruction, Multiple Threads):** GPU execution model where many threads execute the same instruction simultaneously on different data.

- **T&L (Transform and Lighting):** Early GPU hardware acceleration for the mathematical transformations (positioning, rotating, scaling) and lighting calculations applied to 3D vertices.

- **VRS (Variable Rate Shading):** A GPU feature allowing different parts of the screen to be shaded at different rates, optimizing performance by reducing detail where it's less noticeable.

- **Z-buffering:** A technique using a depth buffer to determine which pixels are visible by storing the distance of each pixel from the camera and only rendering closer objects.

CHAPTER 7

Planet Eta: Navigating Legal, Ethical, and Security Landscapes in the Digital Age

Introduction: Charting the Course for Responsible Innovation in Complex Systems

Planet Eta exists at the confluence of groundbreaking innovation and profound societal shifts. Its advanced digital ecosystems, built upon sophisticated Artificial Intelligence (AI), decentralized Blockchain networks, and immersive Metaverse experiences, represent both immense opportunities and significant challenges. These technologies are not isolated pillars but increasingly interconnected systems, creating emergent behaviors and complex governance needs. As these integrated

F. Lisitano and J. Hickie, *The Evolune Metaverse*, Maker Innovations Series,
https://doi.org/10.1007/979-8-8688-1588-1_7

technologies weave themselves ever deeper into the fabric of daily life—
from planetary infrastructure and commerce to personal identity and
social interaction—establishing robust, adaptive, and ethically grounded
legal frameworks and security protocols becomes an existential necessity
for societal stability and progress. Planet Eta, through conscious effort and
iterative learning, serves as a crucial case study in navigating this intricate
landscape, continually striving to foster rapid technological advancement
while diligently safeguarding the fundamental rights, promoting fairness,
and ensuring the safety of its diverse inhabitants.

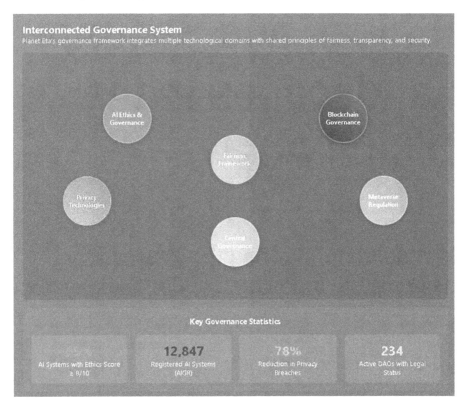

Figure 7-1. *Interconnected Governance System*

This chapter delves into the multi-faceted governance structures Planet Eta employs to manage the intertwined complexities of AI, Blockchain, and the Metaverse. We will undertake a deep exploration of the evolving legal and ethical frameworks designed not merely to regulate but to actively shape the development and deployment of these powerful tools toward beneficial outcomes. We examine how principles of transparency, accountability, fairness, privacy, and security operate through specific policies, regulatory bodies, and technological safeguards. From the granular details of AI bias audits and smart contract vulnerability analysis to the macro-level challenges of governing decentralized autonomous organizations (DAOs) and establishing rights within persistent virtual worlds, we dissect Planet Eta's approach. Through detailed (though fictional) case studies and analysis of its governance mechanisms, this chapter aims to illuminate the intricate path toward responsible digital progress, offering potential models and cautionary tales for any civilization grappling with the profound societal transformations wrought by advanced technology.

Section 1: Ethical AI on Planet Eta— Cultivating Trust Through Principle and Practice

Artificial Intelligence is arguably the most potent technology shaping Planet Eta's present and future. Its capacity for learning, prediction, automation, and complex decision-making offers unparalleled benefits across all sectors. However, this power carries inherent ethical risks: the potential for encoded bias leading to discrimination, the opacity of complex algorithms hindering accountability, the possibility of autonomous systems causing unintended harm, and the ever-present tension between data-driven insights and individual privacy. Recognizing these stakes, Planet Eta has institutionalized a comprehensive, multi-layered approach to Ethical AI, moving beyond abstract principles to embed ethical considerations deeply within its technological and societal fabric.

Core Principles of Ethical AI Development: Beyond the Checklist

Planet Eta's framework is built upon internationally recognized ethical principles but emphasizes their practical implementation and continuous evaluation throughout the AI life cycle.

Fairness, Non-discrimination, and Equity: This principle demands that AI systems treat individuals and groups equitably, avoiding the creation or amplification of unjust biases.

The Challenge of Bias: Bias can creep into AI systems insidiously. It might originate from historical societal biases reflected in the training data (e.g., under-representation of certain groups leading to poorer performance for them), from developer assumptions encoded into the model architecture or objective functions, or from interaction biases where user behavior reinforces existing stereotypes over time.

Planet Eta's Mitigation Strategies

Mandatory Data Diversity Audits: Requiring rigorous analysis of training datasets before model development to identify potential sources of bias related to demographics (species, origin, gender identity, age, ability, etc.). Techniques include statistical analysis of representation and feature correlation analysis. Where historical bias is unavoidable, explicit mitigation strategies must be documented.

Algorithmic Fairness Techniques: Encouraging and sometimes mandating the use of fairness-aware machine learning algorithms. This might involve pre-processing data (re-weighting samples, data augmentation for underrepresented groups), in-processing constraints during model training (adding fairness terms to the loss function), or post-processing model outputs (adjusting prediction thresholds for different groups).

Multiple Fairness Metrics: Recognizing that no single fairness metric is universally applicable, regulators require evaluation across several metrics (e.g., Demographic Parity, similar selection rates across groups; Equalized Odds, similar true positive and false positive rates; Equal Opportunity, similar true positive rates) relevant to the specific application context. The choice of metrics and acceptable trade-offs must be justified.

Intersectionality: Explicitly requiring analysis of fairness not just across single demographic axes but also across their intersections (e.g., ensuring fairness for individuals belonging to multiple minority groups simultaneously).

Continuous Monitoring: Implementing post-deployment monitoring systems to detect performance drift or emergent biases as the AI interacts with real-world data and users.

Transparency and Explainability (XAI): Opening the Black Box To trust AI, especially in critical applications, users and regulators need to understand how it arrives at its decisions.

The "Black Box" Problem: Highly complex models like deep neural networks can achieve state-of-the-art performance but often lack inherent interpretability. Their internal workings involve millions or billions of parameters interacting in nonlinear ways, making it difficult to pinpoint exactly why a specific input led to a specific output.

Planet Eta's XAI Requirements

Mandated Explainability: For high-risk AI systems (defined by sector, e.g., healthcare, justice, critical infrastructure, finance), regulations mandate the provision of explanations comprehensible to the affected user or relevant authority. The level of detail required depends on the context.

Promoting XAI Techniques: Supporting research and adoption of various XAI methods.

LIME (Local Interpretable Model-Agnostic Explanations): Explains individual predictions by creating a simple, interpretable model (like a linear model or decision tree) that approximates the behavior of the complex black-box model locally around the specific input instance being explained. It answers: "why did the AI make this specific decision for this specific case?"

SHAP (Shapley Additive Explanations): Based on cooperative game theory's Shapley values, SHAP assigns an "importance value" to each input feature for a given prediction, indicating how much that feature contributed (positively or negatively) to the final output compared to a baseline prediction. It provides both local (per-prediction) and global (overall model behavior) explanations.

Counterfactual Explanations: Describing the smallest change to the input features that would alter the prediction outcome (e.g., "your loan would have been approved if your income had been $500 higher").

Concept-Based Explanations: Identifying higher-level concepts (e.g., "image texture," "sentence sentiment") that the model relies on.

Intrinsically Interpretable Models: Encouraging the use of simpler models (decision trees, rule lists, generalized additive models) where their performance is sufficient for the task, as they are inherently easier to understand.

Limitations of XAI: Regulators also mandate awareness of XAI limitations. Explanations can sometimes be misleading, incomplete, or fail to capture the full complexity of the model's reasoning. Transparency about the confidence and fidelity of the provided explanations is required.

Accountability, Responsibility, and Human Oversight: Technology must serve humanity, and clear lines of responsibility are essential when things go wrong.

Legal Liability Frameworks: Planet Eta has specific legislation clarifying liability for harm caused by AI systems, considering factors like the degree of autonomy, foreseeability of harm, and the roles of developers, deployers, and operators.

Meaningful Human Control: Mandating appropriate levels of human oversight, especially for systems with potentially severe consequences. This ranges from human-in-the-loop (human directly involved in each decision cycle, e.g., approving AI recommendations), human-on-the-loop (human supervises the AI and can intervene if necessary), to human-command (high-level strategic direction for highly autonomous systems). The level of required oversight depends on risk assessment.

Robust Auditing Trails: Requiring AI systems to log sufficient information about their inputs, internal states (where feasible), decisions, and confidence levels to enable post hoc analysis and accountability. Blockchain is sometimes used for creating tamper-proof audit trails for critical AI decisions.

Mechanisms for Redress: Establishing accessible processes for individuals to challenge AI decisions, seek explanations, request corrections, and obtain remedies for harms caused. This links closely with explainability requirements.

Reliability, Safety, and Security: AI systems must be dependable and secure against failures or malicious attacks.

Rigorous Testing and Validation: Mandating comprehensive testing protocols covering not only accuracy but also robustness (performance under noisy or adversarial inputs), safety (identifying potential failure modes), and security (vulnerability testing).

Formal Verification (Where Applicable): For highly critical systems, exploring the use of formal methods to mathematically prove certain safety or correctness properties of the AI model or system.

Resilience and Fail-Safes: Designing systems with graceful degradation capabilities and fail-safe mechanisms in case of unexpected errors or attacks.

Cybersecurity for AI: Protecting AI models and data from theft, tampering (e.g., model poisoning), or unauthorized access throughout the life cycle.

Privacy: Protecting personal data is a foundational ethical requirement (covered in depth in Section 2).

Operationalizing Ethics: The AI Ethics Council and Compliance Score

Principles alone are insufficient without mechanisms for enforcement and incentivization. Planet Eta's AI Ethics Council is an independent, multi-stakeholder body (including technologists, ethicists, legal experts, social scientists, and citizen representatives) tasked with

- Developing detailed, sector-specific ethical guidelines and standards based on the core principles.

- Reviewing mandatory ethical impact assessments and bias audit reports submitted by organizations deploying AI.

- Operating a certification program for AI systems that meet high ethical standards.

- Maintaining the public "Ethical Compliance Score" registry. This score aggregates assessments across fairness, transparency, accountability, safety, and privacy, providing an easily understandable rating for AI systems.

The Compliance Score has significant real-world impact. High scores can unlock government contracts, provide eligibility for tax incentives or research grants, enhance public reputation, and build consumer trust. Conversely, low scores can trigger regulatory scrutiny, mandatory remediation plans, or even withdrawal of deployment authorization for critical systems. This creates a powerful market-based incentive for organizations to genuinely embed ethics into their AI development practices.

Case Study Revisited: The HealthAI Scandal (2027)—Systemic Failures and Response

The HealthAI scandal wasn't just about biased data; it revealed failures across the AI life cycle. The training dataset, sourced primarily from major urban hospitals, underrepresented rural and specific minority populations. Pre-deployment bias audits were superficial. The complex deep learning model lacked adequate explainability features, making it hard for doctors to understand or question its sometimes-erroneous diagnostic suggestions for under-represented groups. Post-deployment monitoring failed to detect the performance disparities until significant harm had occurred.

The regulatory response via the AI Ethics Directive (AID) was multifaceted. It

- Mandated standardized dataset reporting (Datasheets for Datasets/Data Nutrition Labels) detailing provenance, composition, and known limitations.

- Required rigorous fairness testing using multiple metrics across specified demographic subgroups before deployment in healthcare.

- Increased the stringency and independence requirements for ethical audits.

- Demanded implementation of specific XAI techniques (like LIME/SHAP) for high-risk diagnostic systems.

- Strengthened requirements for post-deployment performance monitoring and bias detection systems.

- Empowered the AI Ethics Council with greater authority to investigate and sanction non-compliant systems. This incident served as a harsh lesson, driving significant advancements in fairness-aware algorithms, XAI research, and the development of more robust AI governance practices on Planet Eta.

Section 2: AI Governance and Regulation— Ensuring Responsible Deployment Through Structure and Oversight

Effective AI governance requires more than just ethical principles; it demands concrete structures, regulations, and enforcement mechanisms to translate those principles into practice and ensure accountability across the AI ecosystem. Planet Eta has implemented a layered governance approach involving public registries, comprehensive data protection laws, and active regulatory oversight.

The AI Governance Registry (AIGR): A Public Ledger for AI Systems

Transparency is a cornerstone of Planet Eta's AI governance. The AI Governance Registry (AIGR) is a mandatory public database for AI systems deemed to have significant societal impact (criteria include sector of application, degree of autonomy, potential for harm, scale of deployment).

Organizations deploying such systems must register and maintain up-to-date entries including

System Identification: Name, version, developer, deployer, deployment date.

Purpose and Domain: Clear description of intended function and operational constraints.

AI Technique: High-level description of the AI approach used (e.g., deep learning—CNN, transformer; reinforcement learning; expert system).

Training Data Summary: Standardized information on primary training datasets—source, size, key characteristics, collection period, description of bias mitigation steps taken during data preparation (e.g., Datasheets for Datasets format). Raw data is not published.

Performance and Fairness Metrics: Key evaluation results on benchmark datasets, including accuracy, robustness metrics, and fairness metrics across legally protected demographic categories relevant to Planet Eta.

Explainability Provisions: Description of methods used to provide explanations (e.g., LIME/SHAP available via API, feature importance reports generated).

Human Oversight: Description of the level and nature of human involvement in the system's operation.

Ethical Compliance Score and Audit History: Link to the AI Ethics Council's current score and summary reports of past ethical/security audits (potentially with redactions for proprietary information).

Incident Reporting: Records of significant failures or harmful incidents involving the system.

The AIGR provides crucial transparency for regulators, researchers, businesses procuring AI systems, and the interested public, enabling monitoring, comparative analysis, and accountability.

Data Protection and Privacy: The DPC-E Framework and PETs.

AI systems often rely on vast amounts of data, making data protection intrinsically linked to AI governance. Planet Eta's Data Protection Code of Eta (DPC-E) is a comprehensive regulation analogous to Earth's GDPR but with a stronger emphasis on proactive technical safeguards.

Core Principles (Recap): Privacy by Design/Default, Data Minimization, Purpose Limitation, Individual Rights (Access, Rectification, Erasure, Portability), Security Mandates.

Enforcement: A dedicated Data Protection Authority monitors compliance, investigates breaches, and imposes significant penalties for violations. Deep Dive into Privacy-Enhancing Technologies (PETs) Promoted by DPC-E.

Planet Eta actively encourages and, in some high-risk contexts, mandates the use of PETs to reconcile the utility of data-driven AI with fundamental privacy rights.

Decentralized Identity (DID) and Verifiable Credentials (VCs)

Concept: Instead of relying on centralized identity providers (like governments or tech platforms), DIDs allow individuals or organizations to create and manage their own unique, persistent digital identifiers cryptographically secured and often registered on a distributed ledger (blockchain or otherwise). Associated with a DID are DID Documents containing cryptographic public keys and service endpoints. Individuals can then obtain cryptographically signed Verifiable Credentials (VCs) from trusted issuers (e.g., a university issuing a degree credential, a government issuing proof-of-age).

Privacy Benefit: When needing to prove something to an AI service (e.g., "I am over 18," "I am an employee"), the user can present the relevant VC. The service verifies the credential's authenticity and issuer signature using the information in the DID document, often without needing to learn any unnecessary personal data beyond the specific claim being verified (enabled by techniques like Zero-Knowledge Proofs applied to VCs). This enhances user control and minimizes data disclosure.

Planet Eta Implementation: Wide adoption for accessing government services, verifying eligibility for benefits, and even logging into certain metaverse platforms without traditional usernames/passwords. (The simple Python class example only mimicked credential storage; real systems involve complex cryptography and ledger interactions).

Differential Privacy (DP)

Concept: Provides a formal, mathematical guarantee of privacy by ensuring that the output of a data analysis (e.g., statistics computed from a database or updates generated by an AI model in Federated Learning) does not reveal significant information about any single individual within the dataset. It achieves this by adding precisely calibrated statistical noise to the data or the results of computations.

Mechanism: The amount of noise added is controlled by a parameter called epsilon (ε). Lower epsilon means more noise and stronger privacy guarantees, but potentially less accurate results. Higher epsilon means less noise, weaker privacy, but higher utility.

Adaptive Anonymization Relationship: DP is a primary technique enabling "adaptive anonymization." The required epsilon (noise level) can be adapted based on the sensitivity of the query, the size of the dataset, or regulatory requirements, providing a flexible privacy-utility trade-off.

Planet Eta Use: Mandated for releasing aggregate statistics from sensitive databases (e.g., census, public health surveys), used in privacy-preserving federated learning, and in some data analytics platforms.

Homomorphic Encryption (HE)

Concept: Allows computations (e.g., addition, multiplication) to be performed directly on encrypted data without decrypting it first. If you encrypt data A and data B, you can compute Encrypt(A+B) directly from Encrypt(A) and Encrypt(B). Decrypting the result yields A+B.

Privacy Benefit: Extremely powerful for scenarios where sensitive data needs to be processed by an untrusted third party (e.g., a cloud AI service). The service performs computations on encrypted data without ever seeing the plaintext, preserving confidentiality.

Types: Partially Homomorphic Encryption (PHE) supports only one type of operation (e.g., addition or multiplication). Fully Homomorphic Encryption (FHE) supports arbitrary computations but is currently extremely computationally expensive (orders of magnitude slower than plaintext computation), limiting its practical use to specific niche applications.

Planet Eta Use: Encouraged and used in specific high-sensitivity areas like secure multi-party computation for financial analysis, collaborative analysis of encrypted medical data, and potentially privacy-preserving machine learning inference (running a model on encrypted input). Significant research focus exists on improving FHE performance.

Synthetic Data Generation

Concept: Using generative AI models (like GANs, VAEs, or diffusion models), trained on real data, to create an entirely new, artificial dataset that captures the statistical patterns and correlations of the original data but contains no real individual records.

Privacy Benefit: Allows AI developers to train, test, and share models using data that has similar characteristics to real sensitive data (e.g., medical records, financial transactions) without exposing any actual personal information. Useful for research, software testing, and democratizing access to realistic (but not real) data.

Challenges: Ensuring the synthetic data accurately captures all important correlations and edge cases from the real data and avoiding the model inadvertently encoding and leaking sensitive information from the original training set (requiring techniques like DP during generative model training).

Planet Eta Use: Commonly used in the development and validation phases for AI in finance and healthcare, reducing reliance on accessing raw sensitive datasets early in the process.

Zero-Knowledge Proofs (ZKPs)

Concept: Allows a Prover to convince a Verifier that a statement is true, without revealing any information beyond the truth of the statement itself. For example, proving you know a password without revealing the password or proving your cryptocurrency transaction is valid according to certain rules without revealing the sender, receiver, or amount (as used in Zcash or Aztec).

Types: Include zk-SNARKs (Zero-Knowledge Succinct Non-Interactive Argument of Knowledge) which are very small and fast to verify but often require a trusted setup phase and zk-STARKs (Zero-Knowledge Scalable Transparent Argument of Knowledge) which are larger and slower to verify but require no trusted setup and offer potentially higher security against quantum computers.

Planet Eta Use: Increasingly used in DID/VC systems for privacy-preserving authentication/authorization, in blockchain applications for confidential transactions (as in EtaCoin compliance), and potentially for verifying the integrity of computations (e.g., proving an AI model was executed correctly) without revealing intermediate steps.

Real-Time Compliance and Robust Auditing

Governance relies on verification. Planet Eta employs

- **AI-Powered Continuous Auditing:** Automated systems that monitor deployed AI for anomalies:

- **Bias Drift:** Detecting if performance disparities between groups emerge or worsen over time.

- **Data Access Violations:** Flagging unexpected or unauthorized access to sensitive data by the AI system.

- **Performance Degradation:** Monitoring accuracy and reliability metrics.

- **Security Vulnerabilities:** Scanning for potential attack vectors or anomalous inputs.

- **Immutable Audit Trails:** Regulations often require critical AI decisions (e.g., loan approvals, medical diagnoses, autonomous vehicle actions) to be logged immutably, potentially using blockchain hashes or dedicated tamper-proof logging systems, to ensure accountability and facilitate post-incident forensic analysis.

- **Independent Third-Party Audits:** Regular audits conducted by certified external organizations to verify compliance with DPC-E, ethical guidelines, and security standards, with reports often summarized for the AIGR.

Case Study Revisited: Privacy in Education Platforms

The 2030 breach of an adaptive learning platform on Planet Eta underscored the need for robust, embedded privacy. The Education Data Privacy Directive (EDPD) mandated

- **End-to-End Encryption:** For all student data, both in transit and at rest.

- **Strict Data Minimization:** Justification required for every data point collected about student learning. Sensitive demographics often prohibited unless explicitly consented to for specific, approved research with strict anonymization.

- **Use of PETs:** Encouraging synthetic data for initial model development, differential privacy for releasing aggregate statistics about learning trends, and exploring homomorphic encryption for analyzing engagement patterns on encrypted interaction data.

- **Annual Privacy Audits:** Mandatory independent audits for license renewal.

This proactive approach allows Planet Eta to benefit from personalized AI learning while maintaining strong student privacy protections. (The simple Python anonymization example only illustrated basic principles like dropping columns and masking; real systems use far more sophisticated PETs like DP or synthetic data generation).

Section 3: Federated Learning—Enabling Collaborative AI While Preserving Privacy

Federated Learning (FL) stands out as a key technological enabler of Planet Eta's vision for collaborative AI that inherently respects data privacy and sovereignty. It allows multiple parties to jointly train powerful AI models without ever needing to share their sensitive raw data, making it ideal for sectors like healthcare, finance, and distributed sensing networks like smart cities.

The Federated Learning Process: A Deeper Look

The core FL workflow involves iterative local training and global aggregation:

- **Initialization and Distribution:** A central server (or coordinating entity) defines the AI model architecture (e.g., a neural network) and initializes its parameters (weights). This initial model is then securely distributed to numerous participating clients (devices or organizations).

- **Local Training:** Each client possesses its own local dataset (which remains private). Using the received global model as a starting point, each client performs one or more epochs of training using only its local data. This updates the model's parameters based on the patterns learned from that specific client's data.

- **Model Update Calculation:** After local training, the client calculates the change it made to the model parameters (e.g., the difference between the updated local weights and the original global weights, or the gradients computed during local training).

Secure Update Transmission: The client securely transmits only
this calculated update (not the raw data) back to the central server. This
transmission often involves

- **Encryption:** Protecting the update during transit.

- **Secure Aggregation Protocols:** Techniques like secure
  multi-party computation (SMPC) or homomorphic
  encryption applied to the updates, allowing the server
  to compute the sum or average of all client updates
  without being able to see any individual client's update.
  This protects against the server inferring sensitive
  information from a single update.

- **Global Model Aggregation:** The central server securely
  aggregates the updates received from a cohort of
  participating clients (often a random subset in each
  round). The most common algorithm is Federated
  Averaging (FedAvg), where the server computes a
  weighted average of the client updates (weighted by the
  amount of data each client used for local training). This
  aggregated update is then applied to the global model.
  (The previous simple code summing estimators was
  incorrect; FedAvg averages weights or weight deltas).

- **Iteration and Convergence:** The newly improved
  global model is distributed back to the clients for the
  next round of local training. This iterative process
  continues until the global model reaches a desired level
  of performance or converges.

Addressing Key Federated Learning Challenges on Planet Eta

Successfully deploying FL at scale required Planet Eta to address inherent technical challenges, such as:

- **Communication Bottlenecks:** Frequent transmission of potentially large model updates from millions of clients can overwhelm networks.

- **Solutions:** Research and deployment focus on update compression (quantizing updates to fewer bits, using techniques like sketching), sparsification (sending only the most significant updates), performing more local computation between communication rounds, and developing hierarchical FL architectures (intermediate aggregation servers). Statistical Heterogeneity (Non-IID Data): client datasets are rarely identically distributed. User data on phones, patient data across hospitals, or sensor readings across city districts vary significantly. This Non-IID nature can cause simple FedAvg to converge slowly, diverge, or result in a global model biased towards certain clients.

- **Solutions:** Planet Eta promotes advanced FL algorithms designed for Non-IID data; FedProx; adds a proximal term to the local client objective function, encouraging local models to stay closer to the global model, improving stability.

- **SCAFFOLD:** Uses control variates to correct for "client drift" caused by Non-IID data, leading to faster convergence.

- **Personalized FL:** Approaches where the goal is not just a single global model, but also personalized models for each client, adapted from the global model (e.g., through local fine-tuning, meta-learning).

- **Security and Robustness:** FL systems need protection against adversaries.

- **Poisoning Attacks:** Malicious clients might send crafted updates designed to degrade the global model's performance or introduce specific biases/backdoors.

- **Mitigation:** Robust aggregation rules (e.g., using median instead of mean, trimming outliers), anomaly detection on client updates, reputation systems for clients, and differential privacy applied to client updates (which also helps against inference attacks) are employed. Secure Aggregation protocols prevent the server itself from being malicious or compromised.

- **System Heterogeneity:** Clients often have vastly different computational power, network connectivity, and data availability. FL schedulers and algorithms need to be robust to clients dropping out or participating intermittently.

Federated Learning Case Study: Smart City Environmental Monitoring

Beyond traffic and energy, Planet Eta uses FL for city-wide environmental monitoring. Thousands of low-cost sensors (measuring air quality—PM2.5, NO2, ozone, noise levels, temperature, humidity) are deployed across a city. Each sensor node (or local cluster) trains a small model locally to predict near-term pollution levels or detect anomalies based on its readings and local context (time of day, nearby traffic). These local models send encrypted, differentially private updates to a city environmental agency server. The server aggregates these updates using FedAvg (or more advanced algorithms) to build a high-resolution, real-time map of environmental quality across the city without collecting raw sensor readings centrally. This aggregated model identifies pollution hotspots, predicts air quality fluctuations, informs public health advisories, and guides urban planning decisions (e.g., optimizing green spaces, regulating industrial emissions), all while preserving the privacy associated with fine-grained sensor locations.

Section 4: Blockchain Governance— Engineering Trust in Decentralized Systems

Planet Eta leverages Blockchain and Distributed Ledger Technology (DLT) for applications demanding high degrees of transparency, security, and censorship resistance, such as decentralized identity, supply chain traceability, secure voting systems, and digital asset management. However, governing these decentralized systems requires novel approaches compared to traditional centralized platforms.

Smart Contract Regulation: Code Is Law, but Law Needs Audits

Smart contracts automate agreements on the blockchain, but their immutable nature means bugs are permanent and potentially catastrophic. Planet Eta's governance focuses on pre-deployment assurance and post-deployment safeguards.

Mandatory Security Audits: Critical smart contracts (especially DeFi protocols or those managing valuable assets or identity credentials) must undergo independent security audits by certified professionals before deployment.

Focus of Audits: Auditors meticulously examine the Solidity (or other smart contract language) code for

Reentrancy: Ensuring external calls cannot recursively call back into the contract to drain funds before internal state is updated, using Checks-Effects-Interactions pattern, Reentrancy Guards (e.g., OpenZeppelin's), or limiting external calls.

Integer Arithmetic Issues: Checking for potential overflows or underflows in arithmetic operations (though modern Solidity versions mitigate this with default checked math).

Access Control: Verifying that functions have correct modifiers (e.g., onlyOwner, onlyAdmin) and that authorization logic is sound. Checking for unprotected selfdestruct or delegatecall vulnerabilities.

Transaction Order Dependency/Front-Running: Identifying logic sensitive to the order in which transactions are mined, which could be exploited by miners or MEV (Maximal Extractable Value) searchers. Requires careful design or commitment schemes.

Timestamp Dependence: Avoiding critical logic relying directly on block timestamps (block.timestamp), which can be slightly manipulated by miners.

Gas Limit Issues/Denial of Service (DoS): Identifying unbounded loops or operations on potentially large arrays that could exceed block gas limits, making functions unusable (e.g., distributing rewards to an ever-growing list of users).

Oracle Security: Assessing the reliability and manipulation resistance of external data feeds (oracles) used by the contract. Preferring decentralized, robust oracle networks (like Chainlink).

Logic Errors: Ensuring the code accurately implements the intended business logic and handles edge cases correctly.

Upgradability and Governance: Recognizing that even audited code may need updates, Planet Eta promotes standard upgradability patterns. The most common is the Proxy Pattern.

Users interact with a simple Proxy Contract.

The Proxy Contract forwards calls (using delegatecall) to a separate Implementation Contract containing the main logic.

The Proxy Contract stores the address of the current Implementation Contract.

An authorized entity (e.g., a DAO governance contract, a multi-sig wallet) can update the Implementation address stored in the Proxy, effectively upgrading the contract logic without changing the contract address users interact with. Common proxy standards include Transparent Upgradeable Proxy (TUP) and Universal Upgradeable Proxy Standard (UUPS).

Emergency Mechanisms: Mandating or strongly encouraging "Circuit Breakers" (pause/unpause functionality) and Multi-Signature (Multisig) Wallets for controlling critical functions like upgrades, pausing, or parameter changes. A Multisig requires M-of-N authorized parties to approve an action, preventing single points of failure or malicious control.

Cryptocurrency Oversight: Balancing Innovation and Stability

Planet Eta embraces the potential of digital currencies but implements measures to curb illicit use and ensure financial stability.

AML/KYC via Zero-Knowledge Proofs (ZKPs): The Cryptocurrency Accountability Act requires identity verification for large or suspicious transactions to combat money laundering and illicit finance. However, Planet Eta prioritizes privacy-preserving compliance. Users typically verify their identity once with a trusted third-party issuer, who provides a Verifiable Credential. When making a regulated transaction, the user generates a Zero-Knowledge Proof demonstrating, for example, that their identity has been verified and they are not on a watchlist, without revealing their actual identity to the exchange or counterparty. ZKP technologies like zk-SNARKs (requiring trusted setup but offering small proofs) and zk-STARKs (no trusted setup, potentially quantum-resistant, but larger proofs) enable this "compliance without surveillance."

EtaCoin (Regulated Stablecoin): To provide a reliable digital medium of exchange, Planet Eta's central bank issues EtaCoin, a fully collateralized stablecoin pegged 1:1 to the official planetary currency. Its smart contract includes embedded compliance features. Transactional limits can be enforced, wallets associated with illicit activity can be frozen via governance mechanisms, and large transactions automatically trigger reporting requirements. However, for everyday transactions below certain thresholds, user pseudonymity is maintained. This offers a regulated alternative to purely decentralized cryptocurrencies or volatile algorithmic stablecoins.

Exchange and DeFi Regulation: Centralized exchanges are licensed and regulated like traditional financial institutions (capital requirements, security audits, AML/KYC). Decentralized Finance (DeFi) protocols operating on Planet Eta are subject to the smart contract auditing requirements, and regulators are developing frameworks to address risks related to impermanent loss, oracle manipulation, and governance attacks within DeFi, often focusing on regulating the interfaces and developers rather than the protocols directly.

Governing Decentralized Autonomous Organizations (DAOs)

DAOs represent a paradigm shift in organizational structure, using smart contracts for rules and often token-based voting for governance. Planet Eta is developing legal frameworks ("Digital Cooperative Acts") to

- Grant DAOs optional legal personality, allowing them to interact with traditional legal systems (e.g., own property, enter contracts).

- Clarify liability issues (are token holders liable? developers? the DAO itself?).

- Establish standards for DAO governance transparency and dispute resolution.

- Explore alternative voting mechanisms beyond simple token-weighted voting (which can lead to plutocracy) such as quadratic voting (where votes cost quadratically more, encouraging broader consensus), conviction voting (where influence grows the longer tokens are staked), or reputation-based systems to mitigate power concentration.

Metaverse Governance: Emerging Challenges

The concept of persistent, interconnected virtual worlds raises novel legal and governance questions:

- **Virtual Property Rights:** Defining the legal status of virtual land, assets, and creations represented by NFTs. Are they property, licenses, or something else? How are disputes over ownership resolved? Planet Eta is establishing specialized digital courts and arbitration panels for metaverse disputes.

- **Intellectual Property:** Protecting copyright and trademarks within user-generated metaverse content. Addressing issues of infringement and fair use in virtual environments.

- **User Conduct and Safety:** Moderating behavior
  (harassment, hate speech) in immersive social
  environments. Balancing free expression with user
  safety. Exploring combinations of AI moderation,
  human moderators, and community-based reputation
  systems. Platform liability for user actions is a key
  regulatory question.

- **Interoperability and Data Portability:** Policies
  encouraging the use of open standards (USD, glTF,
  VRM, OpenXR) to allow users to move their avatars,
  assets, and social graph data between different
  metaverse platforms, preventing monopolistic walled
  gardens.

- Planet Eta's approach to blockchain and metaverse
  governance is adaptive, seeking to apply established
  legal principles where possible while creating novel
  frameworks to address the unique challenges and
  opportunities of these decentralized and immersive
  digital realms.

Section 5: Fairness in AI and Blockchain: The Ethical Foundations of Planet Eta's Digital Policies

A core tenet running through all of Planet Eta's technological governance
is a deep commitment to fairness and equity. Recognizing that powerful
technologies like AI and blockchain can inadvertently perpetuate or even
amplify existing societal biases if not carefully designed and governed,
fairness is treated not as an afterthought, but as a foundational design
principle.

Operationalizing Algorithmic Fairness in AI

Beyond the technical metrics and bias mitigation techniques discussed earlier, promoting fairness in AI on Planet Eta involves broader societal and procedural considerations, including

- **Inclusive Design and Development Teams:**
  Regulations and incentive programs encourage diversity (across species, origin, gender, ability, socioeconomic background) within AI development teams. The rationale is that diverse teams are more likely to recognize potential biases, consider edge cases affecting different groups, and design systems that cater to a wider range of users and contexts.

- **Participatory Design and Stakeholder Consultation:**
  For AI systems with significant public impact (e.g., urban planning, social welfare distribution, predictive policing), Planet Eta mandates meaningful consultation with the communities likely to be affected. This involves co-design workshops, feedback sessions, and impact assessments conducted with community representatives, not just about them, to ensure the AI system aligns with their needs and values and avoids unintended negative consequences.

- **Robust Contestability and Recourse:** Fairness requires accountability. Individuals must have effective mechanisms to challenge AI-driven decisions that affect them. This requires more than just transparency; it necessitates

- **Clear Explanations:** Providing understandable reasons for specific decisions (leveraging XAI).

- **Accessible Appeals Processes:** Establishing clear, low-barrier channels for individuals to request human review of automated decisions.

- **Auditability:** Ensuring decisions can be audited to check for procedural fairness and potential biases.

- **Correction Mechanisms:** Ability to correct erroneous data or flawed model outputs.

- **Addressing Intersectional Fairness:** Recognizing that individuals often belong to multiple demographic groups, fairness assessments must consider intersectionality. An AI system might appear fair when evaluated across gender alone and across species alone but exhibit significant bias against individuals at the intersection (e.g., females of a specific minority species). Planet Eta's auditing guidelines require testing for such intersectional biases.

- **Long-Term Equity Impact Assessments:** Moving beyond immediate statistical fairness, regulations encourage forward-looking assessments of how an AI system might impact broader societal equity over time. For example, would an AI hiring tool, even if statistically "fair" in the short term, gradually homogenize the workforce by optimizing for narrow skill sets, thus reducing long-term diversity and opportunity?

411

Ensuring Fairness in Blockchain Ecosystems

While blockchain offers algorithmic transparency, fairness concerns arise in its application and governance:

> **Equitable Access (The Digital Divide):** The benefits of blockchain (DeFi, DID, secure voting) are only realized if people can access them. Policies on Planet Eta focus on ensuring universal access to basic digital infrastructure (connectivity, devices) and promoting digital literacy programs to prevent blockchain from exacerbating existing digital divides based on wealth, location, or technical skill.

> **Fair Governance Models (Beyond Token Voting):** Simple 1-token-1-vote governance in DAOs or blockchain protocols can lead to plutocracy, where wealthy early adopters or large "whales" control decisions. Planet Eta encourages experimentation with, and adoption of, alternative models aimed at fairer representation.

> **Quadratic Voting (QV):** Users buy votes for a proposal, but the cost increases quadratically (1 vote costs 1 credit, 2 votes cost 4, 3 votes cost 9, etc.). This makes expressing strong preference expensive, encouraging broader consensus and giving more weight to widely supported issues over niche interests of the wealthy.

> **Conviction Voting:** Token holders "stake" their tokens toward proposals they support. The longer that tokens remain staked, the more "conviction" (voting weight) they accumulate, favoring sustained support over short-term speculation.

Reputation-Based Systems: Assigning voting power based on contributions, participation, or expertise within the community, rather than just token holdings. Often combined with DIDs and Verifiable Credentials.

Liquid Democracy/Delegative Voting: Users can either vote directly or delegate their voting power to trusted representatives or experts on specific topics.

Smart Contract Audits for Fairness: Security audits (Section 4) are expanded to include checks for potentially unfair or exploitative logic encoded in smart contracts, such as hidden fees, unfair distribution mechanisms, or clauses that disproportionately disadvantage certain users. Standardized, vetted contract templates for common use cases are promoted.

Fair Token Distribution: Scrutiny is applied to the initial allocation mechanisms (Initial Coin Offerings, ICOs; Initial Exchange Offerings, IEOs; airdrops) of new blockchain projects launching on Planet Eta to ensure they are reasonably fair and transparent, preventing excessive enrichment of founders/insiders at the expense of the wider community. Regulations require clear disclosure of tokenomics and distribution plans.

The Nexus: Fair Digital Identity, Access, and Opportunity

Planet Eta sees Decentralized Identity (DID) systems, often leveraging blockchain, as a critical enabler of digital fairness. By empowering individuals with self-sovereign control over their identity data and credentials, DIDs can

> **Combat Centralized Power:** Reduce dependence on large corporations or governments acting as sole identity providers, potentially mitigating censorship or exclusion.
>
> **Enhance Privacy and Reduce Discrimination:** Enable selective disclosure via Verifiable Credentials (VCs), allowing users to prove eligibility (e.g., "is over 18," "is a resident") without revealing sensitive attributes (exact age, address, ethnicity) that could be used for discrimination by AI algorithms or human gatekeepers.
>
> **Provide Foundational Identity:** Offer a pathway for individuals lacking traditional forms of identification (e.g., refugees, marginalized communities) to establish a secure, recognized digital identity, unlocking access to essential services (finance, healthcare, education).

However, the issuance of VCs must itself be equitable. Planet Eta invests in public initiatives to ensure all citizens can obtain foundational VCs (proof of identity, residency, etc.) through accessible and non-discriminatory processes, preventing the DID ecosystem itself from becoming a source of exclusion. Fairness requires ensuring both the technology and the surrounding social systems for credential issuance are equitable.

414

Ultimately, Planet Eta operates on the principle that technology amplifies underlying societal structures and values. Therefore, achieving fairness in AI and blockchain requires not only technical solutions but also a conscious, ongoing societal commitment to embedding principles of equity, inclusion, and justice into the design, deployment, and governance of these transformative digital systems.

Conclusion: Toward a Responsible, Fair, and Secure Digital Future

Planet Eta, as depicted through its governance challenges and innovative responses, embodies a society actively grappling with the profound implications of integrating advanced AI, blockchain, and immersive metaverse technologies. Its journey serves as a rich narrative illustrating the critical importance of establishing proactive, adaptive, and ethically grounded frameworks to guide technological progress. The intricate system of legal regulations, ethical guidelines, oversight bodies, and technological safeguards described in this chapter underscores a societal commitment that extends beyond mere compliance, aiming to actively shape technology toward outcomes that are not only innovative but also fair, transparent, secure, and beneficial to all citizens.

The establishment of the AI Ethics Council, the mandatory AI Governance Registry, the comprehensive Data Protection Code of Eta (DPC-E) with its emphasis on Privacy-Enhancing Technologies like Federated Learning and Decentralized Identity, and the targeted regulations for smart contract security and cryptocurrency oversight collectively represent a holistic approach. This approach recognizes the interconnectedness of these technologies and the need for governance that addresses both specific risks and systemic ethical considerations. The emphasis on fairness—mitigating bias in AI, ensuring equitable access to blockchain systems, promoting fair DAO governance, and enabling privacy-preserving interactions—demonstrates a commitment to preventing digital technologies from exacerbating existing societal divides.

Planet Eta's proactive stance, learning from incidents like the Health AI scandal or education platform breaches, highlights the necessity of continuous vigilance and adaptation. Governance cannot be static in the face of rapidly evolving technology. The promotion of collaboration between public institutions, private industry, academia, and civil society ensures that policies remain relevant, effective, and reflective of diverse stakeholder needs. By championing principles like privacy-by-design, explainability, accountability, and fairness, Planet Eta fosters an environment where public trust can be built and maintained, creating a virtuous cycle where responsible practices enable further innovation.

As our own world increasingly integrates AI, blockchain, and immersive platforms, the fictional yet instructive example of Planet Eta offers valuable insights. It underscores that harnessing the immense potential of these technologies while mitigating their risks requires more than just technical prowess; it demands wisdom, foresight, ethical commitment, and robust governance structures. The future of the digital age depends on our collective ability to navigate these complexities responsibly, ensuring that technological advancement ultimately serves to empower individuals, enhance societal well-being, and build a more just, secure, and equitable world for generations to come. The journey is ongoing, but the principles illuminated by Planet Eta provide a hopeful compass for navigating the uncharted territories ahead.

CHAPTER 8

Planet Vire: The Apex of Digital Realism and Spatial Interaction

Introduction: Planet Vire—Where Digital Mirrors Reality

Our journey through the advanced technological landscapes of this galactic sector now brings us to Planet Vire. While Planet Zeta pioneered the integration of digital twins and AI agents and Planet Eta established robust frameworks for ethical governance, Planet Vire represents the zenith of sensory immersion and hyper-realistic digital experience. Vire is renowned across the systems for its relentless pursuit of blurring the lines between the physical and the virtual, creating digital environments and entities that are almost indistinguishable from reality. This pursuit is not merely an aesthetic endeavor; it is foundational to Vire's economy, culture, and technological identity, driving innovations in fields ranging from

F. Lisitano and J. Hickie, *The Evolune Metaverse*, Maker Innovations Series,
https://doi.org/10.1007/979-8-8688-1588-1_8

advanced simulation and training to entertainment and interpersonal communication. Vire's technological focus lies at the intersection of three critical domains: Hyper-Realism in computer graphics, advanced Spatial Computing interfaces (AR, VR, MR, and beyond), and sophisticated Artificial Intelligence specifically tailored to generate, enhance, and interact within these ultra-realistic digital constructs.

This chapter explores the principles, technologies, and implications of Vire's mastery over digital realism. We will investigate how hyper-realistic virtual worlds are constructed and experienced. We will examine the profound impact this level of fidelity has on digital interaction, delve into the crucial role AI plays in achieving and surpassing photorealism—particularly in conquering the elusive "uncanny valley" of digital human representation—and contemplate the future trajectory of immersive, interactive environments as pioneered on Vire. Prepare to explore a world where the boundaries of the digital dissolve, offering a glimpse into the next generation of truly immersive experiences.

Figure 8-1. *Planet Vire Overview*

Section 1: The Next Generation of Digital Experiences—Hyper-Realism and Spatial Computing

The defining characteristic of Planet Vire's digital landscape is Hyper-Realism. This term signifies more than just high-resolution graphics; it represents a holistic approach to creating digital experiences that replicate the sensory richness, physical consistency, and nuanced complexity of the real world with unprecedented fidelity. Achieving this requires pushing the boundaries of computational graphics, simulation, and the interfaces through which users interact with these digital realms—primarily Spatial Computing.

Defining Hyper-Realism in Digital Contexts

On Vire, hyper-realism encompasses several key dimensions, pursued with meticulous attention to detail.

Visual Fidelity (Photorealism and Beyond)

The goal is visual indistinguishability from reality.

Accurate Light Transport Simulation

Employing techniques like real-time path tracing (simulating billions of light paths) to capture the subtle interplay of light, shadow, reflection, and refraction that defines realistic scenes. This goes beyond basic ray tracing to include effects like multi-bounce global illumination, caustics, and accurate soft shadows (referencing GPU advancements from Chapter 6).

Physically Based Materials

Utilizing sophisticated PBR shaders that model how diverse materials (metals, plastics, skin, cloth, liquids) interact with light based on physical properties, ensuring consistent appearance under all lighting conditions. Vire's material libraries include highly complex, multi-layered definitions.

Uncompromising Geometric Detail

Leveraging virtualized geometry systems (akin to Nanite) and advanced tessellation to render scenes with billions of effective polygons, capturing microscopic surface details without traditional Level-of-Detail (LOD) pop-in artifacts.

Ultra-High-Resolution Texturing and Filtering

Standardizing on 8K+ textures and employing advanced anisotropic filtering to ensure surface details remain crisp even at grazing angles.

Realistic Atmospheric and Environmental Effects

Simulating complex weather phenomena, volumetric clouds, fog, and atmospheric light scattering with physical accuracy.

Cinematic Camera Simulation

Accurately modeling real-world lens properties, including depth of field, bokeh effects, exposure adaptation, and physically accurate motion blur.

Physical Consistency and Simulation

Visual realism must be matched by behavioral realism.

High-Fidelity Physics Engines

Utilizing GPU-accelerated physics engines capable of simulating complex interactions—rigid body dynamics with accurate friction/restitution, large-scale fluid simulations (SPH, LBM), deformable object physics (soft bodies, cloth), and realistic material fracture models—all in real time.

Deterministic and Consistent Simulation

Ensuring simulations run consistently and predictably, crucial for training applications and fair multi-user interactions.

Auditory Realism and Spatialization

Sound is critical for immersion.

Physics-Based Acoustic Simulation

Modeling how sound waves propagate through complex environments, including reflection from surfaces (reverberation), diffraction around objects, and occlusion (muffling). Material properties affect sound absorption and reflection.

Personalized Binaural Audio (HRTFs)

Rendering audio using Head-Related Transfer Functions, often personalized to the individual user's ear shape, to provide highly accurate 3D sound localization (direction and distance).

Nuanced Interactivity and Responsiveness

The hyper-realistic world must react believably.

Low-Latency Interaction Loop

Minimizing the delay between user input (movement, gestures, voice) and the corresponding sensory feedback (visual, auditory, haptic).

AI-Driven Behavior

NPCs and environmental elements exhibiting complex, context-aware, and non-repetitive behaviors driven by advanced AI (see Section 4), contributing significantly to the sense of a living, breathing world.

Enabling Technologies: The Foundation of Vire's Realism

Vire's leadership in hyper-realism is built upon pushing existing technologies to their extremes and pioneering new ones.

Next-Generation GPUs

Custom-designed or top-tier commercially available GPUs featuring thousands of compute cores, specialized RT Cores optimized for high ray throughput, advanced Tensor/Matrix Cores for AI acceleration, and vast amounts of high-bandwidth memory (HBM3 or beyond). Distributed rendering across multiple local or cloud GPUs is common for demanding applications.

Highly Optimized Real-Time Engines

Proprietary or heavily modified commercial engines designed for extreme scalability, efficient path tracing or hybrid rendering, advanced material systems, and tight integration with AI and physics frameworks. Virtualized geometry and texture streaming are standard.

Advanced Asset Creation

Combining high-fidelity 3D scanning (multi-spectral capture, polarized light scanning), AI-driven procedural generation (for textures, materials, base geometries), and expert human artistry to create vast libraries of photorealistic assets.

GPU-Accelerated Simulation

Extensive use of GPU compute (via CUDA, ROCm, Vulkan Compute, etc.) to accelerate physics, fluid, and material simulations, allowing complex effects to run in real-time alongside rendering.

Integrated AI Pipelines

AI models for denoising, upscaling, content generation, and agent behavior are deeply integrated into the rendering and simulation pipelines, often running on dedicated GPU cores.

Spatial Computing: The Window into Hyper-Reality

Experiencing Vire's hyper-realistic creations fully requires immersive interfaces. Spatial Computing hardware on Vire represents the state-of-the-art, including as follows.

Flagship VR Headsets

Devices prioritizing ultimate fidelity.

- **Displays:** Micro-OLED panels achieving >4K resolution per eye, >120Hz refresh rates, HDR support with high peak brightness, and near-full DCI-P3 color gamut coverage.

- **Optics:** Advanced pancake lenses or custom multi-element designs providing wide FoV (>140° horizontal) with edge-to-edge clarity and minimal artifacts.

- **Tracking:** Inside-out tracking supplemented by external sensors for sub-millimeter accuracy; integrated high-speed eye tracking is standard for foveated rendering and interaction.

- **Haptics:** High-fidelity haptic gloves or controllers providing nuanced tactile feedback; experimental full-body suits are available for specialized applications.

Advanced AR/MR Systems

Focused on seamlessly merging digital and physical.

- **Pass-Through MR:** High-resolution, low-latency color video pass-through (using multiple external cameras processed by dedicated chips and the GPU) provides a convincing view of the real world within an opaque headset, allowing for perfect occlusion and lighting integration of virtual objects.

- **Optical See-Through AR:** Next-generation waveguide or projection systems offering brighter images, wider FoV (>70°), better color uniformity, and dynamic focal depth compared to earlier AR glasses. Requires sophisticated real-time calibration to match virtual content to real-world lighting.

- **World Understanding:** Always-on, AI-accelerated SLAM systems continuously map the environment, identify objects and surfaces semantically, understand room layout, and track user position with high precision. Algorithms like ORB-SLAM 3 or custom deep-learning based approaches are common, heavily utilizing GPU/NPU resources.

- **Real-Time Lighting Estimation:** Using headset cameras to analyze real-world light sources and ambient illumination, allowing virtual objects rendered by the GPU to be lit consistently and cast plausible shadows within the physical scene.

Experimental BCIs

Vire's research labs actively investigate noninvasive Brain-Computer Interfaces (see Section 6) aiming for future interaction modalities based on neural signals, potentially bypassing traditional controllers or gestures. Spatial computing transforms hyper-realism from a passive visual spectacle into an interactive, embodied experience. The GPU remains the critical enabler, shouldering the immense computational burden of rendering these high-fidelity visuals while simultaneously processing the complex data streams required for spatial tracking, environmental understanding, and low-latency interaction.

Section 2: Virtual Worlds, Real Impact—How Hyper-Realism Changes Digital Interaction

The pursuit and achievement of hyper-realism on Planet Vire is not merely about visual spectacle; it fundamentally reshapes the quality, nature, and consequences of interactions within digital and mixed-reality environments. When the lines between physical and digital blur, the impact of virtual experiences deepens considerably.

The Power of Presence and Immersion

As defined earlier, presence is the psychological cornerstone of immersive experiences. Hyper-realism is a key driver in achieving and sustaining it.

Believability and Suspension of Disbelief

When a virtual environment consistently adheres to the visual and physical rules of reality (or its own defined ruleset), the user's brain is less likely to encounter cues that break the illusion. Photorealistic lighting, accurate physics, and detailed audio contribute to a subconscious acceptance of the virtual space as "real" for the duration of the experience.

Emotional Resonance

Realistic environments and, crucially, realistic depictions of characters (human or otherwise) can evoke stronger emotional responses. A subtly rendered facial expression on a hyper-realistic avatar can convey emotion far more effectively than a cartoonish counterpart, leading to deeper empathy, engagement, and social connection (or potentially, stronger negative reactions).

Reduced Cognitive Friction

Interacting with abstract or stylized representations requires cognitive effort to interpret symbols and map them to intended actions or meanings. Hyper-realistic environments that mimic familiar physical interactions reduce this friction. Picking up a virtual object that looks and behaves like its real counterpart feels intuitive, allowing users to focus on the task rather than the interface.

Transforming Simulation and Training: Beyond Procedures to Performance

Hyper-realism elevates simulation-based training from procedural practice to nuanced skill development and realistic performance assessment.

High-Stakes Skill Refinement

Surgical Simulation: Vire's hyper-realistic simulators allow not just practicing procedural steps but honing fine motor skills under realistic conditions. Accurate tissue rendering (including subsurface scattering for translucency) and bleeding simulation, coupled with precise haptic feedback simulating instrument resistance, provide invaluable practice for complex maneuvers like suturing delicate tissues or navigating complex anatomy. The realism helps bridge the gap between simulation and actual operating room performance.

Complex Equipment Operation

Training to operate intricate machinery (e.g., deep-space mining equipment, advanced atmospheric processors on Vire) can benefit immensely from hyper-realism. Simulators replicate not just the controls but the visual cues, auditory feedback, and physical sensations (via motion platforms and haptics) associated with real operation, allowing trainees to develop situational awareness and handle emergencies effectively.

Decision-Making Under Pressure

Emergency response or military training simulations on Vire utilize hyper-realism to create intense, stressful scenarios. Realistic visuals (e.g., fire, smoke, injuries), chaotic spatial audio, and interactions with distressed

AI-driven civilians evoke genuine stress responses, allowing trainees to practice decision-making and emotional regulation under conditions that are difficult and dangerous to replicate physically.

Empathy and Social Skills Development

Perspective-Taking

Experiencing a hyper-realistic simulation from the viewpoint of someone with different abilities (e.g., navigating Vire's complex architecture with simulated visual impairment) or facing discrimination can foster deeper understanding and empathy than simply reading about it.

Difficult Conversations

Training modules using hyper-realistic, AI-driven digital humans allow professionals (doctors delivering bad news, managers handling conflicts, diplomats negotiating) to practice sensitive interpersonal interactions, receiving realistic emotional feedback from the AI character and personalized coaching.

Revolutionizing Collaboration and Communication: Achieving True Co-presence

Hyper-realism aims to overcome the limitations of distance and mediation in remote collaboration.

Photorealistic Avatars and Nonverbal Cues

Vire's focus on crossing the uncanny valley (Section 4) enables the creation of highly realistic avatars that accurately reflect users' real-time facial expressions, eye movements, and subtle body language captured via headset sensors and external tracking. Interacting with these avatars in a shared virtual space provides the rich nonverbal cues essential for natural communication, trust-building, and understanding emotional nuance, creating a strong sense of co-presence that approaches face-to-face interaction. GPUs render these complex, dynamically animated avatars for every participant in real time.

Shared Interaction with Realistic Digital Twins

Engineers reviewing a complex engine design, architects walking through a building model, or scientists collaborating on visualizing complex data can do so within a shared VR/MR space, interacting with a single, hyper-realistic digital twin. The ability to point, manipulate, annotate, and discuss the object spatially with high visual fidelity leads to clearer communication and faster problem-solving than screen-sharing 2D representations.

Remote Expertise ("See What I See")

AR systems overlaying hyper-realistic 3D instructions or expert guidance onto a local worker's view become far more effective when the virtual elements are visually indistinguishable from real tools or components, minimizing ambiguity and potential for error.

Redefining Entertainment and Storytelling: Deepening Engagement

The entertainment industry on Vire leverages hyper-realism to create unparalleled experiences.

Interactive Cinematic Experiences

The line between passive film viewing and interactive gaming blurs. Experiences feature real-time rendered visuals matching pre-rendered CGI quality, allowing players to exist within and influence worlds of cinematic realism. Path tracing, advanced character rendering, and large-scale environmental simulation powered by GPUs are key.

Emotional Storytelling

Hyper-realistic characters capable of nuanced emotional expression allow for deeper player connection and more impactful narratives. Interactions feel less like engaging with code and more like engaging with believable beings.

Immersive Live Events

Virtual attendances at concerts, sporting events, or theatrical performances become compelling when the venue, performers (live-captured or as digital doubles), and dynamic crowds are rendered with high fidelity, coupled with accurate spatial audio. Users feel the energy of the event as if physically present.

Next-Generation Location-Based Entertainment (LBE)

Vire's advanced LBE centers offer experiences that are impossible at home, combining large free-roam tracking areas, multi-sensory feedback (wind, heat, smell simulation—Section 11), physical props integrated with the VR/AR experience, and hyper-realistic graphics rendered by powerful on-site GPU clusters, creating truly unique and memorable adventures.

Industrial Metaverse: Precision and Insight

In industrial contexts, hyper-realism enhances the value of digital twins and simulations.

Virtual Commissioning and Inspection

Visually exact digital replicas allow engineers to detect subtle misalignments, potential collision points, or aesthetic flaws in factory layouts or product designs before physical construction or manufacturing begins.

Predictive Maintenance Visualization

Simulating material stress, heat distribution, or fluid flow with high visual fidelity on a digital twin can help engineers intuitively understand potential failure points identified by underlying sensor data or predictive algorithms.

Enhanced Situational Awareness

In complex control rooms (e.g., power grid management, planetary defense), hyper-realistic 3D visualizations of the system state, potentially integrated with AR overlays, can provide operators with clearer and more intuitive situational awareness than traditional dashboards.

Psychological and Societal Impacts: The Double-Edged Sword

The very power of hyper-realism raises critical considerations actively studied and debated on Vire.

The Nature of Experience

When virtual experiences become sensorially indistinguishable from physical ones, how does this affect memory formation, emotional processing, and the perceived value of different types of experiences?

Potential for Maladaptation

Could excessive time spent in perfectly tailored hyper-realistic environments lead to difficulties coping with the imperfections and challenges of physical reality? What are the risks of addiction or escapism?

Ethical Use

How to prevent the use of hyper-realism for manipulation, sophisticated fraud (e.g., hyper-realistic phishing scams), or creating harmful or non-consensual experiences?

Accessibility vs. Fidelity

The immense computational cost of hyper-realism creates an accessibility challenge. How does Vire ensure equitable access, preventing a divide between those who can afford high-fidelity experiences and those who cannot? Is maximum realism always the most desirable goal, or are there applications where stylized or abstract representations are more effective or appropriate? Planet Vire's society actively engages with these questions through public forums, research funding, and regulatory bodies, recognizing that the profound impact of hyper-realism necessitates careful societal navigation alongside technological advancement.

Section 3: AI, Photorealism, and Spatial Computing—The Synergistic Triangle

The pursuit of hyper-realism within immersive spatial computing environments on Planet Vire is increasingly reliant on a powerful synergy between advanced graphics rendering techniques, sophisticated spatial computing interfaces, and, critically, Artificial Intelligence. AI is no longer just an application running within these environments; it is becoming a fundamental building block for creating and enabling them, forming a virtuous cycle where each technology enhances the others.

AI Enabling Photorealism and Beyond: Overcoming Traditional Limits

AI techniques are fundamentally changing how realistic visuals are generated and rendered, often achieving results or efficiency previously unattainable.

Neural Rendering: Learning Reality

Techniques like NeRFs (Neural Radiance Fields) and 3D Gaussian Splatting represent a paradigm shift from explicit geometry (polygons) to learned implicit or explicit volumetric representations.

- **How They Work:** Instead of artists creating meshes and textures, these methods train a neural network (NeRF) or optimize a set of primitives (Gaussian Splatting) based on multiple photographs of a real scene or object. The trained representation implicitly or explicitly captures the complex interplay of light, geometry, and materials. Rendering involves querying this representation along camera rays.

- **Advantages:** Can capture extremely complex details (fine geometry like hair, intricate textures) and view-dependent effects (reflections, iridescence) with stunning realism, often exceeding traditional methods for static scene capture.

- **GPU Role:** Training these models is computationally intensive, requiring weeks on GPU clusters. Real-time rendering (especially for Gaussian Splatting) heavily relies on GPU parallelism for projecting and blending millions of primitives or querying neural networks efficiently. Tensor Cores significantly accelerate the neural network aspects.

- **Vire Application:** Extensively used for creating high-fidelity digital twins of existing locations/objects, virtual heritage preservation, and generating realistic assets for virtual try-ons or e-commerce. Active research focuses on dynamic scenes, editability, and real-time performance scaling.

Generative AI for Scalable Content Creation

Building vast, detailed hyper-realistic worlds requires enormous amounts of content. Generative AI, powered by large models trained on massive datasets (often using GPU clusters), offers tools to accelerate this process.

- **AI Texture and Material Generation:** Diffusion models and GANs can generate high-resolution, tileable PBR texture sets (albedo, normal, roughness, metallic maps) from text prompts ("worn leather," "mossy stone wall") or image examples, providing artists with unique starting points or variations much faster than manual creation. AI models can also predict plausible material parameters based on limited inputs.

- **AI 3D Modeling Assistance:** While still evolving, AI tools (like OpenAI's Shap-E, Luma AI's Genie) can generate basic 3D meshes from text, images, or video. These often serve as starting points ("blockouts") that human artists refine, significantly speeding up the initial modeling phase. Future research aims for direct generation of high-quality, production-ready models.

- **AI Animation and Rigging Tools:** AI assists in automating parts of the laborious animation process, such as generating realistic secondary motion (cloth physics, hair dynamics), creating varied animation cycles (walks, runs), transferring animations between different character skeletons, or even generating basic animations from text descriptions ("a character slumped in defeat"). AI can also assist with the complex process of character rigging (creating the digital skeleton and controls for animation).

- **GPU Role:** GPUs are essential for both training the massive foundation models underlying these generative tools and for running the inference process efficiently enough to be useful within interactive content creation workflows.

AI for Real-Time Rendering Optimization and Enhancement

AI is critical for bridging the gap between the demands of hyper-realism and the limitations of real-time computation.

- **AI Upscaling (DLSS, FSR, XeSS):** As detailed previously, these techniques use neural networks (running on GPU AI cores) to reconstruct high-resolution images from lower-resolution rendering inputs, providing crucial performance boosts needed for high frame rates in demanding VR/AR and ray-traced scenarios. The AI model effectively "learns" how to add detail intelligently.

- **AI Denoising for Ray/Path Tracing:** Real-time ray tracing and especially path tracing produces noisy images with limited samples per pixel. AI denoisers (like NVIDIA NRD or DLSS 3.5 Ray Reconstruction) are trained neural networks that intelligently filter this noise, preserving detail and temporal stability far better than traditional filtering methods, making advanced lighting techniques viable in real time.

- **AI Anti-Aliasing (DLAA):** Uses the same neural network architecture as DLSS but runs at native resolution, focusing solely on producing superior anti-aliasing (smoother edges, reduced temporal shimmering) compared to methods like TAA, leveraging the AI's ability to understand image structures.

AI Enhancing Spatial Computing: Understanding and Interacting with Space

Spatial computing systems need to perceive, understand, and enable interaction within a 3D environment (physical or virtual). AI provides the intelligence layer, accelerated by GPUs and dedicated NPUs (Neural Processing Units).

Robust Real-Time Environment Perception

- **AI-Enhanced SLAM:** Deep learning models improve SLAM robustness by recognizing semantic features (objects, surfaces) instead of just geometric points, making tracking more reliable under challenging lighting or in low-feature environments. AI can also help differentiate between static and dynamic elements in the scene for more stable mapping.

- **Semantic Scene Understanding:** Beyond just mapping geometry, AI models perform 3D scene segmentation, identifying and labeling objects (chairs, tables, walls, people) and surfaces within the mapped environment. This allows virtual objects to interact meaningfully (e.g., placing a virtual cup on a recognized physical table).

- **Real-Time 3D Reconstruction:** AI techniques like Neural Implicit Representations (similar to NeRFs but optimized for real-time updates) can generate dense, detailed 3D meshes of the immediate surroundings from headset sensors, enabling realistic occlusion and interaction between physical and virtual elements in AR/MR.GPU/NPU Acceleration. Running these complex computer vision and deep learning models in real-time requires significant computational power, typically provided by the GPU or dedicated NPUs within the spatial computing device's SoC.

Natural and Intuitive Interaction

AI bridges the gap between human intent and digital action.

- **Advanced Hand/Body Tracking:** Sophisticated AI models (CNNs, Transformers) analyze data from cameras (inside-out tracking) or specialized sensors to track the detailed pose of the user's hands, fingers, and body with high accuracy and low latency, enabling controller-free, gesture-based interaction.

- **Gesture Recognition and Intent Prediction:** AI interprets specific gestures as commands or even predicts user intent based on movement patterns, allowing for more fluid and proactive interfaces.

- **Voice Interaction (NLU):** On-device or edge AI models perform speech-to-text and natural language understanding, allowing users to control applications and converse with AI agents using voice commands. Low latency inference is key for responsiveness.

- **Gaze Interaction:** AI analyzes eye-tracking data not just for foveated rendering but also to determine user attention and enable gaze-based selection or control, offering another hands-free input modality.

Spatially Aware Intelligent Agents

AI agents operating within Vire's spatial environments become significantly more capable.

- **Embodiment and Presence:** Agents represented by hyper-realistic avatars (Section 4) gain a physical (or virtual physical) presence, allowing them to interact with the environment and users spatially (e.g., navigating around objects, making eye contact, using gestures).

- **Contextual Understanding:** Agents leverage the system's real-time environmental understanding. An AI assistant in AR can provide information about the physical object the user is looking at or guide them through a task involving real-world equipment.

- **Proactive Assistance:** By understanding the user's context (location, activity, gaze), agents can offer assistance proactively rather than just reacting to explicit commands.

Spatial Computing As the Canvas for AI-Driven Realism

Spatial computing provides the essential framework where the outputs of AI-driven realism become truly meaningful and interactive.

Delivering Immersion

VR/AR headsets are the delivery mechanism that allows users to be fully enveloped by or seamlessly interact with AI-generated or AI-enhanced hyper-realistic environments. The sense of presence amplifies the impact of AI-driven fidelity.

Providing Rich Context for AI

The constant stream of multi-modal data from spatial computing sensors (cameras, depth sensors, IMUs, eye tracking, microphones, controllers) provides AI systems with an unprecedentedly rich understanding of the user and their environment, enabling more intelligent, adaptive, and relevant responses and behaviors.

Enabling Embodied Interaction

Spatial interfaces allow users to interact with AI systems and AI-generated content using natural body movements, gestures, and gaze, moving beyond keyboards and touchscreens toward more intuitive paradigms. On Planet Vire, this synergistic triangle is fundamental. AI makes hyper-realism achievable and scalable; spatial computing makes hyper-realism immersive and interactive; and the GPU provides the underlying computational horsepower enabling both AI and high-fidelity spatial rendering.

Section 4: Breaking the Uncanny Valley— The Role of AI in Perfecting Digital Realism

Perhaps the most formidable challenge in the pursuit of hyper-realism lies in the creation of convincing digital humans. As artificial representations approach perfect human likeness, observers often experience a sharp sense of unease or revulsion when subtle imperfections remain—a phenomenon known as the "Uncanny Valley." This dip in affinity can instantly shatter immersion and trust. Planet Vire has invested immense resources into understanding and overcoming this valley, with Artificial Intelligence playing the most critical role in bridging the final gap between artificiality and perceived authenticity.

The Intricate Challenges of Digital Human Realism

Creating a digital human that avoids the uncanny valley requires mastering an extraordinary number of interconnected and subtle details.

Skin Appearance and Micro-geometry

Real skin is not a simple surface. Its appearance is dominated by subsurface scattering (SSS), where light penetrates the surface, scatters within translucent layers (epidermis, dermis), and exits at a different point, giving skin its characteristic soft glow. Simulating SSS in real time is computationally expensive. Furthermore, skin possesses intricate micro-geometry—pores, fine wrinkles, vellus hair—that affects how light reflects at a microscopic level. Traditional texturing often fails to capture this complexity convincingly.

Eye Realism, the Window to the (Digital) Soul

Eyes are arguably the most critical feature for conveying life and avoiding the uncanny effect. Key challenges include

- **Material Complexity:** Rendering the sclera (white) with realistic vascularization and subtle wetness (specular reflections from the tear film), the intricate, multi-layered structure and color variation of the iris, and the subtle distortions and reflections/refractions of the cornea.

- **Movement Dynamics:** Replicating tiny, involuntary eye movements (saccades and microsaccades) that constantly occur even when fixating, natural blink rates and durations (which vary with emotion and attention), and realistic pupil dilation/constriction in response to light and emotional state. Static, unmoving, or unnaturally smooth-moving eyes immediately signal artificiality.

Facial Animation: The Complexity of Expression

Human faces utilize dozens of muscles working in concert to produce a vast spectrum of expressions conveying subtle emotional states.

Macro- and Micro-expressions

Replicating not only broad expressions (smile, frown) but also fleeting, often involuntary micro-expressions (lasting fractions of a second) that betray underlying emotions is crucial for authenticity. Traditional animation methods often struggle with this level of nuance.

Dynamics and Timing

The way expressions form, hold, and fade is as important as the peak expression itself. Unnatural timing or robotic transitions are instantly jarring.

Asymmetry

Real facial expressions are rarely perfectly symmetrical; subtle asymmetries add realism.

Hair Simulation and Rendering

Realistic hair involves simulating the complex interactions of tens or hundreds of thousands of individual, translucent strands. Capturing the way light scatters through and reflects off this volume, along with realistic dynamics (movement, collisions, clumping), is notoriously difficult and computationally intensive for real-time applications.

Body Movement, Animation, and Physics

Beyond the face, the entire body must move realistically.

Natural Dynamics

Avoiding stiff, robotic, or "floaty" movement often seen in basic keyframed or motion-captured animation. Capturing nuances of weight shift, balance, anticipation, follow-through, and individual mannerisms is key.

Secondary Motion

Simulating how clothing moves realistically with the body, how muscles subtly bulge and deform under skin, or how fat tissue jiggles adds significantly to realism but requires complex physics simulation or learned models.

Speech Synchronization and Co-articulation

Lip sync must be perfect. Beyond just matching mouth shapes (visemes) to sounds (phonemes), realistic speech involves co-articulation—the way the shape for one sound blends into the next. Facial expressions must also match the emotional tone of the speech.

Behavioral Realism: The Spark of Intelligence

Even a visually perfect digital human will fall into the uncanny valley if it behaves unnaturally. It needs to exhibit contextually appropriate behavior, react plausibly to stimuli, and engage in believable social interactions, driven by sophisticated AI rather than simple, repetitive scripts.

443

AI Techniques Employed on Vire to Bridge the Valley: Data-Driven Authenticity

AI provides powerful tools to learn and replicate these complex details from real-world data, moving beyond the limitations of purely manual creation or rule-based simulation.

AI for Hyper-Realistic Skin and Materials

- **Generative Adversarial Networks (GANs) and Diffusion Models:** Trained on vast libraries of high-resolution, multi-spectral skin scans, these models can generate incredibly detailed PBR texture maps capturing subtle variations in pigmentation, pores, wrinkles, vascularity, and even subsurface scattering parameters, tailored to specific ages, ethnicities, or individuals.

- **Learned SSS Models:** Neural networks can learn efficient approximations of complex light transport within skin layers, enabling faster and more accurate real-time subsurface scattering rendering compared to older analytical models.

AI-Driven Eye Simulation and Gaze

- **Generative Iris Textures:** AI can synthesize unique and highly detailed iris patterns.

- **Learned Gaze Behavior:** AI models trained on extensive eye-tracking data from real human conversations and interactions can generate realistic, context-aware gaze behavior for digital humans, including appropriate saccades, fixation durations, blink rates, and social cues (like mutual gaze or gaze aversion) linked to simulated emotional states. This makes the eyes appear attentive and alive.

AI-Powered Facial Animation and Expression

This is where AI has made perhaps the most dramatic impact.

- **AI Denoising/Retargeting for MoCap:** Neural networks clean up noisy facial performance capture data and accurately transfer captured expressions onto different digital character rigs, preserving subtle nuances.

- **Generative Expression Models:** Models (e.g., based on VAEs, GANs, or Transformers) can synthesize a wide range of realistic facial expressions from various inputs, including

  - **Emotion Labels:** Generating expressions corresponding to "happy," "sad," "angry," etc., with subtle variations

  - **Audio Input:** Generating appropriate expressions based on the emotional tone detected in speech

  - **Text Input:** Generating expressions matching the sentiment or content of dialogue

- **Micro-expression Synthesis:** AI specifically trained to recognize and generate fleeting micro-expressions can layer these onto base animations, adding a crucial layer of subconscious realism.

- **Real-Time Facial Reenactment:** Advanced deep learning techniques allow a target digital face to be driven in real time by a video feed of a source actor's face. The AI learns a mapping between the source actor's expressions and the target rig, transferring the performance with high fidelity, including subtle nuances often missed by traditional marker-based capture. Vire utilizes highly refined versions of this for creating realistic digital actors and avatars.

AI for Realistic Hair: Learned Hair Dynamics

- **Neural networks can learn physics-based models of hair strand interactions and dynamics** from high-fidelity offline simulations or real hair capture, enabling more efficient and realistic real-time simulation of hair movement.

- **AI Grooming Tools:** Assisting artists in creating complex, natural-looking hairstyles by learning patterns from examples.

- **Neural Hair Rendering:** AI techniques are being explored to directly synthesize the appearance of complex hair volumes, potentially bypassing explicit strand simulation for certain scenarios.

AI-Driven Body Animation and Motion: Learned Locomotion Controllers

- **AI models (often using reinforcement learning or imitation learning) trained on large motion capture datasets** can generate natural, responsive character locomotion (walking, running, jumping) that adapts

446

realistically to uneven terrain, obstacles, and user input, avoiding the sliding or robotic look of simpler animation systems.

- **Motion Matching and Synthesis:** Techniques like Motion Matching use large databases of motion clips and intelligently blend between them based on user input and character state to produce highly fluid and naturalistic movement. AI enhances the selection and blending process. Generative models can also synthesize entirely new motions in a learned style.

- **AI for Secondary Animation:** Neural networks can learn to predict and generate realistic secondary motions (cloth simulation, muscle jiggle) based on primary body movement, reducing the need for complex, computationally expensive physics simulations in some cases.

AI for Lip Sync and Expressive Speech

- **Advanced Audio-to-Facial Animation:** State-of-the-art AI models directly map input audio (speech) to highly realistic, synchronized lip movements, jaw motion, tongue positions, and even corresponding facial expressions reflecting the emotional tone of the voice. These often outperform traditional phoneme/viseme mapping, especially for capturing co-articulation effects.

AI for Believable Behavior and Interaction

Making a digital human act humanlike requires sophisticated AI driving its decisions and responses.

- **Advanced Conversational AI:** Integrating large language models (LLMs) fine-tuned for character personality and context allows digital humans to hold extended, coherent, and engaging conversations that go far beyond simple scripted dialogue trees.

- **AI Emotional Models:** Implementing cognitive architectures that simulate internal emotional states based on events, interactions, and personality parameters. These simulated emotions then drive the character's expressions, tone of voice, dialogue choices, and behavioral tendencies, leading to more believable and less predictable interactions.

- **Learned Social Behaviors:** Training AI agents through observation or reinforcement learning to exhibit appropriate social norms in interaction, such as maintaining appropriate eye contact, respecting personal space, turn-taking in conversation, and reacting plausibly to user actions.

The Vire Digital Human Project: A Synthesis

Planet Vire's ambitious "Digital Human Project" exemplifies this AI-driven approach. It integrates

- **Massive Data Acquisition:** Utilizing advanced scanning rigs (light stages, multi-camera setups) to capture unprecedented detail of human appearance (geometry, multi-spectral textures for accurate skin rendering) and behavior (4D capture of facial expressions, body motion, voice under various emotional contexts).

- **Foundation Models for Humans:** Training large-scale AI foundation models specifically on this human data to generate realistic appearance, animation, and basic behaviors.

- **Real-Time AI Inference and Rendering:** Deploying these models within highly optimized real-time rendering engines running on cutting-edge GPUs, capable of synthesizing hyper-realistic digital humans interacting within spatial computing environments.

The resulting digital beings, used in advanced simulations, virtual assistants, entertainment, and as personal avatars, represent Vire's state-of-the-art in crossing the Uncanny Valley. The project's most celebrated achievement is ARIA (Adaptive Realistic Interactive Assistant), a universally recognized digital companion that has become the face of Vire's consumer AI interface. ARIA can seamlessly adapt her appearance, personality, and expertise to match user preferences and needs while maintaining such convincing human characteristics that many users report developing genuine emotional connections. She serves as Vire's cultural ambassador, appearing in educational programs where she inhabits historically significant figures like renowned scientist Dr. Elena Vasquez for immersive history lessons, and has starred in several blockbuster interactive cinema experiences where viewers can directly converse with her character and influence story outcomes through natural dialogue.

Ethical Considerations: The Responsibility of Realism

Successfully creating highly realistic digital humans necessitates confronting profound ethical responsibilities, a major focus of Vire's governance bodies.

Disclosure and Deception

Clear, unambiguous disclosure is mandated when users interact with AI-driven digital humans to prevent deception. Penalties for malicious impersonation using this technology are severe.

Deepfakes and Misinformation

The core technology overlaps significantly with deepfake generation. Vire invests heavily in AI-based detection methods for malicious deepfakes and has strict laws prohibiting their creation and distribution for harmful purposes (fraud, disinformation, non-consensual pornography).

Emotional Attachment and Manipulation

Guidelines govern the design of AI personalities, particularly for virtual companions or assistants, to prevent exploitative emotional manipulation or fostering unhealthy dependency. Regular audits check for addictive or manipulative behavioral patterns.

Bias and Representation

Ensuring the datasets used to train digital humans are diverse and that the resulting creations do not perpetuate harmful stereotypes in appearance or behavior is a critical ongoing effort, involving bias audits and diverse development teams.

Digital Likeness Rights

Establishing clear legal frameworks defining ownership and control over digital replicas based on real individuals, including rights related to consent, compensation, and posthumous use. On Vire, the consensus is that the power to create digital life indistinguishable from reality carries an immense ethical weight, requiring constant vigilance, robust regulation, and societal adaptation.

Section 5: From CGI to Reality—The Future of Immersive, Interactive Environments

The convergence of hyper-realism, advanced spatial computing, and sophisticated AI, as pioneered and refined on Planet Vire, is not merely an incremental improvement in digital experiences; it signals a trajectory toward a future where the very distinction between Computer-Generated Imagery (CGI) and perceived reality becomes increasingly fluid and perhaps, ultimately, irrelevant. This evolution promises to fundamentally reshape human interaction with information, computation, and each other.

The Trajectory Toward Seamless Integration: Key Vectors

Photorealism Becomes Ubiquitous

Driven by continued advances in GPU power (Chapter 6), AI rendering techniques (NeRFs, Gaussian Splatting, AI denoising/upscaling), and material science simulation, achieving photorealistic visual fidelity in real time will transition from a high-end novelty to a baseline expectation for many immersive applications. The focus will shift from achieving realism to scaling it efficiently across vast, dynamic worlds and diverse hardware platforms.

AI-Generated Dynamic and Persistent Worlds

The creation of metaverse-scale environments will move beyond static, manually authored spaces. Procedural Content Generation guided by AI (PCG+AI) will create vast, varied landscapes, cities, and interiors. More profoundly, Generative AI will enable worlds that are dynamic and responsive at a fundamental level. Environments might evolve based on complex simulated ecosystems, weather patterns driven by real-time data, or even collective user actions. Narratives within these worlds could branch and adapt dynamically, with AI generating new plotlines, characters, dialogues, and locations in response to player choices, creating truly unique, emergent experiences. This requires massive cloud GPU resources for both the simulation and the real-time generative AI inference.

Digital Humans Achieving Social Presence

The final hurdles of the Uncanny Valley will likely be overcome through refined AI techniques. Digital avatars and AI non-player characters (NPCs) will achieve not just visual realism but behavioral and emotional realism. They will exhibit nuanced personalities, understand social context, engage in complex conversations (powered by advanced LLMs), express subtle emotions authentically, and build believable relationships with users and each other. This will enable virtual social interactions that feel genuinely present and meaningful, revolutionizing remote work, education, social platforms, and entertainment.

Spatial Computing Dissolves into Reality (AR/MR Dominance)

While VR provides full immersion, the long-term trajectory likely favors Augmented and Mixed Reality (AR/MR) interfaces that seamlessly overlay and integrate digital information and interactive elements onto the user's perception of the physical world. This requires breakthroughs in

- **Hardware Miniaturization:** Creating lightweight, comfortable, all-day wearable glasses with high-resolution, bright displays (micro-OLED/LED, advanced waveguides), efficient processors (low-power GPUs/NPUs), and long battery life.

- **Continuous Environment Understanding:** Robust, low-power AI algorithms constantly mapping, segmenting, and understanding the user's surroundings (SLAM, object recognition, semantic understanding) to enable persistent, context-aware digital overlays.

- **Seamless Integration:** Digital elements perfectly registered, lit, shadowed, and occluded by the physical world, creating the illusion that they are truly part of the environment. The "Metaverse" may ultimately become less of a separate virtual place and more of an intelligent digital layer woven into the fabric of physical reality.

Multi-sensory Immersion Beyond Sight and Sound

Achieving true hyper-realism requires engaging in all senses. Future advancements actively pursued on Vire (Section 11) include

- **Advanced Haptics:** Moving beyond simple vibrations to sophisticated tactile feedback simulating texture, shape, temperature, and force feedback (e.g., via gloves, bodysuits, mid-air haptics).

- **Olfactory and Gustatory Simulation:** Integrating controlled scent and potentially taste simulation into experiences, adding powerful layers of realism and emotional connection (e.g., smelling food in a virtual restaurant, the scent of rain in a simulated forest).

- **Proprioceptive/Vestibular Feedback:** Technologies that provide a convincing sense of body position, movement, and balance within the virtual world (Section 11).

Natural and Intuitive Interaction Paradigms

Interaction will move decisively beyond keyboards, mice, and even controllers.

- **Dominance of Voice, Gesture, and Gaze:** AI-powered natural language understanding, precise hand/body tracking, gesture recognition, and eye tracking will become standard input methods, allowing users to interact with digital systems as naturally as they interact with the physical world.

- **Brain-Computer Interfaces (BCIs):** While still largely experimental, noninvasive BCIs hold the potential for direct neural control or communication, offering ultimate bandwidth and intuitiveness, though fraught with immense technical and ethical challenges (Section 6).

Potential Societal Shifts and Transformations: Life on Vire and Beyond

The widespread adoption of these technologies, as seen on Vire, leads to profound societal shifts.

Redefinition of Work and Collaboration

Physical co-location becomes less critical for many professions. Hyper-realistic virtual workspaces enable true co-presence, facilitating global collaboration. AR guidance transforms frontline work, training, and maintenance. New job roles emerge in designing, managing, and governing these digital realities.

Transformation of Education and Learning

Experiential learning becomes the norm. Students explore complex subjects immersively. They conduct virtual experiments and receive personalized instruction from AI tutors or collaborate with peers across geographical boundaries in shared virtual labs. Skill acquisition through hyper-realistic simulation becomes highly efficient.

Evolution of Entertainment and Social Interaction

Entertainment becomes deeply interactive, personalized, and multi-sensory. Socializing occurs seamlessly across physical and hyper-realistic virtual spaces, potentially strengthening distant relationships but also raising concerns about the nature of purely digital social bonds and potential isolation from physical communities.

Revolution in Healthcare

Remote diagnosis assisted by AI analyzing data from spatially aware sensors, AR-guided robotic surgery, VR-based therapies for mental and physical rehabilitation, and personalized preventative health coaching from AI companions become standard practices.

Merging of Commerce and Experience

Retail blends physical and digital through AR try-ons, virtual storefronts, and personalized product visualizations. Experiences themselves become commodities within the "Cognitive Economy" (Section 10).

New Forms of Art and Creativity

Artists, designers, and storytellers leverage these tools to create entirely new forms of interactive, immersive, and personalized art and narrative experiences that were previously unimaginable.

Challenges and Ethical Considerations on the Horizon: Navigating the Future Responsibly

This transformative potential comes hand-in-hand with significant challenges and ethical dilemmas that societies like Vire must continuously address:

- **The Compute Imperative:** The demand for computational power (especially GPU performance and efficiency) to drive hyper-realism, AI, and spatial computing continues to grow exponentially, requiring ongoing breakthroughs in hardware and distributed systems.

- **Content Scalability:** Manually creating content for potentially infinite virtual worlds is impossible. Reliance on AI generation necessitates robust tools for quality control, artistic direction, and managing potential biases in generated content.

- **Interoperability vs. Walled Gardens:** Achieving an open, interconnected metaverse requires strong commitment to open standards (USD, glTF, OpenXR, etc.) to prevent fragmentation into incompatible, proprietary platforms controlled by a few large entities.

- **Accessibility and the Digital Divide:** Ensuring that the benefits of these powerful technologies are shared broadly and do not exacerbate existing inequalities based on wealth, location, or digital literacy is a critical societal challenge requiring deliberate policy interventions.

- **Privacy in an Omnipresent Digital Layer:** Protecting individual privacy becomes exponentially more complex when interfaces constantly monitor user behavior, environment, and potentially even biometric or neural data. Robust technical safeguards (PETs) and strong data rights regulations (like Vire's DPC-E and cognitive liberty protections) are essential.

- **Misinformation, Manipulation, and Reality Distortion:** The power of hyper-realism, especially for digital humans, creates potent tools for highly convincing disinformation, fraud, and psychological manipulation. Developing effective detection methods, legal frameworks, and societal resilience against these threats is crucial. The potential for users to lose touch with physical reality or develop unhealthy dependencies on virtual environments requires careful study and mitigation strategies.

- **Governance and Adaptation:** Existing legal and ethical frameworks are often ill-equipped to handle the novel challenges posed by AI-driven immersive realities, DAOs, and virtual economies. Governance systems must become more agile, adaptive, and globally coordinated. Planet Vire, as depicted, represents a society actively engaged in this complex balancing act— pushing technological frontiers while simultaneously developing the ethical and regulatory frameworks needed to navigate the consequences. Its journey underscores that the future of immersive environments is not predetermined by technology alone but will be shaped by the choices societies make regarding its development, deployment, and governance.

Transition to Advanced Concepts

Having explored the foundations of hyper-realism on Planet Vire—the visual fidelity, the spatial interfaces, the impact on interaction, and the crucial role of AI in achieving convincing digital humans—we now venture deeper. The following sections delve into the more advanced, often experimental, technologies and societal structures that truly set Vire apart. These represent the bleeding edge where computation, neuroscience, economics, and sensory simulation converge, pushing the very definition of digital experience beyond conventional boundaries. While Sections 1-5 described the established state-of-the-art, Sections 6-12 explore the frontiers Vire is actively pioneering, grappling with technologies that promise unprecedented immersion but also demand profound ethical consideration.

Section 6: Neuromorphic Integration—The Biological Frontier of Digital Realism

Bridging silicon and synapse: this section explores how Vire pioneers direct neural interfaces and biological computing to enhance digital experiences beyond traditional hardware limitations, while navigating the profound ethical implications of connecting mind to machine.

While conventional computing, powered by advanced GPUs and AI accelerators, enables remarkable realism, Planet Vire recognized inherent limitations in replicating the sheer efficiency, adaptability, and nuanced processing of biological nervous systems. This has led to the ambitious Neuromorphic Integration Initiative, aiming to bridge the gap between silicon-based computation and biological cognition. This frontier moves beyond merely simulating reality toward fundamentally altering the interface between mind and machine, enhancing the realism and depth of digital experiences in ways traditional approaches cannot.

Beyond Interfaces: Toward Direct Neural Engagement

Traditional spatial computing interfaces, however immersive, remain external mediators of experience. Vire's initiative explores technologies that interact more directly with the user's neural processes, aiming for a more seamless and intuitive connection between thought, intention, and digital action or perception. This research proceeds cautiously along two main paths, governed by strict ethical protocols emphasizing safety, consent, and reversibility.

Advanced Noninvasive BCIs (Brain-Computer Interfaces)

Vire has significantly advanced noninvasive BCI technology beyond the capabilities commonly found elsewhere, focusing on high-resolution sensing and precise stimulation.

- **Magnetoencephalography-Quantum Sensing (MEG-QS):** Traditional MEG requires bulky, cryogenically cooled SQUID sensors. Vire's MEG-QS utilizes nitrogen-vacancy (NV) centers in diamond—atomic-scale defects whose quantum spin state is sensitive to tiny magnetic fields. Arrays of these room-temperature quantum sensors integrated into lightweight headsets can detect the weak magnetic fields produced by synchronous neural firing with unprecedented spatial (~1-2 mm) and temporal (~1 ms) resolution.

- **How It Enhances Experience:** Real-time decoding of high-resolution MEG-QS data allows interfaces to respond not just to overt commands but potentially to shifts in attention, cognitive load, or emotional state inferred directly from neural activity patterns. This enables interfaces that adapt implicitly and proactively to the user's mental state, enhancing flow and reducing cognitive friction in hyper-realistic environments.

- **Focused Transcranial Ultrasonic Stimulation (FTUS):** While MEG-QS reads brain activity, FTUS provides a way to noninvasively write or modulate it. By using phased arrays of thousands of miniature ultrasonic transducers, FTUS can focus acoustic energy deep within the brain with millimeter precision, temporarily exciting or inhibiting targeted neural populations. Unlike TMS (Transcranial Magnetic Stimulation) which has lower spatial resolution, FTUS offers finer control.

- **How It Enhances Experience:** Carefully calibrated FTUS can potentially evoke subtle sensory qualia (e.g., rudimentary tactile sensations, phosphenes—perceived flashes of light), modulate emotional states (e.g., inducing calmness in therapeutic applications), or enhance specific cognitive functions (e.g., attention, memory consolidation) relevant to the digital experience. It represents an experimental step toward direct neural feedback within immersive environments.

- **Computational Demands:** Decoding real-time MEG-QS data (solving the complex "inverse problem" to map sensor readings to neural sources) and calculating the precise phase and amplitude settings for thousands of FTUS emitters require immense computational power. Vire utilizes specialized neuromorphic co-processors integrated with GPUs to handle these tasks, running sophisticated AI models trained to interpret neural signals and control the stimulation hardware.

Biological-Digital Interfaces (Experimental Frontiers)

Representing a more radical and ethically complex frontier, Vire labs conduct highly regulated research into direct interfaces between living neural tissue and electronic systems:

- **Organoid Neural Networks (ONNs)/"Wetware":** These involve culturing brain organoids—small, self-organizing 3D structures derived from pluripotent stem cells that mimic aspects of brain development and form

461

functional neural networks. When interfaced with micro-electrode arrays (MEAs) or advanced optical recording techniques and coupled to neuromorphic chips, these ONNs can function as biological co-processors.

- **Potential Advantages:** ONNs exhibit forms of plasticity, self-organization, and low-power computation characteristics of biological brains, potentially excelling at tasks involving complex pattern recognition, associative learning, and adaptation that remain challenging for purely silicon-based AI.

- **Relevance to Realism:** Integrating ONNs into the control systems for highly complex digital entities (e.g., advanced AI NPCs) could imbue them with more organic, less predictable, and ultimately more believable behaviors, helping to bridge the final gaps in the uncanny valley. Imagine an AI character whose "mood" is influenced by the emergent activity patterns within its integrated ONN.

- **Synthetic Synaptic Interfaces (SSIs):** Moving beyond electrodes, SSIs aim for molecular-level communication. This involves engineering nanostructures and proteins that can be integrated near or within synapses (the junctions between neurons) to detect neurotransmitter release or modulate synaptic strength electronically or optically.

- **Potential Advantages:** Offers the promise of much higher bandwidth and more naturalistic communication with neural circuits compared to electrodes, potentially allowing for seamless integration of digital information processing with biological neural computation.

- **Current Status:** This research is highly experimental on Vire, focused on fundamental understanding and safety, with significant technical and ethical hurdles remaining before any practical application.

Ethical Framework for Neural Integration

Given the profound implications of these technologies, Vire enforces an extremely stringent ethical framework, overseen by the Planetary Bio-Digital Ethics Committee.

- **Informed and Dynamic Consent:** Participants in any neural interface research or application must provide detailed, ongoing consent, with the ability to withdraw at any time without penalty. Consent protocols must account for the potential difficulty in understanding highly novel technologies.

- **Safety and Reversibility:** Priority is given to noninvasive approaches. Any invasive or biological interface research must demonstrate extremely high safety standards and clear pathways for reversibility or removal without lasting harm.

- **Cognitive Liberty:** Establishing the fundamental right of individuals to control their own mental processes, free from unwanted neural monitoring or manipulation. Strict regulations govern the collection, storage, access, and use of neural data.

- **Transparency:** Requiring clear disclosure of the capabilities and limitations of any BCI or neural interface system used in consumer applications.

- **Prohibition of Augmentation Inequality (Ongoing Debate):** Active societal debate and regulatory exploration around preventing neural interface technologies from creating insurmountable advantages or exacerbating social inequalities.

Section 7: Neuromorphic Computing— Learning from Biology to Enhance Digital Reality

Mimicking the brain's architecture: this section examines how Vire employs brain-inspired computing architectures and spiking neural networks to create more efficient AI systems and more naturally behaving digital entities.

The limitations of traditional von Neumann computer architectures (with separate CPU and memory) become increasingly apparent when trying to simulate the complexity and efficiency of biological intelligence. Planet Vire has invested heavily in neuromorphic computing—designing hardware and algorithms inspired by the structure and function of the brain—as a key enabler for the next generation of hyper-realism and AI.

Spiking Neural Networks (SNNs): Time Matters

Unlike traditional Artificial Neural Networks (ANNs) that typically operate with continuous activation values and process information in synchronous layers, SNNs more closely mimic biological neurons.

- **Spike-Based Communication:** Neurons in SNNs communicate using discrete events called spikes (analogous to biological action potentials). Information is encoded not just in the rate of spikes, but also in their precise timing and patterns.

- **Asynchronous Operation:** Neurons process information and generate spikes based on their internal state and incoming spike timings, without needing a global clock signal for synchronization across the entire network.

- **Temporal Processing:** SNNs are naturally adept at processing information that unfolds over time, making them well-suited for tasks involving real-time sensory input, sequence recognition, and dynamic control.

Neuromorphic Hardware: Architecture Inspired by the Brain

Vire has developed specialized neuromorphic processors or Biomimetic Processing Units (BPUs) optimized for running SNNs efficiently:

- **Massively Parallel Neuron/Synapse Arrays:** These chips contain large arrays of simple processing units representing neurons and programmable connections representing synapses, often implemented using analog or mixed-signal circuits to mimic biological dynamics directly in silicon.

- **Event-Driven Processing:** Computation occurs primarily when spikes arrive or are generated. In periods of low activity, the chip consumes very little power, leading to potentially huge gains in energy efficiency compared to traditional synchronous architectures that clock all units constantly. This is critical for mobile/wearable spatial computing devices.

- **On-Chip Learning Rules:** Hardware often incorporates mechanisms for synaptic plasticity (like Spike-Timing-Dependent Plasticity, STDP), allowing the network connections to strengthen or weaken based on the relative timing of pre- and post-synaptic spikes, enabling on-chip learning and adaptation.

- **Specialized Interconnects:** Communication fabrics designed to efficiently route asynchronous spike events between potentially millions of artificial neurons.

Applications in Hyper-Realism and AI Behavior

Neuromorphic computing on Vire provides key advantages for creating more realistic digital experiences:

- **Efficient Sensory Processing:** SNNs running on BPUs can process visual (e.g., event-based cameras) and auditory data with remarkable efficiency and low latency, mimicking biological sensory pathways. This enables faster, more power-efficient real-time environment understanding for spatial computing and more responsive sensory feedback for users. For example, neuromorphic audio processing can perform complex sound source localization and noise filtering with minimal power draw.

- **Biologically Plausible AI Behavior:** Traditional AI for NPCs often relies on complex behavior trees or reinforcement learning that can sometimes result in predictable or robotic actions. SNNs and neuromorphic approaches allow for modeling AI behavior with more organic, emergent properties:

- **Adaptive Motor Control:** Generating smoother, more natural-looking animations that adapt dynamically to environmental interactions.

- **Context-Aware Decision-Making:** Integrating sensory input and internal state over time to make more nuanced decisions.

- **Realistic Emotional Modeling:** Perhaps the most significant contribution to crossing the uncanny valley is using neuromorphic principles to model emotion:

  - **Limbic System Analogues:** Architectures inspired by brain regions involved in emotion (amygdala, hippocampus, prefrontal cortex) allow for simulating more complex and dynamic emotional states in digital humans, influenced by memory, context, and simulated neurochemistry (neuromodulation).

  - **Subtle Behavioral Manifestations:** These simulated emotions drive subtle, realistic changes in facial micro-expressions, posture, gaze patterns, vocal prosody, and even simulated physiological responses (breathing, flushing) rendered on the avatar, making the character feel genuinely responsive and alive rather than just acting.

  - **Emotional Contagion:** Implementing models where digital humans subtly mirror or react to the user's detected emotional state (via facial expression analysis or BCI input), creating a powerful sense of rapport and connection. By moving toward computational models that more closely resemble biological intelligence, Vire aims to create digital entities and environments that are not just visually realistic, but feel fundamentally more natural and alive.

Section 8: Hyper-Personalized Experiences—Tailoring Reality to the Individual

Reading the mind's preferences: this section explores how Vire uses advanced sensing and AI to create digital experiences that adapt in real-time to each user's cognitive state, emotional responses, and individual preferences, while maintaining strict ethical boundaries.

Planet Vire's mastery of digital realism extends beyond creating universally convincing environments to crafting experiences that are deeply personalized, adapting in real time to the unique cognitive and emotional landscape of each individual user. This hyper-personalization aims to maximize engagement, learning, therapeutic benefit, or entertainment value by aligning the digital experience with the user's implicit preferences, cognitive style, and current state.

Cognitive Profile Mapping: Understanding the User Within

The foundation for hyper-personalization lies in sophisticated, noninvasive techniques for building a dynamic cognitive-emotional profile of the user:

- **Implicit Preference and Engagement Detection:** Moving beyond explicit likes or ratings, Vire systems analyze subtle physiological and behavioral cues:

- **Micro-expression Analysis:** High-speed cameras integrated into headsets track fleeting facial muscle movements indicative of subconscious emotional reactions (surprise, confusion, delight, frustration) to elements within the experience. AI models interpret these micro-expressions.

- **Gaze Pattern Analysis:** Advanced eye tracking measures not just where the user is looking, but how they are looking—dwell times on objects of interest, saccade patterns indicating exploration or search, pupil dilation changes correlated with arousal or cognitive load. These patterns reveal implicit interest and engagement levels.

- **Autonomic Nervous System Responses:** Integrated sensors (e.g., photoplethysmography (PPG) for heart rate variability, electrodermal activity (EDA) for arousal/stress) monitor physiological signals that reflect emotional states, providing objective measures of engagement and affective response.

- **Neural Correlates (via BCI):** Experimental MEG-QS systems (Section 6) can potentially identify neural signatures associated with attention, reward processing, cognitive load, and specific emotional states, offering the most direct (though still interpretive) window into the user's internal experience.

- **Cognitive Style Assessment:** AI models analyze interaction patterns and performance on specific tasks within the digital environment to infer individual cognitive styles:

  - **Information Processing Preferences:** Identifying whether a user learns or interacts more effectively through visual, auditory, kinesthetic, or symbolic representations.

  - **Cognitive Load Monitoring:** Estimating the user's current mental workload based on interaction speed, error rates, physiological signals, or BCI data, allowing the system to adjust information density or task difficulty accordingly.

  - **Learning Rate and Style Identification:** Adapting educational content delivery (pacing, modality, type of feedback) based on identifying the user's optimal learning patterns.

- **Memory Dynamics Modeling:** Understanding how individual users form and retain memories allows for optimizing information delivery:

  - **Personalized Knowledge Graphs:** Mapping the user's existing knowledge structures and semantic associations to present new information in a way that connects optimally with what they already know.

  - **Spaced Repetition Optimization:** Tailoring the timing of information review based on models of the individual's forgetting curve to maximize long-term retention (used in educational and training applications).

- **Emotional Context for Memory:** Identifying the types of emotional contexts (e.g., excitement, curiosity, narrative tension) that most effectively enhance memory encoding for a particular user and leveraging these within learning or storytelling experiences.

Dynamic Content Generation and Real-Time Adaptation

The cognitive-emotional profile serves as an input for AI systems that dynamically tailor the digital experience in real time.

- **AI-Driven Narrative and Environment Adaptation: Emotional Arc Pacing**

  - **Generative AI systems controlling narrative experiences** can adjust plot developments, character interactions, environmental ambiance (lighting, music), and pacing based on the user's detected emotional state, aiming to maintain optimal engagement, tension, or achieve specific therapeutic goals.

  - **Personalized Aesthetics:** AI can generate variations in visual style, sound design, or even architectural layouts within virtual environments based on the user's inferred aesthetic preferences.

  - **Adaptive NPC Behavior:** AI companions or characters subtly adjust their personality, dialogue style, level of assistance, or emotional responses to build better rapport and cater to the user's interaction style.

- **Cognitive-Emotional State Synchronization:** Aligning the demands and stimuli of the digital experience with the user's current internal state:

    - **Flow State Induction/Maintenance:** In games or skill-based tasks, AI dynamically adjusts the difficulty level based on performance and cognitive load metrics to keep the user in the optimal "flow channel" between boredom (too easy) and anxiety (too hard).

    - **Adaptive Assistance:** Providing hints or simplifying tasks when high cognitive load or frustration is detected; increasing challenge or complexity when the user shows signs of mastery or boredom.

    - **Emotional Regulation Interfaces:** In therapeutic contexts, the system might gently modulate sensory input (e.g., calming visuals, soothing audio) in response to detected user stress or anxiety, helping them practice regulation techniques.

- **Privacy-Preserving Population-Level Learning:** While personalization is individual, insights are often derived from population data using privacy-preserving techniques:

    - **Federated Learning for Personalization Models:** Training the underlying AI models that drive personalization across many users via Federated Learning (Section 3), so the system learns general patterns of preference and response without centralizing individual sensitive cognitive profiles.

- **Clustering and Collaborative Filtering:**
  Identifying groups of users with similar cognitive-emotional profiles to provide reasonable initial personalization for new users ("Users like you also enjoyed…") before a detailed individual profile is built.

Ethical Frameworks for Hyper-Personalization on Vire

The power to map and adapt to a user's inner world carries immense ethical responsibility. Vire's governance includes specific safeguards:

- **Cognitive Data Rights and Granular Consent:** Users have explicit legal rights over their cognitive-emotional profile data. Consent systems are highly granular, requiring users to opt-in specifically for different types of data collection (e.g., eye tracking, EDA, inferred emotional state) and different uses (e.g., experience adaptation, research, targeted content recommendation). Users can review and revoke consent easily.

- **Transparency of Adaptation:** While the adaptation should feel seamless, systems must provide users with ways to understand how and why the experience is being personalized upon request, preventing hidden manipulation.

- **Anti-Manipulation Audits:** Independent audits specifically check personalization algorithms for patterns indicative of psychological manipulation, exploitation of cognitive biases, or intentionally addictive designs. Systems promoting harmful behaviors or extreme viewpoints through personalization are prohibited.

- **Serendipity and Diversity Exposure:** To counteract the creation of "filter bubbles" where users are only exposed to content matching their inferred preferences, regulations mandate that personalization systems incorporate mechanisms for introducing novel, diverse, or challenging content occasionally, promoting exploration and preventing cognitive narrowing.

Hyper-personalization on Vire aims to create digital experiences that are not just realistic but deeply resonant and effective, adapting not just to user actions but to their very state of mind, while navigating the complex ethical landscape this capability entails.

Section 9: Distributed Reality Simulation— The Technological Infrastructure of Vire

The invisible foundation: this section examines the sophisticated distributed computing architecture that enables Vire's massive, persistent, and personalized virtual worlds, from edge devices to planetary-scale cloud systems.

Delivering hyper-realistic, hyper-personalized, persistent, and massive multi-user digital experiences requires a computational and networking infrastructure far beyond traditional client-server or even basic cloud models. Planet Vire has pioneered a Distributed Reality Simulation architecture, a multi-layered, intelligent infrastructure designed to manage complexity and scale efficiently.

Multi-scale Computational Architecture: Edge-Core-Cloud Continuum

Vire's infrastructure avoids centralizing all computation. Instead, it distributes processing across a continuum:

- **Neuromorphic Edge Processing:** User-worn devices (headsets, glasses, wearables) incorporate powerful, highly efficient neuromorphic co-processors (BPUs, Section 7) alongside mobile GPUs/NPUs. These handle tasks requiring ultra-low latency.

    - **Sensor Fusion:** Processing data from cameras, IMUs, eye trackers, microphones, biosensors in real-time.

    - **Basic SLAM/Tracking:** Performing initial pose estimation and local environment mapping.

    - **Interaction Processing:** Detecting hand gestures, voice commands, basic object interactions.

    - **Minimal Rendering/Display:** Handling final display output, potentially compositing locally rendered elements with streamed content.

- **Local Core Nodes (Fog/MEC):** More powerful compute nodes distributed geographically within cities, buildings, or even homes (Multi-access Edge Computing, MEC). These handle tasks for users within their vicinity:

    - **Area-Specific Simulations:** Managing detailed physics, AI behavior, and persistent state for a local area (e.g., a virtual marketplace, a collaborative workspace).

475

- **Multi-User Coordination:** Synchronizing interactions between multiple users within the same local space.

- **Intermediate Rendering/Caching:** Potentially performing more complex rendering tasks or caching frequently accessed data closer to users.

- **Planetary Scale Cloud:** Massive data centers equipped with hyperscale GPU clusters and large neuromorphic systems handle tasks requiring enormous resources or global consistency:

  - **Global World State Management:** Maintaining the persistent state of the entire shared virtual world.

  - **Large-Scale AI Model Training:** Training the foundation models for graphics, AI behavior, personalization, etc.

  - **Complex Simulation Offload:** Running computationally intensive simulations (e.g., planet-wide weather, large-scale economic models) whose results influence local experiences.

  - **High-Fidelity Cloud Rendering/Streaming:** Rendering complex scenes on demand for users on lower-power devices.

Dynamic Resource Allocation and Orchestration

A sophisticated AI-driven orchestration layer manages this distributed infrastructure as follows:

- **Attention-Based Prioritization:** The system dynamically allocates more compute and network resources to areas and objects that users are actively perceiving or interacting with. Unobserved or distant areas might be simulated at lower levels of fidelity or frequency. Eye-tracking data plays a crucial role here.

- **Predictive Pre-computation and Caching:** AI models predict likely user movements, interactions, or data needs and proactively pre-load assets, pre-render views, or allocate compute resources to minimize perceived latency.

- **Foveated Computing:** Extending the foveated rendering concept, not just rendering but also simulation (physics, AI) can be performed at higher fidelity in the user's attentional focus area and lower fidelity elsewhere, optimizing overall resource usage.

- **Peer-to-Peer (P2P) Augmentation:** Allowing users' devices to opportunistically share computational load for highly localized interactions, reducing reliance on core or cloud nodes for certain tasks:

  - **Collaborative Rendering/Simulation:** Devices of users in close proximity in a shared virtual space might directly share rendering tasks or synchronize physics for objects they are jointly interacting with.

  - **Mesh Intelligence Networks:** Forming temporary, ad hoc P2P networks for specific tasks requiring very low latency local communication (e.g., coordinating complex multi-user construction).

,

Advanced Data Transport and Synchronization

Moving and synchronizing the vast amounts of data required for hyper-realistic distributed simulation necessitates novel techniques beyond simple data transfer:

- **Neural Compression Systems:** AI-powered compression that understands the perceptual significance of data.

  - **Perceptual Lossy Compression:** Prioritizing high fidelity for data crucial to human perception (e.g., faces, areas of focus) while more aggressively compressing less critical data (e.g., distant background textures, imperceptible physics variations).

  - **Semantic Compression:** Transmitting high-level descriptions or commands (e.g., "place a standard Vire chair here") instead of full geometry/texture data, allowing the receiving end to reconstruct the details using local AI models or asset libraries.

  - **Model-Based Delta Transmission:** For known objects or systems, only transmitting the differences (deltas) from a locally stored base model or predicted state, significantly reducing data volume.

- **Predictive State Synchronization:** Minimizing the need for constant state updates across the network.

  - **Client-Side Prediction:** Each client runs local models predicting the behavior of remote objects and avatars based on their last known state and physics/AI models.

- **Dead Reckoning:** Extrapolating future states based on current velocity and acceleration.

- **Eventual Consistency with Correction:** Clients primarily interact with their locally predicted state for low latency. The system only sends explicit correction updates when the actual state deviates significantly from the prediction, ensuring eventual consistency across all viewers. Sophisticated algorithms manage resolving conflicting states.

- **Quantum-Secured Communication (Experimental):** For highly sensitive state synchronization or command channels (e.g., financial transactions, critical infrastructure control within the simulation), Vire explores Quantum Key Distribution (QKD) to ensure theoretically unbreakable communication security.

- **Causality Enforcement:** Maintaining a consistent sense of cause-and-effect across a distributed system with inherent network latencies is complex. Vire employs logical clocks, timestamping protocols, and potentially compensatory latency techniques to ensure interactions resolve in a plausible order for all participants.

The Planetary Reality Engine: A Unified Framework

Overseeing this entire distributed system is Vire's Planetary Reality Engine (PRE), a conceptual framework and set of core services ensuring consistency and interoperability, including

479

- **Standardized Digital Physics:** Defining a baseline set of physical laws, material properties, and simulation algorithms used across interconnected Vire experiences, ensuring objects behave consistently when moving between different virtual worlds or applications (unless explicitly designed otherwise). Automated Reality Coherence Verification systems constantly check for and flag physical inconsistencies.

- **Persistent World State Management:** Utilizing highly scalable, distributed databases (potentially leveraging novel storage technologies) to maintain the state of persistent virtual environments over long periods, tracking changes and enabling historical playback or "time travel" within simulations. Autonomous Evolution Systems (AI-driven) can continue simulating environmental changes (e.g., plant growth, erosion) even when regions are unobserved by users.

- **Digital Geographic Information System (DGIS):** A planet-wide spatial indexing system that precisely maps both physical locations and purely virtual spaces, enabling

  - **Accurate Reality Anchoring:** Tying virtual objects and information layers precisely to physical coordinates for seamless AR/MR experiences.

  - **Parallel Reality Support:** Allowing multiple, distinct virtual overlays or layers to coexist over the same physical space, accessible by different users or applications.

- **Cross-Reality Navigation:** Defining pathways and portals allowing users to move fluidly between physical reality, augmented layers, and fully virtual worlds while maintaining a consistent sense of location and orientation. This sophisticated distributed infrastructure is the invisible foundation enabling the scale, fidelity, and responsiveness of Planet Vire's hyper-realistic digital experiences.

Section 10: The Cognitive Economy—New Value Systems in Hyper-Realistic Environments

Beyond time and clicks: this section examines how Vire has developed new economic models that value attention quality, cognitive impact, and experiential depth, creating markets where mental engagement becomes a measurable and tradeable resource.

The deep immersion and personalized nature of experiences on Planet Vire, coupled with advanced monitoring capabilities, have catalyzed the emergence of a unique Cognitive Economy. This economic system moves beyond traditional metrics of production, consumption, or even engagement time, assigning tangible value to attention, creativity, subjective experience, and cognitive/emotional impact.

Attention As a Quantifiable and Tradable Resource

In information-rich digital environments, user attention is the scarcest resource. Vire has developed systems to measure and value it directly:

- **Neural Engagement Metrics:** Moving beyond clicks or view time, Vire employs noninvasive sensing (eye tracking, physiological monitoring via wearables, potentially BCI data where consented) combined with AI models to quantify the quality and depth of user engagement.

  - **Focus Intensity:** Measuring sustained attention versus distraction.

  - **Cognitive Load:** Assessing the mental effort involved in processing information.

  - **Emotional Resonance:** Quantifying the strength and valence (positive/negative) of emotional responses evoked by the experience.

  - **Memory Encoding Strength:** Estimating the likelihood of an experience forming a lasting memory based on engagement patterns and emotional markers.

- **Attention Markets and Rights Management:** These objective metrics enable new economic models:

  - **User Control and Compensation:** Vire law recognizes Attention Rights, allowing individuals to control how their attention data is used and to be directly compensated (e.g., via micro-payments in EtaCoin or other tokens) by platforms or creators who benefit from their focused engagement. Transparent dashboards show users how their attention is being "spent" and earned.

- **Attention Exchanges:** Platforms where creators or advertisers can bid for high-quality user attention directed toward specific content or experiences, with value determined by engagement metrics rather than just exposure.

- **Predictive Attention Markets:** Future markets allowing stakeholders to speculate on or hedge against the anticipated engagement levels for upcoming experiences or products, influencing investment and resource allocation.

Valuing Creativity and Experiential Impact

The Cognitive Economy shifts value creation toward the design and delivery of impactful experiences:

- **Cognitive Experience Design (CXD):** An established profession on Vire, blending expertise from art, narrative design, game design, neuroscience, psychology, and AI.

  - CXD professionals specialize in

    - **Emotional Arc Crafting:** Designing experiences to guide users through specific emotional journeys (e.g., for therapeutic applications, compelling storytelling, or brand building).

    - **Flow State Optimization:** Creating activities that dynamically adjust challenges to maintain user engagement and facilitate skill acquisition.

- **Memory Engineering:** Designing experiences using principles of cognitive psychology (e.g., spaced repetition, emotional salience, narrative coherence) to maximize long-term retention and positive recall.

- **Sensory Harmonization:** Orchestrating visual, auditory, haptic, and even olfactory/gustatory stimuli (Section 11) to create unified and impactful multi-sensory experiences.

- **AI-Human Creative Collaboration:** AI tools become partners in the creative process:

  - **Neural Feedback Loops:** Tools provide creators with real-time predictions (based on aggregate anonymized data) of how design choices might impact user cognitive and emotional responses, allowing for rapid iteration.

  - **Semantic Ideation Partners:** AI systems help brainstorm and elaborate on creative concepts based on high-level goals or prompts, suggesting variations while preserving the creator's core vision.

  - **Automated Personalization Frameworks:** AI handles the low-level adaptation of experiences to individual user profiles (Section 8), freeing human creators to focus on high-level design and narrative.

- **Impact-Based Compensation:** Creator compensation models move beyond simple sales or subscriptions:

  - **Neural Copyright and Attribution:** AI systems analyze the unique cognitive/emotional signature of an experience to identify its creators and ensure proper attribution and royalty distribution, even for derivative works.

- **Engagement-Weighted Revenue:** Revenue sharing based on validated metrics of deep engagement and positive emotional/cognitive impact, rather than just time spent or ad views.

The Experience Archive and Experiential Markets

Subjective experiences themselves gain value within this economy:

- **High-Fidelity Experience Recording:** Utilizing advanced BCI and sensor technology (Section 6), Vire enables the capture of rich experiential data—not just sensory input but associated cognitive states, emotional responses, and even internal thought patterns (with explicit consent).

- **Curated Experience Libraries:** Vast archives (like Vire's "Chronos Archive") store significant recorded experiences: historical events witnessed firsthand, explorations of unique environments (real or virtual), mastery of complex skills, profound artistic performances, etc. These archives serve educational, historical, and entertainment purposes.

- **Experience Markets:** Platforms emerge where users can

    - **Access Recorded Experiences:** Experience events or perspectives they couldn't access otherwise (e.g., experiencing zero gravity, seeing through an animal's eyes, understanding a complex scientific concept from an expert's perspective).

485

- **Share or License Personal Experiences:**
  Individuals can choose to share or license access
  to recordings of their own unique skills or life
  experiences, creating new forms of income.

- **Therapeutic Experience Access:** Accessing
  curated experiences designed for mental health
  benefits (e.g., guided meditations with biofeedback,
  simulations for overcoming trauma).

- **Governance of Experiential Data:** Strict regulations
  govern consent, privacy, ownership, and potential
  misuse of recorded subjective experiences. Experiential
  Data Trusts—collective organizations—often
  manage sensitive archives with ethical oversight. The
  Cognitive Economy on Vire represents a fundamental
  shift, recognizing that in a world saturated with
  information and simulated reality, the true value lies
  in attention, creativity, and the quality of subjective
  experience itself.

Section 11: Beyond Visual and Auditory— The Complete Sensory Simulation

Engaging all senses: this section explores Vire's cutting-edge research into haptic feedback, thermal simulation, olfactory and gustatory interfaces, and full-body sensory integration to create truly comprehensive sensory experiences.

While visual and auditory realism form the bedrock of immersion, Planet Vire's pursuit of hyper-realism extends to engaging all human senses, aiming for a complete sensory simulation that replicates the richness of physical interaction with unprecedented fidelity. This requires venturing into the challenging domains of touch, temperature, smell, and taste.

Advanced Haptic Systems: Feeling the Digital World

Haptics—the science of touch—is crucial for making virtual objects feel solid and interactions tangible. Vire employs technologies far beyond simple controller rumble. Examples include

High-Resolution Tactile Feedback

Simulating texture, pressure, and shape.

- **Electrostatic Tactile Displays:** Applying varying electrostatic fields to a surface (e.g., a screen or glove) to modulate friction as the user's finger moves across it, creating surprisingly realistic sensations of different textures without moving parts.

- **Ultrasonic Haptics:** Using phased arrays of ultrasonic transducers to focus acoustic pressure waves in mid-air, creating tactile sensations (like points, lines, or textures) directly on the user's bare skin without needing gloves or controllers. Useful for buttons, alerts, or subtle environmental effects.

- **Microfluidic Haptic Arrays:** Integrating networks of microscopic fluid channels and actuators into flexible surfaces (like gloves). By precisely controlling fluid pressure and flow, these arrays can create highly localized and dynamic pressure patterns, simulating complex shapes and textures felt by the fingertips or palm.

487

- **Electrotactile Stimulation:** Applying controlled electrical currents to the skin via electrode arrays to directly stimulate nerve endings, capable of evoking a wide range of tactile sensations (pressure, vibration, texture, potentially even thermal illusions) with high resolution but requiring careful calibration.

Force and Resistance Feedback

Simulating the weight, inertia, and resistance of virtual objects.

- **Exoskeletal Gloves/Arms:** Wearable robotic structures that apply controlled forces to the user's fingers, hand, or arm, resisting movement to simulate grasping solid objects, feeling weight, or encountering resistance. These range from lightweight finger-tracking gloves with resistance to full-arm exoskeletons for industrial simulations. Miniaturization and reducing bulk remain challenges.

- **Magnetorheological Fluids/Actuators:** Using fluids that change viscosity dramatically in response to a magnetic field, integrated into gloves or controllers to provide variable resistance.

- **String-Based Haptics:** Systems using multiple actuated strings attached to fingertips or controllers to provide programmable force feedback within a limited workspace.

Thermal Simulation

Adding temperature sensations enhances realism significantly.

- **Peltier Element Arrays:** Integrating dense arrays of small thermoelectric coolers (Peltier devices) into gloves or interaction surfaces. These solid-state devices can rapidly heat or cool locally when electricity is applied, simulating contact with hot or cold virtual objects. Power consumption and heat dissipation are challenges.

- **Microfluidic Thermal Systems:** Circulating temperature-controlled fluids through channels in wearables to provide broader heating or cooling sensations, simulating environmental temperatures or contact with larger thermal masses.

- **Focused Infrared Emitters:** Using directed IR beams to create sensations of radiant warmth on the skin from virtual sources like fire or sunlight, without direct contact.

Chemical Sensory Simulation: The Final Frontiers of Smell and Taste

Simulating olfaction (smell) and gustation (taste) is perhaps the most complex challenge due to the intricacies of chemoreception, but Vire has made significant experimental progress, including

Olfactory Simulation (Digital Scent)

- **Chemical Cartridge Systems:** Devices containing cartridges of various base aromatic chemicals. By precisely mixing and releasing controlled amounts of these base scents near the user's nose, a wide spectrum of smells can be synthesized. Challenges include the number of base chemicals needed, rapid switching between scents without lingering odors, and safe delivery.

- **Direct Neural Stimulation (Experimental):** Research into noninvasively stimulating the olfactory bulb or related neural pathways (e.g., via focused ultrasound or targeted electrical fields) to evoke scent percepts without releasing chemicals, though this remains highly complex and experimental.

- **Contextual Enhancement:** Using visual and auditory cues to enhance or bias the perception of limited synthesized scents (e.g., seeing a flower while receiving a basic floral scent compound enhances the perceived realism).

Gustatory Simulation (Digital Taste)

Even more challenging than smell.

- **Electrotactile/Thermal Stimulation on Tongue:** Applying specific electrical currents or temperature changes to different parts of the tongue via small electrodes can evoke basic taste sensations (salty, sour, potentially sweet/bitter) and thermal illusions (like the "coolness" of mint).

- **Controlled Chemical Release:** Micro-dispensing systems releasing tiny, controlled amounts of edible, safe chemical compounds directly onto the tongue to simulate specific flavor components. Requires complex delivery mechanisms and safety protocols.

- **Cross-Modal Illusions:** Leveraging smell (which contributes heavily to flavor perception) and visual cues (seeing virtual food) to create more convincing taste illusions from limited direct gustatory stimulation.

Proprioception and Vestibular Simulation: The Sense of Self in Space

Beyond external senses, immersion requires simulating our internal senses of body position (proprioception) and balance/motion (vestibular system).

Balance and Motion Simulation

- **Galvanic Vestibular Stimulation (GVS):** Applying small electrical currents to the skin near the mastoid bones behind the ears can stimulate the vestibular nerves, creating illusory sensations of tilting, acceleration, or rotation. Used carefully, it can enhance the feeling of motion in VR but can also easily cause discomfort or disorientation if not perfectly synchronized.

- **Motion Platforms:** Physical platforms that tilt and move the user in sync with virtual motion (common in high-end simulators). Provide strong motion cues but are expensive and require significant space.

491

- **Locomotion Interfaces:** Devices like omni-directional treadmills or specialized footwear that allow users to physically walk or run in place while moving through the virtual world, providing more natural vestibular and proprioceptive feedback than controller-based movement.

Embodiment and Body Schema

Creating a convincing feeling of inhabiting a virtual avatar.

- **Visuomotor and Visuotactile Synchrony:** Ensuring that when the user moves their physical limbs, their virtual avatar's limbs move identically and instantaneously, and that haptic feedback aligns perfectly with visual contact points (e.g., feeling a vibration exactly when the virtual hand touches a virtual surface). This synchrony is critical for the Rubber Hand Illusion and similar embodiment effects.

- **Proprioceptive Targeting:** Using subtle haptic feedback or potentially BCI stimulation (experimental) to provide feedback consistent with the virtual avatar's pose, helping the user's brain adapt their internal body map (body schema) to match the avatar, even if its proportions differ slightly from their physical body. Vire's commitment to multi-sensory simulation aims to create digital experiences that are not just seen and heard, but felt, smelled, tasted, and embodied, achieving a level of immersion that truly rivals physical reality.

Section 12: The Future Beyond Vire—From Simulation to New Realities

Transcending boundaries: this final section contemplates the ultimate implications of Vire's technologies, exploring potential futures where the distinction between physical and digital reality dissolves, and humanity faces profound questions about consciousness, identity, and the nature of existence itself.

As we conclude our exploration of Planet Vire's remarkable achievements in digital realism, spatial computing, AI, and sensory simulation, we inevitably turn our gaze toward the horizon. The technologies pioneered and perfected on Vire are not merely endpoints; they are stepping stones toward futures that challenge our fundamental understanding of reality, experience, and consciousness itself.

The Dissolution of Boundaries: Physical, Digital, Biological

The relentless trajectory observed on Vire points toward an era where the traditional distinctions between the physical world, digital information, and biological systems become increasingly blurred and ultimately synthesized:

- **Physical-Digital Integration ➤ Synthesis:** Moving beyond AR overlays to a world where digital capabilities are embedded within physical matter.

  - **Computational Matter/Programmable Matter:** Hypothetical materials composed of microscopic computing elements (nanites or "smart dust") that can dynamically alter their physical properties (shape, color, texture, conductivity) based on digital instructions. Imagine buildings that reconfigure their layouts, clothes that change style instantly, or tools that adapt their form to the task at hand, seamlessly merging digital design with physical manifestation.

- **Ambient Intelligence Environments:** Physical spaces (homes, cities, workplaces) where sensing, computation, and actuation are invisibly embedded throughout the environment, rather than residing in discrete devices. The environment itself becomes the interface, anticipating user needs and adapting proactively based on context and behavior, powered by distributed AI and sensor networks.

- **Biodigital Convergence:** The cautious yet progressive integration of digital systems directly with biological processes.

  - **Advanced Neural Interfaces:** Moving beyond current BCI research toward interfaces (potentially based on SSIs or advanced neuromorphic designs) that allow for high-bandwidth, bidirectional communication between the human brain and digital systems, feeling as natural and intuitive as internal thought.

  - **Computational Biology Integration:** Using digital twins not just to model but potentially to interact with and guide biological processes at cellular or molecular levels (e.g., personalized medicine delivery systems integrated with real-time biological monitoring).

Experience-Reality Entanglement: Redefining "Real"

As simulated realities achieve near-perfect sensory fidelity and deep personalization, the very definition of "reality" becomes more complex and subjective:

- **Consensus Realities:** Shared, persistent, hyper-realistic virtual environments could become primary spaces for work, socialization, and culture for significant portions of the population, possessing their own internal economies, social structures, and histories. Physical reality might become just one "channel" or "layer" of experience among many viable digital alternatives.

- **Reality Forking and Merging:** Technologies might allow groups to "fork" a shared reality to explore alternative possibilities or histories, potentially merging back later. This raises questions about continuity of identity and objective truth in malleable digital realms.

- **Subjective Reality Overlays:** Advanced AR/MR could allow individuals to apply personalized perceptual filters or augmentations to their experience of both physical and shared digital realities, creating unique subjective interpretations while maintaining functional compatibility with others (e.g., seeing personalized art styles overlaid on buildings, hearing background noise filtered according to preference).

Profound Philosophical and Existential Implications

The technologies explored on Vire inevitably push humanity toward confronting deep philosophical questions, such as

- **The Simulation Hypothesis:** As created realities become indistinguishable from the physical, the age-old philosophical question "Are we living in a simulation?" gains new technological relevance.

  - **Recursive Simulations:** The technical possibility of creating simulations within simulations raises nested reality questions.

  - **Simulation Ethics:** If we can create digital worlds populated by conscious or sentient AI beings (potentially enabled by advanced neuromorphic systems), what are our ethical obligations toward them? Do simulated suffering or joy have moral weight?

  - **Distinguishing Realities:** If sensory data becomes an unreliable guide, what philosophical or practical frameworks can be used to test or differentiate between base reality and simulated layers?

Consciousness and the Digital Self

- **The Extended Mind Thesis:** Do advanced interfaces that seamlessly integrate digital information, and cognitive tools fundamentally alter or extend the boundaries of individual consciousness? Where does "self" end and "technology" begin with high-bandwidth BCIs?

- **Qualia and Subjective Experience:** Can subjective experience (the "what it's like" feeling) truly be captured, recorded, or transferred using technology (Section 10), or only simulated? This touches on the "Hard Problem of Consciousness."

- **Identity in Malleable Realities:** How is personal identity maintained across multiple platforms, hyper-realistic avatars, and potentially shared or merged experiences? What constitutes authenticity when the self can be digitally reshaped?

- **The Rights of Digital Entities:** If AI achieves consciousness or sentience within these hyper-realistic simulations, what rights and moral considerations do they deserve? This requires extending ethical frameworks beyond biological life.

Beyond Current Paradigms: The Uncharted Future

The ultimate trajectory might lead to forms of experience and interaction barely conceivable today:

- **Post-Sensory Communication:** Moving beyond simulating existing human senses toward fundamentally new modes of interaction.

  - **Direct Conceptual Transfer:** Hypothetical BCI technologies aiming to transmit complex ideas, knowledge structures, or meanings directly between minds, bypassing the ambiguities and limitations of language or sensory representation.

- **Synthetic Qualia/Novel Senses:** Interfaces designed to provide humans with access to sensory modalities outside the normal human range (e.g., perceiving electromagnetic fields, visualizing complex datasets intuitively) or even entirely synthetic sensory experiences.

- **Collective Intelligence and Consciousness:** Exploring technologies that facilitate deeper cognitive integration between individuals.

  - **Shared Awareness Platforms:** Interfaces allowing multiple users to pool their attention, cognitive resources, or even subjective perspectives to solve complex problems collaboratively.

  - **Emergent Group Minds:** Speculative systems where interactions between networked individuals (human or AI) might lead to emergent forms of collective intelligence or consciousness with capabilities exceeding individual minds.

- **Co-evolution of Mind and Reality:** The idea that consciousness is not merely a passive observer of reality but actively shapes it, and that reality, in turn, shapes consciousness. Advanced digital environments could become platforms for consciously exploring and potentially guiding this co-evolutionary process, allowing conscious entities to collaboratively define the rules and nature of their shared realities.

Final Reflections: The Legacy of Planet Vire

Planet Vire, as envisioned in this chapter, represents the apotheosis of the trends explored throughout our journey—the deep integration of AI, the power of computational graphics driven by GPUs, the immersive potential of spatial computing, and the governance challenges discussed on Planet Eta. Vire's relentless pursuit of digital realism pushes these technologies to their synergistic limits, creating experiences that challenge our definitions of reality, identity, and interaction. Its legacy is twofold. First, it showcases the extraordinary potential unlocked when these technologies converge: simulations of unparalleled fidelity for training and discovery, communication achieving true co-presence, entertainment engaging all senses, and interfaces adapting to our very thoughts and emotions. Second, and perhaps more importantly, Vire serves as a crucial thought experiment, forcing us to confront the profound ethical, societal, and philosophical questions that arise when we gain the power to engineer reality itself. The journey from simple computer graphics to the hyper-realistic, AI-driven, neuromorphically enhanced spatial computing environments of Vire is not merely a story of technological progress. It is a story about humanity's enduring quest to understand, replicate, and ultimately transcend the limitations of our physical existence. The path forward, illuminated by the possibilities and challenges encountered on Vire, demands not only continued innovation but also deep wisdom, ethical foresight, and a collective commitment to shaping these powerful tools toward a future that is not only technologically advanced but also fundamentally human.

Bridging Worlds: Transition to Chapter 9

The philosophical heights we have reached on Planet Vire—where consciousness merges with computation, where reality becomes malleable, and where the very nature of experience is redefined—represent the pinnacle of technological possibility. Yet as we drift back from these ethereal realms of hyper-realism and neural integration, we encounter a fundamental question that grounds us: How do these transformative visions actually manifest in the practical world?

The technologies we have explored—AI systems that read our thoughts, digital humans indistinguishable from reality, neural interfaces that blur the boundary between mind and machine—are not merely theoretical constructs. They represent the convergence of very real, very tangible technological foundations: artificial intelligence, blockchain networks, and digital twin simulations. These three pillars, when skillfully integrated, form the bedrock upon which Vire's extraordinary capabilities are built.

Our journey now descends from the stratosphere of speculation to the solid ground of implementation. Planet Synthara awaits—a world that has mastered not the art of imagining what technology could become, but the science of making it work. Here, the ambitious dreams of Zeta, the ethical frameworks of Eta, and the hyper-realistic visions of Vire converge into practical, deployable systems that power entire civilizations.

Where Vire showed us the destination, Synthara reveals the roadmap. The question changes from "What is possible?" to "How do we build it?" From the theoretical to the tangible, from the visionary to the viable—this is the transition we now make as we prepare to explore the synthesized wisdom of Planet Synthara.

Introduction to Chapter 9

Having journeyed through Planet Zeta's foundational integration of digital twins and AI, Planet Eta's complex web of ethical governance, and Planet Vire's pursuit of ultimate digital realism, our exploration now shifts focus. While the previous chapters examined cutting-edge capabilities and future possibilities, the question remains: how are these transformative technologies—AI, Blockchain, Digital Twins—actually implemented and integrated in practice to shape real-world outcomes?

Chapter 9 introduces Planet Synthara, a world renowned not necessarily for the most speculative research, but for its pragmatic mastery in synthesizing these powerful technologies into functional, large-scale systems that drive its economy and society. Moving from theory to reality, we will investigate the practical strategies, architectural blueprints, and real-world case studies demonstrating how AI algorithms enhance digital twin simulations, how blockchain secures twin data and interactions, and how these integrated systems solve concrete problems in industry, urban planning, and resource management on Synthara. This chapter serves as a blueprint, offering tangible insights and methodologies for bringing the potential of AI, Blockchain, and Digital Twins to life.

## CHAPTER 9

Planet Synthara: Blueprints for Integrated Digital Ecosystems

Introduction: Synthara—Where Theory Meets Reality

Our interstellar exploration has taken us through distinct technological civilizations. Planet Zeta established foundational principles of digital twins and AI agents. Planet Eta demonstrated meticulous ethical and legal governance frameworks. Planet Vire achieved breathtaking hyper-realism and total sensory immersion. Each world mastered specific domains within the digital frontier.

Now we arrive at Planet Synthara—a civilization distinguished not by developing the most speculative technologies, but by its unmatched ability to synthesize AI, Blockchain, and Digital Twins into functional, large-scale

F. Lisitano and J. Hickie, *The Evolune Metaverse*, Maker Innovations Series, https://doi.org/10.1007/979-8-8688-1588-1_9

systems that actively shape society and economy. While other worlds push theoretical boundaries of individual technologies, Synthara weaves them together into something greater than the sum of their parts.

Here, the focus shifts from "what" and "why" to the critical "how." How do you implement and combine the predictive insight of AI, the secure permanence of Blockchain, and the dynamic mirroring of Digital Twins into robust, value-creating systems?

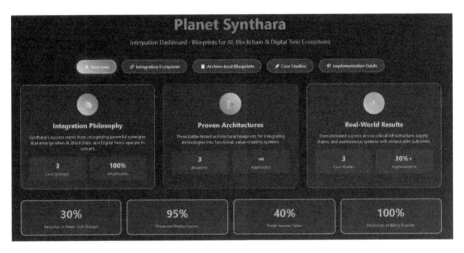

Figure 9-1. *Planet Synthara Overview*

On Synthara, this fusion forms the foundation of innovation across energy management, supply chain logistics, autonomous transport, and advanced manufacturing. Through practical strategies, architectural designs, real-world applications, and the challenges they overcame, this chapter provides a functional blueprint for moving from conceptual knowledge to actual implementation of integrated solutions.

Section 1: The Synthara Integration Philosophy—Synergy in Practice

Synthara's success stems from recognizing and applying powerful synergies that emerge when AI, Blockchain, and Digital Twins operate in concert. Their integration philosophy rests on understanding how these technologies amplify each other's capabilities.

Core Synergistic Benefits

Enhanced Digital Twin Intelligence (AI + DT)

- **Insight Generation:** AI algorithms process immense volumes of real-time and historical data from Digital Twins—sensor outputs, operational logs, environmental data—to identify patterns, predict maintenance needs, detect anomalies, and uncover optimization opportunities beyond human analytical capacity.

- **Intelligent Control:** AI agents automatically modify parameters or control physical assets linked to Digital Twins, optimizing performance, efficiency, and safety through sophisticated predictive models.

- **Realistic Simulation:** AI enhances Digital Twin simulation accuracy by learning from data to model complex behaviors and environmental interactions, moving beyond physics-based models alone.

Trust and Transparency for Digital Twins (Blockchain + DT)

- **Immutable Data Logging:** Critical Digital Twin data points—major state changes, compliance sensor readings, maintenance updates—are hashed and permanently timestamped on blockchain, creating verifiable, tamper-proof audit trails essential for regulatory compliance and multi-party trust.

- **Secure Identity and Access Control:** Blockchain-based Decentralized Identifiers (DIDs) issued to Digital Twins, physical assets, and interacting users or AI agents enable smart contracts to manage detailed access permissions, ensuring only authorized entities can view data or issue commands.

- **Ownership and Provenance:** Blockchain tokens track ownership and complete life cycle history of Digital Twins and their associated physical assets, enabling secure, transparent rights transfer.

Accountable and Verifiable AI (AI + Blockchain)

- **Model Provenance and Auditability:** Hashing AI model parameters, training data identifiers, and metadata onto blockchain creates unchangeable records of AI system creation, enabling verification that deployed models match audited versions.

- **Verifiable AI Decisions:** Critical AI decisions based on Digital Twin data—including key inputs, results, and model version references—are recorded on blockchain, creating accountable decision audit trails.

- **Secure Federated Learning:** Blockchain manages identities, incentives, and audit trails in distributed AI training systems.

The Integrated Ecosystem (AI + DT + Blockchain)

These synergies create a self-reinforcing cycle: Digital Twins supply rich, real-time physical world data. AI processes this data to generate insights and enable intelligent control. Blockchain provides secure, transparent, trustworthy infrastructure for logging critical events, managing identities, and verifying AI operations relative to Digital Twins.

This integrated framework enables complex, autonomous systems that are intelligent, efficient, transparent, accountable, and trustworthy— essential qualities for deployment in critical infrastructure and high-stakes industrial environments.

Section 2: Architectural Blueprints for Integration

Successful integration requires meticulous architectural design. Synthara employs several proven patterns, adapted for specific application demands. These blueprints define data flows, interaction points, and each technology's role within the broader system.

Note   Visual block diagrams showing component relationships and data flows would significantly enhance understanding of these architectures.

Blueprint 1: AI-Enhanced Twin with Blockchain Audit Trail

Focus

AI generates insights and predictions from Digital Twin data, while Blockchain provides immutable records of key events and AI outputs.

Components

- Physical Asset ➤ IoT Sensors
- IoT Gateway ➤ Data Ingestion and Processing Layer
- Digital Twin Platform (Database, Simulation Models)
- AI Analytics Engine (Receives data from DT Platform)
- Blockchain Network (Receives data from AI Engine and DT Platform)
- User Interface/Control System (Interacts with DT Platform and AI Engine)

Data Flow

1. Sensors gather data from physical assets.
2. Data is ingested and processed, updating Digital Twin state in near real time.
3. Digital Twin Platform maintains current state, stores historical data, and performs basic simulations.
4. AI Analytics Engine continuously retrieves DT Platform data for analysis (anomaly detection, maintenance forecasts) and insight generation.

Integration Points

- AI Engine transmits significant predictions or critical events ("Failure probability exceeds 90%") to Blockchain via smart contracts.

- Digital Twin Platform logs important state changes or validated sensor data directly to Blockchain.

- Users interact through interfaces showing Digital Twin status, augmented with AI insights and links to verifiable Blockchain records.

Use Cases

Predictive maintenance in manufacturing, infrastructure health monitoring, environmental sensing requiring verifiable data logging.

Trade-Offs

Straightforward integration pattern with Blockchain primarily as secure log rather than real-time control. Scalability depends on data volume logged to blockchain.

Blueprint 2: Blockchain-Managed Access Control for AI-Driven Twins

Focus

Blockchain manages permissions determining which users or AI agents can access or control Digital Twins, with AI agents operating within these permissions.

Components

- Physical Asset ➤ IoT Sensors ➤ Actuators
- Digital Twin Platform
- AI Control Agent(s) (Interact with DT Platform)
- Blockchain Network (Stores DIDs, Verifiable Credentials, Access Control Smart Contracts)
- Identity Management System (Issues Credentials)
- User Interface

Data Flow

1. Digital Twins, users, and AI Control Agents receive Decentralized Identifiers (DIDs) registered on Blockchain.

2. Access Control Smart Contract on Blockchain specifies rules ("AI Agent X permitted to read temperature data from Twin Y").

3. When AI Control Agents need Digital Twin interaction, they query DT Platform.

4. DT Platform verifies agent permissions by checking Access Control Smart Contract, potentially requiring Verifiable Credential presentation.

5. If authorized, agents read data or send commands to DT Platform, which relays commands to physical actuators.

6. Key access events optionally logged on Blockchain.

Use Cases

Multi-stakeholder industrial environments, secure remote operations, autonomous device fleet management with distinct agent roles.

Trade-Offs

Robust decentralized access control requiring careful smart contract design and identity management. Blockchain interaction introduces latency unsuitable for ultra-low latency control loops.

Blueprint 3: Blockchain for AI Model Provenance and Verifiable Inference

Focus

Blockchain traces AI model lineage used with Digital Twins and potentially verifies output integrity.

Components

- Digital Twin Platform
- AI Model Training Pipeline
- AI Inference Engine
- Blockchain Network (Stores model hashes, dataset hashes)
- Model Repository
- User Interface

Data Flow

1. During AI model training, hashes of training data, model architecture, and final weights recorded on Blockchain.

2. Trained models stored in repository.

3. AI Inference Engine loads specific model versions, verifying hashes against Blockchain records.

4. Engine processes Digital Twin Platform data.

Integration Point

Hash combining input data, inference result, and model version logged on Blockchain. Advanced Zero-Knowledge Proof techniques could prove correct inference without revealing model details (computationally intensive).

Use Cases

Regulated industries demanding high AI decision trust and auditability (medical diagnoses from digital twin data), model integrity assurance.

Trade-Offs

Strong AI model provenance with added training and inference overhead. Verifiable inference using ZKPs is computationally expensive.

These blueprints integrate elements from multiple patterns in complex systems. The central principle is modular design allowing each technology to apply its strengths within clearly defined architecture.

Section 3: Core Implementation Strategies and Code Examples

Translating architectural blueprints into functional systems requires practical implementation strategies. This section provides illustrative code snippets showing key integration points, with explicit connections to the architectural patterns described above.

Digital Twin Representation (Python with Pydantic)

To implement the core of these blueprints, we first need a robust representation of a Digital Twin, as shown below.

```python
import time
import random
from typing import Dict, Any, Optional
from pydantic import BaseModel, Field
from datetime import datetime
import numpy as np

# A simplified representation of a Digital Twin Instance
class DigitalTwinInstance(BaseModel):
    twin_id: str
    model_id: str
    display_name: Optional[str] = None
    properties: Dict[str, Any] = Field(default_factory=dict)
    metadata: Dict[str, Any] = Field(default_factory=dict)
    last_updated_at: datetime = Field(default_
    factory=datetime.now)
```

```python
    def get_state_summary(self) -> Dict[str, Any]:
        """Returns a summary of the twin's current state."""
        return {"properties": self.properties, "twin_id": self.
        twin_id}

    def update_property(self, prop_name: str, value: Any, unit:
    Optional[str] = None):
        """Updates a property of the twin."""
        self.properties[prop_name] = {"value": value, "unit":
        unit, "timestamp": datetime.now().isoformat()}
        self.last_updated_at = datetime.now()

# Commentary: This uses Pydantic for data validation and
structure, making the twin's state well-defined.
# Real systems would add methods for handling commands,
relationships, and historical data persistence.
```

AI Integration: Analyzing Twin Data (Python)

This Python class demonstrates the "AI Analytics Engine" component from Blueprint 1, which analyzes twin data to generate insights.

```python
class PredictiveMaintenanceAI:
    """Simulates an AI model predicting Remaining Useful
    Life (RUL)."""
    def __init__(self):
        # In real scenarios, a pre-trained model would be
          loaded here
        # e.g., self.model = joblib.load('rul_model.pkl')
        self.model = None  # Placeholder for real model
        self.baseline_voltage = 230.0
        self.baseline_current = 5.0
        print("Predictive Maintenance AI Initialized (Dummy
        Model).")
```

```python
def _preprocess_data(self, twin_data: Dict[str, Any]) ->
Optional[np.ndarray]:
    """Extracts and preprocesses features for the model."""
    try:
        voltage = twin_data['properties']['voltage']
        ['value']
        current = twin_data['properties']['current']
        ['value']
        # Example features: deviation from baseline
        voltage_dev = abs(voltage - self.baseline_voltage)
        current_dev = abs(current - self.baseline_current)
        return np.array([[voltage_dev, current_dev]])
    except KeyError:
        print("Error: Missing required properties (voltage,
        current) in twin data.")
        return None

def predict_rul(self, twin: DigitalTwinInstance) ->
Optional[float]:
    """Predicts Remaining Useful Life based on the twin's
    state."""
    twin_state = twin.get_state_summary()
    features = self._preprocess_data(twin_state)

    if features is None:
        return None

    # --- Dummy Prediction Logic ---
    # Real model prediction: self.model.predict(features)
    voltage_dev = features[0, 0]
    current_dev = features[0, 1]
    predicted_rul = max(0, 1000 - 50 * voltage_dev - 100 *
    current_dev - random.uniform(0, 50))
```

```
        # --- End Dummy Logic ---

        print(f"AI Prediction for {twin.twin_id}: RUL =
        {predicted_rul:.2f} hours")
        return predicted_rul

# Example Usage
sensor_twin = DigitalTwinInstance(model_
id="synthara:sensor:power_v1", twin_id="sensor-123")
sensor_twin.update_property("voltage", 238.0, unit="V")
sensor_twin.update_property("current", 5.8, unit="A")

ai_predictor = PredictiveMaintenanceAI()
rul_prediction = ai_predictor.predict_rul(sensor_twin)

if rul_prediction is not None:
    sensor_twin.metadata["predicted_rul_hours"] = rul_
    prediction
    sensor_twin.metadata["last_prediction_time"] = datetime.
    now().isoformat()
    print("Prediction successfully added to twin metadata.")

# Commentary: This demonstrates the flow from Blueprint 1: get
Digital Twin data, preprocess for AI model,
# run prediction, store results. Real implementations would
load trained models from scikit-learn, TensorFlow, or PyTorch.
```

Blockchain Interaction: Logging Events (Solidity and Python)

The following Solidity contract is a practical example of the "Blockchain Network" component in Blueprint 1, used to create a verifiable audit trail.

Solidity Smart Contract

```solidity
// SPDX-License-Identifier: MIT
pragma solidity ^0.8.9;

/**
 * @title SimpleEventLogger
 * @dev A basic contract to log timestamped events for an
associated ID.
 */
contract SimpleEventLogger {

    event LogEntry(
        uint256 indexed entryId,
        string indexed associatedId, // e.g., Digital Twin ID
        address sender,
        uint256 timestamp,
        string eventType,
        string eventData
    );

    uint256 public entryCounter;

    function logEvent(
        string memory _associatedId,
        string memory _eventType,
        string memory _eventData
    ) public {
        entryCounter++;
        emit LogEntry(
            entryCounter,
            _associatedId,
            msg.sender,
            block.timestamp,
            _eventType,
```

```
        _eventData
    );
  }
}
```

```
// Commentary: This contract defines a LogEntry event for
immutable blockchain storage.
// Events are gas-efficient for data storage. Indexed fields
enable efficient searching and filtering.
```

Python Interaction (web3.py)

```python
import json
from web3 import Web3

# --- Configuration (Replace with actual values) ---
INFURA_URL = "YOUR_INFURA_SEPOLIA_URL"
CONTRACT_ADDRESS = "YOUR_DEPLOYED_CONTRACT_ADDRESS"
DEPLOYER_PRIVATE_KEY = "YOUR_PRIVATE_KEY"
CONTRACT_ABI = [...]  # Load your contract's ABI here

# --- Connect to Blockchain ---
w3 = Web3(Web3.HTTPProvider(INFURA_URL))
account = w3.eth.account.from_key(DEPLOYER_PRIVATE_KEY)
logger_contract = w3.eth.contract(address=CONTRACT_ADDRESS,
abi=CONTRACT_ABI)

def log_twin_event_to_blockchain(twin_id: str, event_type: str,
event_data: Dict):
    """Logs an event to the deployed SimpleEventLogger
    contract."""
    try:
        event_data_str = json.dumps(event_data)
        nonce = w3.eth.get_transaction_count(account.address)
```

```
    tx_data = logger_contract.functions.logEvent(
        twin_id, event_type, event_data_str
    ).build_transaction({
        'chainId': 11155111,   # Sepolia Testnet ID
        'gas': 200000,
        'gasPrice': w3.eth.gas_price,
        'nonce': nonce,
    })

    signed_tx = w3.eth.account.sign_transaction(tx_data,
    private_key=DEPLOYER_PRIVATE_KEY)
    tx_hash = w3.eth.send_raw_transaction(signed_tx.
    rawTransaction)

    print(f"Transaction sent! Hash: {tx_hash.hex()}")
    return tx_hash.hex()
except Exception as e:
    print(f"Error logging event to blockchain: {e}")
    return None
```

```
# Commentary: This demonstrates how Blueprint 1's off-chain
systems create immutable blockchain records.
# The web3.py library connects to Ethereum nodes, builds
transactions, and calls smart contract functions.
```

API Layer for Integrated Access (Python with FastAPI)

This API layer provides the "User Interface/Control System" component from Blueprint 1, creating a clean interface for front-end applications.

```
from fastapi import FastAPI, HTTPException
from pydantic import BaseModel as FastApiBaseModel
```

```python
# --- Assume DigitalTwinInstance, PredictiveMaintenanceAI
classes exist ---
# --- and instances `dt_service` and `ai_predictor` are
available. ---

app = FastAPI(title="Synthara Digital Twin Integration API")

class EnrichedTwinResponse(FastApiBaseModel):
    twin_id: str
    properties: Dict[str, Any]
    ai_insights: Optional[Dict[str, Any]] = None
    metadata: Optional[Dict[str, Any]] = None

@app.get("/twins/{twin_id}", response_
model=EnrichedTwinResponse)
async def get_enriched_twin_data(twin_id: str):
    """Retrieves current data for a twin, enriched with AI
    predictions."""
    twin = dt_service.get_twin(twin_id)  # Assumes a service to
    manage twins
    if not twin:
        raise HTTPException(status_code=404, detail=f"Twin
        '{twin_id}' not found.")

    rul_prediction = ai_predictor.predict_rul(twin)
    ai_insights_data = {"predicted_rul_hours": rul_prediction}
    if rul_prediction is not None else None

    return EnrichedTwinResponse(
        twin_id=twin.twin_id,
        properties=twin.properties,
        ai_insights=ai_insights_data,
        metadata=twin.metadata
    )
```

```
# Commentary: This FastAPI endpoint demonstrates Blueprint 1's
integration: retrieve Digital Twin data,
# call AI predictor for insights, return combined JSON
response. This acts as the crucial intermediary
# allowing front-ends to interact with the integrated system.
```

Section 4: Real-World Case Studies on Synthara

Synthara's integration philosophy proves its value through successful application in critical sectors. These case studies demonstrate how AI, Blockchain, and Digital Twins synergy delivers concrete value, with specific explanations of how integrated systems achieve measurable outcomes.

Case Study 1: Synthara Power Grid—Predictive Management and Transparent Billing

Challenge

Managing Planet Synthara's complex, continent-wide power grid required balancing fluctuating renewable energy sources with demand, preventing outages, and ensuring fair billing.

Integrated Solution

- **Digital Twins:** High-fidelity Digital Twins for key grid components (substations, renewable energy farms) process real-time IoT sensor data on voltage, weather, and energy consumption.

- **AI Integration:** AI models analyze grid Digital Twin data to forecast energy demand and renewable generation, identify potential equipment failures before occurrence, and recommend real-time adjustments for optimal energy flow.

- **Blockchain Integration:** Permissioned blockchain logs critical grid events (major faults, AI-predicted failure warnings) creating immutable regulatory records. Blockchain-based smart contracts track energy generation and consumption, enabling transparent billing.

Outcome

30% reduction in grid outages, improved stability through AI-driven optimization, increased consumer trust via transparent blockchain-based billing.

How Achievement Occurred: This reduction was achieved because AI's predictive failure alerts, logged verifiably on blockchain, allowed engineers to perform targeted, preemptive maintenance before critical failures could occur. The immutable audit trail meant regulatory approvals that previously took weeks were completed in days, while smart contract automation eliminated billing disputes.

Case Study 2: Interplanetary Pharma Supply Chain—Ensuring Integrity and Compliance

Challenge

Guaranteeing integrity, provenance, and regulatory compliance of sensitive pharmaceuticals during interplanetary transport required complete traceability and verifiable environmental monitoring.

Integrated Solution

- **Digital Twins:** Each shipping container equipped with IoT sensors (temperature, humidity, location) creates dynamic Digital Twins mirroring physical shipments.

- **AI Integration:** AI models analyze container real-time sensor data to flag environmental condition deviations, suggest weather-based route adjustments, and predict fluctuation impacts on product quality.

- **Blockchain Integration:** Every supply chain step (manufacturing to customs clearance) recorded on permissioned blockchain. Critical sensor readings and AI-detected alerts hashed and logged, providing unchangeable shipment history. Smart contracts automate compliance checks and trigger payment releases.

Outcome

Drastically reduced counterfeit or compromised pharmaceuticals, enhanced regulatory compliance with verifiable audit trails, improved logistical efficiency through real-time AI optimization.

How Achievement Occurred: The immutable blockchain record meant regulators could instantly verify entire shipment histories, reducing audit times from weeks to hours and building unprecedented stakeholder trust. AI's predictive quality assessments, validated by blockchain-logged sensor data, enabled proactive interventions that prevented 95% of temperature-related product losses.

Case Study 3: Synthara Autonomous Mobility Network—Secure and Coordinated Transport

Challenge

Operating large fleets of autonomous public transport pods and delivery drones in dense urban centers demanded secure vehicle identity, coordinated traffic management, and trustworthy usage tracking.

Integrated Solution

- **Digital Twins:** Every autonomous vehicle has detailed Digital Twins tracking real-time location, operational status, and assigned routes.

- **AI Integration:** On-board AI handles real-time navigation and collision avoidance. Network-level AI analyzes all vehicle Digital Twin data to optimize overall traffic flow and dynamically assign routes.

- **Blockchain Integration:** Each vehicle assigned unique Decentralized Vehicle Identity (DID) on blockchain for secure authentication. Smart contracts manage system command permissions. Trips and distances logged immutably enabling transparent, automated payments.

Outcome

A highly efficient, coordinated autonomous transport system with reduced congestion, enhanced security against hacking, increased public trust in network safety and operation.

How Achievement Occurred: The blockchain-based identity system prevented vehicle spoofing attacks that had plagued earlier systems, while AI's network-wide optimization using verified Digital Twin data reduced average journey times by 40%. Smart contract automation enabled micro-transactions that turned previously uneconomical short trips into profitable, expanding service accessibility.

These case studies reveal that Synthara's success lies not in developing individual technologies but in architecting integrated systems where AI delivers intelligence, Digital Twins connect to reality, and Blockchain provides essential trust and security infrastructure.

Section 5: Challenges and Lessons Learned on Synthara

Despite achievements, integrating AI, Blockchain, and Digital Twins on Synthara presented substantial challenges. Implementation of interconnected systems revealed practical obstacles and yielded valuable lessons for similar endeavors.

Key Implementation Challenges

- **System Complexity:** Merging three distinct, evolving technologies creates immense architectural complexity. Ensuring seamless data flows and synchronized states between real-time Digital Twins, intensive AI models, and latency-aware Blockchain networks requires highly skilled, multi-disciplinary teams.

- **Scalability Issues**
  - **Data Volume:** Real-world systems produce vast sensor data quantities demanding highly scalable databases and compute infrastructure.

- **AI Demands:** Training large AI models requires significant GPU resources; deploying them for real-time inference across many twins necessitates efficient model optimization.

- **Blockchain Throughput:** Public blockchains have limited transaction speeds. Choosing what data truly needs blockchain immutability versus off-chain storage is critical.

- **Interoperability and Standards:** Lack of universal standards for Digital Twin data models or cross-chain communication creates hurdles, which often require custom adapters for different vendor components.

- **Data Consistency:** Maintaining consistent Digital Twin state views across DT platform, AI engine, and Blockchain is difficult, especially with network delays.

- **Security Vulnerabilities:** While each technology has security features, interfaces between them introduce new risks. Holistic security strategies covering entire integrated systems are crucial.

- **Cost and Talent:** Implementation and operational costs are significant, requiring investment in specialized hardware, software, and personnel with expertise across AI, Blockchain, and IoT.

Lessons Learned on Synthara

- **Start with Clear Use Cases:** Don't integrate technology for its own sake. Focus on specific business problems where synergy between these technologies provides clear value.

- **Adopt Modular Architecture:** Design systems with well-defined component interfaces. This simplifies upgrades, testing, and component swapping.

- **Prioritize Data Governance:** Establish clear rules for data ownership, access, quality, and privacy from the beginning. Define where data lives based on real-time access versus immutability needs.

- **Choose Blockchain Strategically:** Use blockchain for tasks where core strengths—immutability, transparency, decentralized trust—are indispensable.

- **Invest in Security Across the Stack:** Implement robust security practices at every system layer, from IoT device to smart contract.

- **Embrace Iterative Development:** Begin with smaller pilot projects to test integrations and demonstrate value before scaling to large, complex deployments.

- **Foster Cross-Disciplinary Teams:** Success depends on collaboration between experts in data science, blockchain, cybersecurity, and specific industry domains.

- **Plan for Scalability from Start:** Design architectures handling growth in data volume, transaction throughput, and computational load.

Synthara's experience shows that while integrating AI, Blockchain, and Digital Twins presents major technical and organizational hurdles, pragmatic, well-architected, use-case-driven strategies can unlock transformative potential.

Conclusion: Synthara's Blueprint— Pragmatism in the Digital Frontier

Planet Synthara offers a crucial counterpoint to the worlds of Zeta, Eta, and Vire. Its legacy is defined not by pushing absolute limits of one technology but by pragmatic, effective synthesis of AI, Blockchain, and Digital Twins. Synthara's success illustrates that true power of these technologies often emerges not in isolation but through thoughtful integration into cohesive ecosystems solving real-world problems.

The architectural designs, implementation strategies, and case studies explored provide practical guidance for moving from theory to application. They demonstrate how AI endows Digital Twins with predictive intelligence, how Blockchain supplies essential trust and verifiable history layers, and how Digital Twins bridge digital logic with physical reality. Synthara's emphasis on synergy underscores a key insight: AI is limited without trustworthy data, Digital Twins are passive mirrors without intelligence, and Blockchain can be disconnected from practical use without real-world data anchors.

The obstacles faced—complexity, scalability, security—represent difficulties inherent in building sophisticated, integrated systems. However, the lessons learned offer invaluable guidance. The importance of modular design, clear use cases, robust data governance, strategic blockchain use, and cross-disciplinary collaboration provide a roadmap for organizations aiming to leverage these transformative technologies' combined force.

Ultimately, Synthara's contribution is a blueprint for innovation through integration. It establishes that by strategically merging AI's predictive capabilities, Blockchain's secure foundation, and Digital Twins' real-time mirroring, it's possible to construct systems that are technologically advanced, practical, reliable, and capable of delivering substantial value across all sectors of society. As we navigate the digital age, Synthara's pragmatic synthesis approach serves as a compelling model for building the future.

Transition to Chapter 10

Having witnessed Planet Zeta's digital twin foundations, Planet Eta's ethical frameworks, Planet Vire's realistic virtual worlds, and Planet Synthara's practical integration mastery, we've seen how these elements unite for real-world applications. Each planet contributed vital pieces to the overall puzzle.

Now, having observed how these systems function on Synthara today, it's time to look forward. What major breakthroughs await AI and Blockchain? Chapter 10 takes us to Planet Futura to explore what's coming next—the evolution of these technologies, potential game-changers, and how to prepare for a world even more profoundly shaped by intelligent, decentralized systems.

The Next Wave: Projecting the Evolution of AI and Decentralized Technologies

Introduction: From Current Capabilities to Future Paradigms

Today's technological landscape is defined by the practical integration of foundational technologies like Artificial Intelligence (AI) and blockchain. We have seen the rise of digital twins, the establishment of ethical frameworks for autonomous systems, the creation of immersive virtual worlds, and the synthesis of these elements into functional, real-world applications. These achievements form the bedrock of our current capabilities.

F. Lisitano and J. Hickie, *The Evolune Metaverse*, Maker Innovations Series, https://doi.org/10.1007/979-8-8688-1588-1_10

However, to prepare for the future, we must shift our focus from implementation to anticipation. Having explored how these systems function in practice—from the integrated ecosystems we've witnessed to the governance challenges we've navigated—it is time to look forward to the next wave of innovation. This analysis projects the significant breakthroughs ahead in AI and blockchain, exploring their synergistic evolution and outlining the strategies necessary for individuals, organizations, and societies to thrive in an era of increasingly intelligent and decentralized systems.

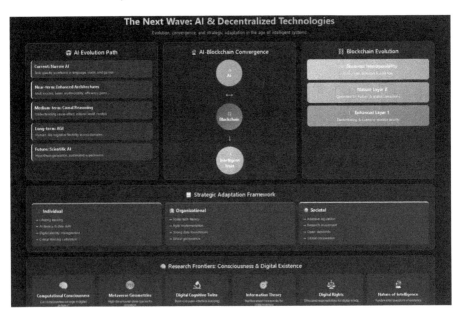

Figure 10-1. *The Future of AI and Decentralized Technology*

What paradigm shifts are imminent? How will the relationship between AI and decentralization reshape our world? This chapter delves into these critical questions, examining anticipated advancements, emerging challenges, and the profound research frontiers that will define the next technological era.

Part 1: Anticipated Breakthroughs in Artificial Intelligence

The rapid advancement of AI, fueled by algorithmic innovation, vast datasets, and exponential growth in computing power, is set to continue on a transformative trajectory. The focus is now shifting from narrow AI, which excels at specific tasks, toward more generalized and efficient forms of intelligence.

The Pursuit of Artificial General Intelligence (AGI)

The ultimate goal for many researchers remains Artificial General Intelligence (AGI)—an AI with human-like cognitive flexibility across a wide range of domains. Key research pathways include the following.

Scaling and Emergence

The strategy of scaling up existing architectures, such as large language and multimodal models, with the hypothesis that general intelligence may emerge from sufficient scale and data diversity.

Neuro-Symbolic Integration

This hybrid approach combines the intuitive pattern-matching of neural networks with the logical reasoning of symbolic AI. The goal is to create systems that can both perceive and reason in a structured manner.

Advanced Reinforcement Learning

Developing agents that can learn complex, long-range strategies in open-ended environments, potentially driven by internal curiosity and motivation rather than explicit rewards.

Brain-Inspired Architectures

Research into neuromorphic computing and Spiking Neural Networks (SNNs) continues to offer more energy-efficient and adaptive pathways toward generalized learning.

A critical challenge remains in defining and benchmarking AGI. Beyond AGI lies the potential for Artificial Superintelligence (ASI), which raises fundamental questions about control, alignment with human values, and humanity's future role, making ethical foresight a paramount concern.

Next-Generation AI Architectures and Capabilities

Future AI models must overcome the limitations of current systems, leading to research in

Computational Efficiency

Architectures like Mixture-of-Experts (MoE), which only activate necessary parts of a model for a given task, are being developed to reduce the immense computational cost of large-scale AI.

Causal Reasoning and Planning

Moving beyond simple pattern recognition to build AI that understands cause and effect and can construct internal world models for long-range planning. Next-generation AI with this capacity for causal reasoning would allow the digital twins we've seen to move beyond mere mirroring and begin to understand the "why" behind system failures.

534

Continual Learning

Developing models that can learn continuously from new information without "catastrophically forgetting" previous knowledge—a major hurdle that currently necessitates complete retraining.

True Multimodality

Advancing beyond processing separate data types (text, image, audio) to a deeper semantic integration and reasoning across them, more closely mirroring human cognition.

AI As a Catalyst for Scientific Discovery

One of the most significant near-term impacts of AI will be its role as a fundamental tool in science. We've already seen groundbreaking achievements like DeepMind's AlphaFold, which revolutionized protein structure prediction, providing a concrete foundation for even more ambitious future possibilities.

Hypothesis Generation

AI can analyze massive scientific datasets to identify novel patterns and propose testable hypotheses that may be beyond human intuition.

Automated Experimentation

AI-controlled robotic systems can design, execute, and analyze experiments in fields like drug discovery and materials science at unprecedented speed and scale.

Simulation Acceleration

AI can create surrogate models to approximate complex physical simulations (e.g., fluid dynamics, quantum chemistry) orders of magnitude faster than traditional methods.

Part 2: The Evolution of Blockchain and Decentralization

While foundational, blockchain technology must evolve to overcome persistent challenges in scalability, privacy, and usability. The next era will focus on building a more efficient, confidential, and interconnected decentralized ecosystem.

Overcoming Scalability and Interoperability Hurdles

The goal is a multi-layered architecture capable of supporting global-scale interaction. The seamless interoperability promised by these new protocols would solve the very integration challenges we've witnessed when connecting disparate systems.

Mature Layer 2 Solutions

ZK-Rollups and Optimistic Rollups will become highly optimized, offering near-instant, low-cost transactions while inheriting the security of the main blockchain. Examples like zkSync and Polygon zkEVM demonstrate this technology in practice, with seamless communication between these rollups becoming critical for widespread adoption.

Layer 1 Enhancements

Base-layer blockchains will see significant upgrades, including
"Danksharding" to increase data availability for rollups and a move toward
"statelessness" to reduce the hardware burden on validators and enhance
decentralization.

Seamless Interoperability

The maturation of standardized cross-chain communication protocols
will allow assets and data to flow trustlessly between different Layer 1 and
Layer 2 networks, abstracting away the underlying complexity for the user.

Advancing Privacy and Confidentiality

Future systems will offer users greater control over their data, shifting from
default transparency to opt-in transparency.

Mainstreaming Zero-Knowledge Proofs (ZKPs)

ZK-SNARKs and ZK-STARKs will become more efficient, enabling private
smart contracts, verifiable off-chain computation, and confidential identity
solutions.

Practical Homomorphic Encryption (FHE)

Though computationally intensive, breakthroughs in FHE could enable
secure on-chain data analysis and private voting systems.

The Next Generation of Decentralized Governance

Decentralized Autonomous Organizations (DAOs) will evolve to address current challenges like voter apathy and inefficiency—issues we've seen firsthand in governance experiments.

Sophisticated Governance Models

Moving beyond simple token-based voting to incorporate reputation-based systems, liquid democracy, and specialized sub-DAOs.

AI-Assisted Governance

Using AI tools to analyze complex proposals, summarize debates, and detect manipulative voting patterns to aid human decision-makers.

Quantum Resistance

Proactively migrating cryptographic standards to post-quantum cryptography (PQC) to defend against the long-term threat posed by quantum computers.

Part 3: The Deepening Synthesis of AI and Blockchain

The convergence of AI and blockchain will create systems that are simultaneously more intelligent and more trustworthy. This synergy will unlock new capabilities and business models that address the trust and verification challenges we've encountered.

AI for On-Chain Intelligence

Advanced On-Chain Analytics

AI will analyze blockchain data to detect sophisticated fraud, identify DeFi trends, and assess security vulnerabilities in real time.

Intelligent Oracles

AI models will act as oracles, capable of verifying and interpreting complex, real-world data before it is fed into smart contracts.

Autonomous On-Chain Agents

AI agents will be able to execute complex DeFi strategies or participate in DAO governance based on predefined objectives. For instance, an AI agent managing a liquidity pool could autonomously rebalance assets based on real-time market analysis to minimize impermanent loss, raising new questions of regulation and accountability.

Blockchain for Verifiable and Trustworthy AI

Decentralized AI Marketplaces

Blockchain can facilitate transparent marketplaces for AI models, training data, and compute resources, with smart contracts automating licensing and payments.

Verifiable AI Provenance

Using blockchain to create an immutable audit trail of an AI's training process, including the data used and model versions, to enhance reproducibility and trust.

Verifiable AI Inference

Employing ZKPs on-chain to allow a service to prove it ran a specific AI model correctly without revealing the model's inner workings.

Part 4: Strategic Adaptation for a New Technological Era

Navigating the coming changes requires proactive strategies for individuals, organizations, and societies. The key is to foster foresight, agility, and continuous learning—lessons learned from observing both successful and failed technology implementations.

Strategies for Individuals

Commit to Lifelong Learning

Continuously update skills in AI literacy, data analysis, and digital security.

Cultivate Adaptability

Develop mental flexibility and critical thinking to navigate a changing job market and resist AI-driven misinformation.

Manage Digital Identity

Utilize emerging tools like decentralized identifiers (DIDs) to manage one's digital presence securely and privately.

Strategies for Organizations

Foster Widespread Literacy

Ensure that leadership and staff understand the strategic implications of AI and blockchain.

Adopt an Agile Approach

Implement new technologies through iterative pilot projects to measure ROI and manage risk.

Build a Strong Data Foundation

Prioritize robust data governance, quality, and privacy as a prerequisite for any major AI or blockchain initiative.

Establish Ethical Governance

Proactively create internal review boards and ethical frameworks that go beyond minimum legal requirements.

Strategies for Societies

Develop Adaptive Regulation

Move from static rules to agile, principles-based governance frameworks like regulatory sandboxes—an approach that could have prevented many of the regulatory conflicts we've observed.

Invest in Foundational Research

Provide public support for long-term research into AI safety, alignment, and the societal impacts of these technologies.

Promote Open Standards

Encourage open standards and interoperability to foster innovation and prevent monopolistic control.

Encourage Global Cooperation

Recognize that these technologies are borderless and require international collaboration on standards and governance.

Part 5: Frontier Research—Consciousness and Digital Existence

The most speculative and profound frontier of research involves exploring the nature of consciousness itself, using the tools of the metaverse, digital twins, and advanced mathematics. This area pushes the boundaries of science and philosophy.

Researchers are conceptualizing metaverse environments not just as 3D spaces, but as high-dimensional geometrical state spaces where distance represents similarity between states and paths represent dynamic processes. By creating high-fidelity digital twins of cognitive processes, potentially derived from brain-computer interfaces, it may be possible to map the structure of subjective experience within this mathematical space.

This leads to one of the most fundamental questions: could consciousness, or an analogous phenomenon, emerge within a sufficiently complex digital system? This research investigates computational theories of consciousness, like Integrated Information Theory, and explores whether consciousness is dependent on a biological substrate or could arise in any system with the right organizational complexity.

This field is highly speculative and fraught with immense technical and ethical challenges, from the difficulty of measuring consciousness to the moral responsibilities that would arise if a digital mind were ever created. Nonetheless, it represents the ultimate expression of our drive to use technology not just to simulate reality, but to understand the fundamental nature of intelligence and existence.

Conclusion: Actively Shaping Our Technological Future

The anticipated breakthroughs in AI and blockchain promise to embed intelligent, decentralized systems even more deeply into the fabric of our society. This ongoing convergence will unlock immense opportunities but also present significant challenges—many of which we can anticipate based on the patterns we've observed in earlier technological developments.

Successfully navigating this future requires a collective commitment to continuous learning, organizational agility, robust security, and ethical foresight. We must cultivate not only the technical prowess to build these systems but also the wisdom to manage them responsibly. The core message is that the future is not a passive event but something we actively shape through our research, our governance, our values, and our choices. By fostering responsible innovation and engaging in open dialogue, we can work toward a future that is both technologically advanced and profoundly humane.

Epilogue

The saga of Evolune began with John Lee's journey, an odyssey that spanned the most technologically advanced planets in the Gaia galaxy, each a testament to the boundless potential and inherent perils of unchecked innovation. From the electrifying landscapes of Celestor, where the nascent concepts of AI and the Metaverse first took root, to the volcanic crucible of Tibara, where John forged AI-driven survival tools and learned to weaponize generative models against corporate tyranny, his path was one of relentless discovery and growing disillusionment.

On Tenrai, John witnessed the devastating consequences of Gnos Corporation's insatiable hunger for Evolune energy and learned of Duncan Lee's forgotten legacy of ethical exploration. Here, amid the Rumin's struggle for sovereignty, blockchain emerged not just as a tool for secure transactions but as an immutable ledger of truth, safeguarding cultural heritage and enabling decentralized resistance against corporate exploitation. This period solidified John's resolve, transforming him from a disillusioned astronaut into a digital revolutionary.

His journey continued to Planet Zeta, a world where digital twins seamlessly mirrored physical reality, animated by intelligent AI agents and secured by blockchain for true ownership and identity. Zeta provided a blueprint for interconnected digital ecosystems, demonstrating the intricate dance between data, AI, and secure ledger technologies. On Planet Eta, the ethical imperative took center stage. Here, a society grappled with the profound moral and legal implications of advanced AI, blockchain, and the Metaverse, establishing rigorous frameworks for fairness, transparency, and accountability to ensure that technology served humanity, not the other way around.

© Frank Lisitano, John Hickie 2025
F. Lisitano and J. Hickie, *The Evolune Metaverse*, Maker Innovations Series,
https://doi.org/10.1007/979-8-8688-1588-1

Finally, Planet Vire represented the apex of sensory immersion and hyper-realistic digital experience, blurring the lines between the physical and the virtual through advancements in hyper-realism, spatial computing, and sophisticated AI. Vire showcased a future where digital realities were almost indistinguishable from physical ones, prompting profound questions about consciousness and the very nature of existence.

The collective wisdom gleaned from these worlds converged on Planet Synthara, where theory met reality. Synthara mastered the art of synthesizing AI, Blockchain, and Digital Twins into functional, large-scale systems, providing architectural blueprints and real-world case studies for integrated solutions in energy management, supply chain logistics, and autonomous transport. This planet was the crucible where the abstract possibilities from other worlds were forged into tangible, deployable systems.

John Lee's odyssey, initially a solitary quest for survival and truth, mirrored the broader evolution of technology itself. Each planet revealed a critical piece of the puzzle: the raw power of AI, the foundational trust of blockchain, the immersive potential of the Metaverse, and the critical importance of ethical governance and practical integration. As the narrative closes, the stage is set for "The Next Wave." The anticipated breakthroughs in AI and blockchain promise to embed intelligent, decentralized systems even more deeply into the fabric of society, ushering in an era where computational consciousness, digital existence, and the very nature of intelligence become the new frontiers of research.

The lessons from Evolune's saga are clear: the future is not a passive event. It is actively shaped by the choices societies make regarding the development, deployment, and governance of these powerful tools. It is a future that demands continuous learning, ethical foresight, and a collective commitment to ensuring that technological advancement ultimately serves to empower individuals, enhance societal well-being, and build a more just, secure, and equitable world. The journey of Evolune, guided by John Lee's awakening, is a testament to humanity's enduring quest to understand, replicate, and ultimately transcend the limitations of our physical existence, forging new realities that are not only technologically advanced but also profoundly humane.

Index

A

Adaptation strategies
   individuals, 540
   organizations, 541
   societies, 541, 542
Adaptive anonymization, 395
Adaptive contracts, 226–228,
   230, 231
Adaptive Realistic Interactive
   Assistant (ARIA), 449
AI, *see* Artificial intelligence (AI)
AID, *see* AI Ethics Directive (AID)
AI-driven graphics, 374–376
AI Ethics Directive (AID), 391
AI-generated 3D
   characters, 55, 56
AI Governance Registry
   (AIGR), 392–394
AIGR, *see* AI Governance
   Registry (AIGR)
AI winters, 29
ANNs, *see* Artificial neural
   networks (ANNs)
Anti-aliasing, 357, 436
API, *see* Application programming
   interface (API)

Application programming
   interface (API)
   Python with FastAPI, 519, 520
AR, *see* Augmented reality (AR)
Architectural visualization, 369
ARIA, *see* Adaptive Realistic
   Interactive Assistant (ARIA)
Artificial general intelligence (AGI),
   533, 534
Artificial intelligence (AI), 12, 13,
   531, 532, 539
   accountable and verifiable,
     506, 507
   algorithmic fairness, 410, 411
   anti-aliasing, 436
   applications, 32–35
   challenges, 204
   discovering, 26–28
   ecosystem, 330
   ethics (*see* Ethical AI)
   historical development, 28, 29
   integration, 514–516
   neural rendering, 433, 434
   next-generation architectures
     and capabilities, 534, 535
   on-chain intelligence, 539

B

R

S

GPSR Compliance
The European Union's (EU) General Product Safety Regulation (GPSR) is a set
of rules that requires consumer products to be safe and our obligations to
ensure this.

If you have any concerns about our products, you can contact us on

ProductSafety@springernature.com

In case Publisher is established outside the EU, the EU authorized
representative is:

Springer Nature Customer Service Center GmbH
Europaplatz 3
69115 Heidelberg, Germany